Counseling the
HOMOSEXUAL

Counseling the HOMOSEXUAL

Michael R. Saia

BETHANY HOUSE PUBLISHERS
MINNEAPOLIS, MINNESOTA 55438
A Division of Bethany Fellowship, Inc.

Copyright © 1988
Michael R. Saia
All Rights Reserved

Published by Bethany House Publishers
A Division of Bethany Fellowship, Inc.
6820 Auto Club Road, Minneapolis, Minnesota 55438

Printed in the United States of America

Library of Congress Cataloging-in-Publication Data

Saia, Michael R., 1950-
    Counseling the homosexual.

    Bibliography: p.
    1. Gays—Pastoral counseling of. 2. Homosexuality—Religious aspects—Christianity. 3. Church work with gays. I. Title.
BV4470.S25 1987   253.5'0880664   87-35524
ISBN 0-87123-989-2 (pbk.)

MICHAEL SAIA has had a teaching ministry with Youth With a Mission for the past sixteen years. He and his wife travel extensively, teaching in YWAM missionary training schools, churches, and seminars. Teaching a variety of subjects, his lectures are tempered by his pastoral concern and counseling experience. His experiences ministering in varied countries and cultural settings provide many illuminating illustrations.

About fifteen years ago, he began witnessing to homosexuals and counseling Christians coming from a homosexual background. This book is a result of his research for this outreach. He and his wife live in Los Angeles, California.

FOREWORD

God does not demand that a person be healed, heterosexually oriented, or happy—God demands *holiness*." When I opened Saia's book and discovered those words, I knew I had happened upon a radical approach to homosexuality— radical and biblical. I like that. The author's statement does not allow any of us, whether homosexual or heterosexual, to walk away deceptively comforted or untouched.

Saia's approach does not *heal* homosexuality, nor even adopt that as a goal. He teaches homosexuals to do what I describe as *telling themselves the truth*. For he knows Jesus' promise, that the truth will set men free, is the only hope for anyone—that includes, but is not restricted to, homosexuals. In this light, God's requirement of *holiness* is as fearsome for the complacently heterosexual as for the complacently homosexual, because it brings both under judgment even as it holds out rich promise.

This book does not commit the grievous mistakes made by many previous books purporting to help homosexuals. Typically, authors have enthusiastically (but, I think, misguidedly) reduced the problem to the simplest terms: it's a demon, it's an illness, it's a sin, it's learned behavior, it's inherited, it's mother's fault, it's father's fault, it's the result of a traumatic early life event, etc. Next, some of these authors have recommended a crisis-like act of ministry: deliverance from evil spirits, prayer for thorough and deep inner healing or healing of memories, an act of repentance, renunciation, etc. Then some go on to recount their successes.

Not Saia. His manual deals at length and in detail with *counseling* procedures for people with sexual-orientation difficulties. And these procedures amount to a well-rounded program of instruction in Christian living, particularly geared to those who are especially tempted by sexual desire for those of their own gender.

This material is biblical! From start to finish, God's love for the sinner, including the homosexual sinner is emphasized. Saia should know. That same divine love has compelled him to spend his evenings hanging out in bars in order to find, meet, and win their "gay-life" denizens. It's a tough ministry. But it has generated experience invaluable for the counselor who wishes to do his work God's way, the hard way, and perhaps, the effective way.

William Backus
Forest Lake, Minnesota
September 22, 1987

CONTENTS

ABOUT THE NAMES

With the exception of my name and my wife's, all names used in illustrations have been changed.

ABOUT THE VOCABULARY

When dealing with the complex subject of homosexuality, it is difficult to maintain a consistent vocabulary. Technically speaking, the word *homosexual* should be applied only to those who are actively involved in homosexual behavior, whereas the term *homosexually oriented* can be applied to those who have a homosexual sexual preference but may or may not be "homosexual" (engaged in the lifestyle). In writing this book, it has been difficult to obtain 100 percent accuracy in the use of these terms. Thus, in some cases, the awkward "homosexually oriented person" has been dropped and replaced by a general designation (e.g., "counselee"), and the word "homosexual" has at times been employed to cover both homosexuals and the homosexually oriented who are not technically "homosexual." In cases of ambiguity, the context should be enough to help the reader understand the exact meaning of the words.

Also, some readers may object to the use of the word *gay* for "homosexual," insisting that the homosexual lifestyle is anything but "gay." In the homosexual community, however, the word "gay" is not understood to mean "happy" but rather, simply "homosexual." Thus, in my synonymous use of the terms, I am not referring to an emotional state, but to sexual activity.

Finally, my use of the words *counselor* and *counselee* is informal. I consider a counselor to be any person who gives counsel, whether that is in an office or over a cup of coffee in a restaurant. The counselee is anyone who receives advice or help from another. Though the book will be used by professional counselors who see their counselees in a clinical setting, it applies as well to any Christian desiring to help homosexuals.

INTRODUCTION

Repent, you faggot!" the street evangelist screamed through his hand-held bullhorn. The loudspeaker made the angry tones of the man's voice all the more irritating, and the crowd began to jeer. Spitting epithets, the crowd moved out of earshot. The evangelist smiled smugly at his own faithfulness to preach the "Good News" in the face of "persecution."

An unlikely scenario? Unfortunately not. This street scene took place in one of our major cities. It highlights the drastic need for change in the attitudes of many in the body of Christ. Due to a dearth of information, and in some cases from false information, Christians often respond without compassion to those whose lives are gripped by homosexuality. Christians who proclaim "God is love" and "Jesus loves everybody" are often the last to show love to people they can only think of as "perverts," "sex deviates," "queers," or "fags."

Without a change of attitude our words will forever fall on the deaf ears of those who are searching desperately for the very thing we hope to offer—unconditional love, the unconditional love of God. To many homosexuals, the "Good News" of Jesus Christ often becomes the "bad news":

God hates homosexuality.
I am homosexual.
Therefore, God hates me.

Our message comes out sounding like this: "If you give up your way of having your need for love met for your entire life, God will forgive you and give you eternal life." The homosexual who hears this "Good News" reasonably responds with "No thanks, buddy" and walks away longing for the love only Christ can give. Was the problem with Christ himself? No, but the only

11

Christ the homosexual may have seen was a well-meaning Christian who exhibited a bad attitude and thus communicated rejection, turning the homosexual away from his only true hope.

Even Christians who do not shout put-downs on the street commonly lack Christ's compassion for homosexuals. One time my friend Bob, who struggled at times with his sexual preference, had accompanied me to a meeting for a study in the Word of God and fellowship with other Christians. "There's not one guy in there I would go to if I needed help with my problem," Bob remarked as we left.

Normally the Bible study included both sexes, but it happened to include only men this particular night. When the subject of homosexuality came up—Bob did not initiate it—everyone in the group seemed to have something to say. People cracked jokes, told stories, and expressed opinions and attitudes. Bob listened in silence, but studied every face. His remark following the study told it all. These Christians said that they loved everyone, but their attitudes did not reflect that love. Thus Bob was cut off from the very people he should be able to look to for comfort, prayer, and support.

People often think they have God's attitude toward homosexuality and homosexuals because they feel revulsion at the mention of the topic. But is this really God's attitude?

The well-dressed businessman who confronted me after a meeting obviously felt I had been far too gracious in my comments about homosexuals and their problems. "How can you talk about homosexuals in that way?" he challenged. "Don't you realize that God says that what they are doing is an abomination?"

"And have you ever lied?" I asked him.

"Why, yes, but . . ."

"And have you ever been proud?"

"Yes, but . . ."

"And yet you feel no revulsion toward yourself even though God says that these activities are an abomination before Him?"

"Well, no . . ." he said, and went on to another subject.

Our opinions and ideas about homosexuality and homosexuals usually reflect the world's perspective, not God's. While we were growing up, most of our thoughts were molded by the world and its thoughts rather than by the truth of God's Word. And since the "whole world is under the power of the wicked one," and that wicked one is the father of lies, most of what we learned was a lie. God does hate sin and He declares that the act of homosexuality is an abomination before Him, only because of His great love for us. God hates sin because it destroys us; our sin does not bring Him to abhor us as individuals.

Christ, though He hated sin, maintained God's attitude toward people and sin. When Jesus went to eat dinner at the house of Simon the Pharisee, the meal was interrupted by the entrance of an uninvited woman. The woman stood behind Jesus, wept on His feet, wiped His feet with her hair, and anointed His feet with perfume.

Simon, seeing this, said to himself, "If this man were really a prophet, he would know that this is a sinner who is touching him."

And Jesus, answering Simon's thoughts, said, "Do you see this woman?"

In Jesus' response lies the difference between the way we see people and the way God sees them. Simon saw a "sinner." Jesus saw a woman. We have to ask ourselves whether we see "sinners" or men and women.

Like Simon's reaction, the revulsion that many people have toward the homosexual may stem from pride: "Well, I'm really better than these sex deviates because at least my sin doesn't include the perversion of homosexuality." But our hearts can deceive us; we need to let God reveal our motives to us so we can deal with the real reasons behind our attitudes toward others.

Unless attitudes in the church change, we cannot help but communicate rejection to the very people we hope to reach. If we do not begin to see men and women instead of "sinners," the world will shout "Hypocrisy!" when we say that we love one another. The hollow ring of our words will be lost in the clamor of sin, and the unbeliever will go away unconvinced that Jesus was sent from the Father.

But how do we change our attitudes?

An attitude is a mental habit that produces an emotional "tone" in a person's life—that is, a person thinks so long in a certain way about a subject that even its mention will bring about a habitual emotional response. For instance, a person with a bad attitude toward work is someone who has thought about work in the wrong way for so long that even the thought of work can bring on negative reactions. If the person can learn to think truthfully about work (i.e., "in all labor there is profit"), then his emotions will eventually follow his thoughts, and a positive attitude will result.

Thus we can change our attitudes by learning to think according to the truth regarding a particular issue. The raw material necessary for changing an attitude, then, is truth, and this comes to us in the form of information.

Accurate information gives birth to compassion, the compassion God wants us to have toward people. Impatience with others and the problems they face frequently reflects a lack of understanding about their background and experiences. It seems as if the more we know about someone, the easier it is to understand why he does the things he does and to have patience with him as he sorts out his problems.

When I was attending Bible school, I boarded in a house with three other Christian men. One of the men, Jim, was notorious for the amount of noise he could make while eating. Most mothers teach their children to close their mouths while chewing, but somehow Jim's mother seemed to have missed this point.

One day, as Jim was enjoying his peanut butter sandwich, I had endured enough. I was about to say something when I felt an impression from the Holy Spirit. "Wait," He said. "Don't say anything just yet." So I decided to wait on God's timing.

Later that same day, Jim and I were visiting one of Jim's unsaved friends. As we sat in the kitchen and discussed our faith in Christ, Jim began to talk about his teeth.

"It's awfully embarrassing," Jim said, almost apologetically, "that I have to make so much noise when I eat."

Well, well, I thought. *I suspect that I am about to learn something.*

"You see," Jim continued, "I only have the front four teeth on both top and bottom, and no teeth from there back. So I have to chew everything in the front of my mouth and I make a terrible racket while I eat. Someday I may get the money to do something about it."

I learned something that day—not only about Jim, but also about compassion and patience. I never again found it as difficult to listen to Jim's chewing. Information had changed me.

Maybe this is why the Lord has such compassion on us—He knows us so well that He even knows better than we do why we behave the way we do. This never excuses bad behavior, of course, but it may help us understand why He has such patience with us.

Understanding the background, experiences, problems, needs and thoughts of the homosexual (or one who has a homosexual sexual preference) can also help us to express compassion, patience, and flexibility when we try to support someone struggling with such problems. Truth will change our attitudes and make us more effective servants of Christ.

As recently as ten years ago it was difficult to find good books on homosexuality written from a Christian perspective. In the last few years a number of good books have been published, and it is commendable that the body of Christ is responding to the need for information on this problem. But zeal to speak to the issue has sometimes resulted in communicating biblical standards of morality without explaining the psychology of homosexuality. Zeal without understanding has brought continuing condemnation to those struggling with a sexual preference distortion and has encouraged the Church to maintain a legalistic, uncompassionate posture toward those it does not understand.

It is my sincere hope that this book will accomplish two ends. First, that the material will effectively equip members of Christ's body to support and counsel those who struggle with homosexuality. I wish to give these counselors practical, step-by-step, principle-oriented information to use in counseling. Second, I hope that the book will serve as an instrument of direction and encouragement to those struggling with temptation toward homosexuality. My desire is that through this information the "struggler" might come to freedom and stability in his walk with Christ and might glorify Christ through a godly life.

PART ONE

DEVELOPMENT OF THE HOMOSEXUAL ORIENTATION

CHAPTER ONE

WE NEED A CHANGE

One Sunday morning my wife Carol and I visited a small but well-attended church known for its lively worship, evangelistic fervor, and good biblical teaching. We were listening to the absorbing message when one statement seemed to stand out from the rest.

"I don't know if we can fully learn this lesson while we are bound in carnal flesh," the speaker said casually, and proceeded to explain his point.

My wife and I turned to look at each other. The look on my wife's face said, "Did I really hear him say that?" Thinking it best not to discuss the matter during the service, we continued listening in silence.

Being teachers ourselves, Carol and I try to give speakers the benefit of the doubt when we hear something questionable in a teaching. It is easy to misunderstand a speaker, so listeners must give speakers much latitude. In this case, though, the preacher proceeded to clarify his point beyond any doubt. He really did mean to say that our problem in this life is our physical body. If only we didn't have a physical body, he taught, everything would be wonderful.

This is a blatant example of a concept called *dualism*. Dualism and other false teachings plague the Church and cripple its efforts to help those in need.

DUALISM

Dualism is the idea that anything physical is evil and anything spiritual is good. This thought, common to Greek and Eastern philosophy but totally foreign to the Scriptures, has been prevalent in the Church since the fourth century and has produced its fruit in countless aspects of Christian thought and conduct. The problem with this teaching is that whoever believes it comes to view anything that has to do with the body as necessarily evil and fit to be rejected. It produces a negative attitude toward such things as mixed swimming or the Christian's involvement in politics and art. Even such basic activities as eating and sleeping suddenly become "evil" because of their relationship to the physical world, and Christians are warned to stay away from them lest they become "worldly."

Sex, because of its immediate involvement with the physical body, is a prime target for this false idea. Viewing sex as somehow evil, dirty or unspiritual has been a common problem through Church history despite the Bible's clarity about the origin, purpose, use, misuse, and importance of our sexual capacities. God saw all that He made and called it "very good," but dualism influences people to call what God made "evil" and so cast a shadow on what God has done. Part of this dualistic response to sex is categorizing sins into special groupings and setting up lists by which one sin can be compared to another with respect to its "relative evil."

That there are degrees of sin and of sanctions for sin is not in question here. God simply never has told us the relationship of one sin to another, probably because He knows better than we do our tendency to make a system of works righteousness out of such a list. He helps us avoid that temptation by commanding abstinance from all sin regardless of relative degree of sanction.

There is one manner in which sexual sins do differ from other sins. Paul the Apostle states that every other sin which a person commits is "apart from the body," but that the one who commits sexual immorality sins against his own body. There is no comparison of relative evil in this statement, only a difference in effect between sexual immorality and all other kinds of sin.

Ultimately, any human attempt to categorize sins brings us to a categorization of people, putting individuals or groups into mental pigeonholes and treating them accordingly. To say "This sinner is worse than that one, so I will love this one and reject that one" is to equate a person's morality with his value. Thus if a person is involved in a sin that is considered "more evil" than another type of sin, it is permissible to treat the person as less valuable or less lovable, or not relate to the person at all. This kind of exclusion must not be part of the lives of Christians committed to loving their neighbors as themselves.

MORALS AND METAPHYSICS

Another important philosophical misconception that plagues the Church hinders us from understanding the homosexual and his inner battles. In philosophy, the division that deals with the area of existence or being is commonly called *metaphysics*. The division dealing with choices and standards for morality, on the other hand, is referred to as *ethics* or *morals*. Questions like "Where did everything come from?" or "Why do things exist?" are classed as questions about metaphysics, while issues having to do with good and evil and how people are to respond to standards of morality are regarded as questions about ethics or morals.

As with dualism, a confusion entered the Church around the end of the fourth century, resulting in a tendency to combine questions about metaphysics and morals into one category. This blurring of distinctions has resulted in much difficulty; some issues require a complete separation of the categories to be able to arrive at valid conclusions concerning either or both of the divisions of philosophy.

Take, for example, the difference between temptation and sin. For many men, the temptation to lust is a frequent concern. But the question inevitably arises about where to draw the "line" between what is temptation and when one becomes involved in the sin of lust. If your metaphysics (what you are) and your morals (what you do) are confused in your mind, it will be very difficult to discern the "line" between temptation and sin. Now, although how a man responds immediately to his perception of a member of the opposite sex may not literally be a physical phenomenon, for all practical purposes the response is in the metaphysical realm. That is, if a man sees a woman walking down the street and there is an attraction to her in his mind, he experiences that attraction as if it were a metaphysical reaction because it can come unbidden to his consciousness. Whether the man goes on to choose to fantasize about the woman determines whether or not he has entered into the sin of lust. Many men walk around under a load of unnecessary condemnation because they do not make a distinction between the immediate reaction in their minds, which should be treated as a metaphysical event, and the choice to fantasize, which is a moral issue and can be sin. Thus many men suffer needlessly because of a confusion in the Church that makes no distinction between what we are and what we do.

Attractions stemming from sexual preference or orientation afford an even clearer illustration of both the confusion in the Church and the way it can affect those struggling with homosexual tendencies.

When a heterosexually oriented man reached puberty and began to be aware of himself as a sexual being, he probably did not ask himself, *Why am I being attracted to girls? Why am I choosing to do such a thing?* In fact, he probably did not think of the event as a choice at all but as a natural occurrence: *After all*, he thought, *I am a man.* He might recognize fantasizing or lust or fornication as sin, but he would not see his attraction to the opposite sex as sin—it is just "there." In other words, he treats his sexual orientation as a fact simply because he does not perceive it as a moral issue. He did not choose to have that particular orientation.

Likewise, if a young man, during the time of his sexual development, should come to realize that he is attracted to the same sex rather than to the opposite, he does not experience this as a moral issue but as a fact. To him, as with the heterosexually oriented man, the preference is simply "there." Remember that we are not discussing at this point why he has the preference or the possible factors involved in its development, but his discovery that his sexual attraction is to his own rather than the opposite sex. I will consider the source (etiology) of the homosexual preference in a later chapter. I am also not dealing here with a person's possible response to his having a homosexual preference, responses which may or may not be sinful.

"When I was thirteen years old, I became aware that I was attracted to men rather than to women," John reported frankly as he gave his testimony to a Christian community. "For me this was a fact and nothing more than a fact. I did not feel guilty about it; actually, I could not feel guilty about it because I did not choose it. It was simply there in my mind.

"However, when I first chose to be involved in a homosexual act," John said, his tone becoming more solemn, "I was overwhelmed with guilt. I knew that I had done something terribly wrong."

At this point the Church usually responds with confusion rather than understanding. "But that's terrible," someone might say. "He shouldn't feel like that. That's abnormal. He must be doing something wrong, something sinful. He needs to repent. If he would thoroughly repent, then he wouldn't have those feelings anymore." And so many Christians confuse what the person is with what the person does and hold the person responsible not only for the sin of homosexuality (the acts the person is responsible for because he chose to commit them), but also for his sexual preference (which he did not choose, but simply is the way his mind happens to work).

I am not trying in any way to say that to have a homosexual preference excuses someone from guilt if he has committed homosexual acts—the preference cannot be used as an excuse for sin. I am also not trying to say someone with such an orientation has no hope of change—there is hope for change, and I will discuss that in a later chapter. But when people do not keep the matter of preference (which, *functionally* is in the realm of metaphysics) and sin (which is moral) separate, a heavy load of false guilt and condemnation is laid on hurting people who are already having a hard enough time feeling good about God and themselves. They know that they are different and desperately want to understand themselves and to be accepted by others, but they are told that they ought to feel guilty for something they did not choose.

As one man put it, "I feel as if God is always breathing down my neck." If, no matter how pure his life is, he has to feel guilty for his attractions, then there is never any relief from guilt. "How would you feel," another man said, "if you had to feel guilty every time you became hungry?" Hunger is not gluttony, and preference is not homosexual sin. But the confused Church has often equated preference and homosexual acts (sin) and held people responsible for something that is not actually a moral issue.

CAN YOU "SPOT 'EM A MILE AWAY"?

"Well, what do you think?" I asked my friend, who had accompanied me to a gay bar to share Jesus with the men there. "Would you have recognized these men as homosexuals if you had seen them on the street?"

"Not a one," he responded. Then he added, musing, "It's not at all what I thought it would be like in here."

My friend's reaction was a common one. The stereotypes he had brought with him in his mind were being broken down by the stark reality of what he was seeing. He expected something different—perhaps men with limp wrists, swivel hips, feminine clothing and affected speech. Instead, he was confronted with men who looked, dressed, acted and spoke the same way he did. He admitted that it was a shocking revelation, but a good one.

The notion that outward appearance or speech shows whether someone is a homosexual is widespread both in the world and in the Church. There is some basis in fact for this notion—some members of the gay community do dress according to the stereotypical image in order to attract attention to themselves. Since this is the exception rather than the rule, though, it is best to reserve all judgment until there is better information available for making an assessment. Actually, the only way to be sure is if the person himself tells you that he has a homosexual preference. There simply is no way to tell on the basis of outward appearance.

Mark, who was working with a major magazine publishing corporation, was lamenting over the difficulty he had in walking on the streets in the city where he was living. "Can I help it if I walk like this? My whole family walks like this. It comes from my heredity and my training." Mark was heterosexually oriented but evidently his manner of walking was mistaken frequently to be an indication that he was gay, and so he often had to deal with the propositions of other men, and Mark was becoming understandably annoyed.

Family members or relatives are often shocked beyond words when they discover (or it is disclosed) that another member of the family has a homosexual orientation. If it were so evident from the way the person dressed or acted, there would not be this surprise. It is because the people really could not tell that they were so amazed at the revelation.

Outward appearance, then, cannot and should not be used as a gauge to judge the sexual preference of another. It was said of Jesus that He would not judge by what His eyes saw or by what His ears heard. He knew people truly according to what He saw in their hearts. Perhaps it would be wise to follow His example in the crucial matter of another person's sexuality.

THEY DON'T WANT TO HEAR

The idea that homosexuals are always dishonest and hardhearted is another fallacy that hinders Christians from effectively reaching the gay community. *You just can't talk to them*, many people think, and so they eventually quit any attempt to preach the Gospel to this segment of our society.

On the contrary, it seems that anyone who has broad contact with homosexuals finds that there exists the same amount of openness to the Gospel among male and female homosexuals that we find in any other portion of society—some are open to hearing about Jesus, some are not. Individual background and experience influences the attitude of the person toward the Gospel message, and making generalizations about how a person will respond ignores the complexity of the situation.

Homosexuals commonly respond to discussions about God with "I pray every day" or "I am a very religious person." True, they may not have a perfect, biblical definition for these terms, but does that then mean that there is nothing valid about their prayer or religious activities? What about Cornelius? Peter did not want to go to the house of a Gentile because Gentiles were "sinners" and "unclean," even "dogs," as Jews often referred to them. And yet the prayers of this unsaved man were remembered before God and God changed Peter's heart and sent him to Cornelius that he might know the truth about Jesus.

A friend and I were walking along a street notorious for its male homosexual prostitutes. Our task that evening was to intercede for the evangelism that would take place the next weekend. It was not our intention to speak to anyone that evening. Our job was to pray.

"Hi, guys!" the cheery voice of a young male prostitute caught our attention. I looked up from the sidewalk long enough to say "Hi," and then looked back down, ready to go on.

"What are you guys doing tonight?" the young man asked, joining us in our walk.

I'll get rid of him, I thought. So I proceeded to tell him quite directly that we were praying, that we would be praying for the people on the street and that we would also pray for him. Much to my surprise, the declaration of our intentions did not deter him in the slightest.

"That's good," he said. "May I walk along with you for a while? I'd like to talk."

During the one-and-a-half-hour conversation that ensued, we learned that this young man had a Bible in his back pocket that he read every day, that he prayed every day, and that he wanted to know more about God. Yet he was selling himself on the street. We cannot tell where a person's heart is by external appearances: not all homosexuals are closed to the Gospel.

THEY ARE BEYOND HOPE

Many churches and some entire denominations have taken the stand that homosexuals cannot become Christians. They reason that God has "given them over" to their sin and therefore there is no way the person can be set free. They take their argument from Romans, chapter one, where Paul discusses the sin of the Gentiles who have never heard the Law or Gospel. Paul concludes that because of their refusal to live according to the light that they have, God has given them over (or up) to their sin. The resultant fruit of this, Paul says, is displayed in the sins they commit. But the list of sins Paul gives includes enough categories to implicate any of us. Why, then, do some Christians single out the sin of homosexuality as an indicator that the person so involved will not or cannot be forgiven? Is there more than one unpardonable sin?

Blasphemy against the Holy Spirit is the only sin listed in the Bible that is called "unpardonable." One would think, then, that Bible-believing Christians would understand that every other sin can be forgiven. But other sins are also treated by Christians as if they were unforgivable—sins like murder, prostitution, homosexuality, bestiality (having intercourse with animals), and divorce without proper grounds. Yet Jesus himself said that every sin, other than blaspheming the Holy Spirit, can be forgiven.

Paul himself writes to the Corinthian church that some of them had been involved in both aggressive and passive male homosexual activity (1 Cor. 6:9–11), and yet they had become Christians just as genuinely as the rest of the brothers and sisters in Corinth. It requires a strange twist of interpretation, then, to attribute to Paul the notion that homosexuals cannot be saved.

This reaction in the Church may be caused in part by the low success rate experienced by many ministers who try to help homosexuals. Two factors explain, in part, this high attrition rate. First, the psychological damage being dealt with is of such a nature that it may be necessary for the person to travel a long, hard road to healing. Some may quit before substantial change is evident in the person's life. Second, Jesus said it is truth that sets people free, but the Church has often tried to help homosexuals without the proper information to attack the problem. Regardless of our practical difficulties, though, God says that a homosexual can be saved, and we must approach the question with that in mind.

THE DEVIL MAKES THEM DO IT

"A snakepit, I've walked into a snakepit, Lord!" The words erupted into my mind involuntarily as I stood in the middle of the floor, unable to move because of the crush of male bodies on every side. This was my first experience sharing my faith in a gay bar, and I did not know as of yet that I was going to enjoy it. The air was thick with cigarette smoke, the music was loud enough, I thought, to destroy anybody's eardrums, and the sense of loneliness was enough to depress the happiest of souls. "Snakepit" was indeed an appropriate description, but even as the word came to my consciousness I heard another familiar voice. "Yes, Michael, the place is like a snakepit, but it's not the men." And with that, Jesus gently reminded me of the truth that we battle not flesh and blood but unseen spiritual forces trying to destroy men.

Just as in any other situation where sin is being committed, when people are involved in the sin of homosexuality, demons are released to operate. Demons can, of course, be working in a homosexual's life. The false idea that creeps in at this point, however, is that every time a person is tempted with homosexual sin, the enemy has done it. Some Christians teach that if a person has a tendency toward homosexuality, then he automatically needs deliverance from demonic bondage. This approach is born of two fallacies.

First, there is an illogical understanding of the situation. If a demon tempts a person to sin, that person is tempted. But that cannot be turned around to say that any temptation to sin is done by a demon. Some Christians find it difficult to accept that a temptation in a person's life could be as strong as some homosexuals (or former homosexuals) find it and still not be demonic. They think that anything causing that much trouble must be a demon. These Christians seem unaware of both the extent of the fallenness of the world and of the role a person's psychological condition can play in temptation to sin. So they blame everything on a demon, thinking that will answer all the questions.

Second, some Christians are convinced that deliverance from demons is the cure for all spiritual ills. Actually, even in cases where a person needs deliverance, deliverance itself does not solve anything. It merely removes some roadblocks so the person can get on with the normal processes of change.

For some men leaving a homosexual lifestyle, deliverance will be necessary. If that is so, then someone should pray with the person and in the authority of Jesus cast the demon(s) out. It should not be supposed, though, that the person will then have no more attraction to those of the same sex and will never again be tempted with homosexuality. This would ignore the person's distorted sexual identity, a psychological and not a demonic problem.

ARE WE AFRAID?

Fear of the topic of homosexuality or of persons who have been involved in homosexuality has been aptly described as "homophobia." But the "homophobic reaction" often extends beyond the bounds of homosexuality or homosexuals. Many people, especially men, are afraid even to share deep emotions with members of the same sex. Others may fear entering into close, committed relationships with members of the same sex. And some believers will ardently avoid any display of physical affection that exceeds what is culturally acceptable.

In some circles, a handshake is the only accepted measure of affection shown between men. Women in this same setting might be allowed to share a short kiss on the cheek. Anything in excess of these displays probably will be taboo, and those who go beyond these standards will be thought of as "having something wrong with them." In such a setting an embrace is usually met with stiffness. While it is possible that this response could originate from deep hurts in a person's past, it is also often true that many people think there is something essentially wrong with sharing any kind of physical affection with someone of the same sex.

Many Christians feel that even being near a homosexual is an indication that something is wrong with them or that the Christian is condoning the activities of the homosexual. And although most Christians realize that there is no validity in guilt by association, they follow a different standard when the issue is homosexuality.

When I tell of some of my experiences witnessing in a local gay bar, people commonly ask, "But don't some of the men think you're gay, too?"

"Actually, most of them do," is my usual response, "but that's their problem, not mine."

For many people, refusing to be weighed down by what others think simply is not enough. The fear of being thought gay will drive many Christians to avoid talking to homosexuals or to avoid locations where they might encounter gays. *I can't let anybody see me with people like that. What will others think of me? Why, they might even think that I was that bad!* Yet Jesus was known as a friend of sinners; He ate and drank with them to the point that He was accused of being a glutton and a drunkard. Can we, who are commanded to live in His love, do less?

"Don't let go of me, please." Bill's embrace seemed to be born more of desperation than of affection. I had just finished a lecture on the healing that can come through love, and Bill had come up afterward to give me a hug. As he clung to me, though, I could tell that something had made him terribly afraid.

"I'll hold you as long as you want, Bill, but could you tell me what's happened to frighten you so?"

"A friend and I went on a short vacation together," Bill started, trying to speak rather than cry, "and everything was fine until we had to sleep in the same bed one night because there was only one bed. Well, in the middle of the night I was awakened by my friend as he tried to approach me sexually. I told him to leave me alone but ended up having to fight him off and eventually jumped out of bed to get away. I slept on the floor the rest of the night, and my friend didn't try to do anything to me the rest of the trip, but I'm still so afraid. Is there something wrong with me that he should approach me like that? I see him every day at work. What should I say to him? I'm still so afraid."

Bill's story is not uncommon. Many have been approached sexually by friends or relatives of the same sex. There are two essential issues here. The first is, "How should I feel about myself?" The second is, "How should I respond to the other person?"

First, there is no need for someone to feel guilty or ashamed because of the actions of another. God has said that every man will be guilty for his own sin and not that of another (Ezekiel 18); God will not hold us responsible for what others do. The proper response to the situation would be grief—grief that God has been hurt by the sin committed, and grief that the other person is troubled and in great need. To be grieved out of love for the other person is appropriate, but guilt and shame are not.

Second, we become afraid of situations or people when we sense our inadequacy to handle the problems confronting us. We look at the problem and realize we lack the power and wisdom to help the other person. And so we become afraid.

But rather than fear, the appropriate response is to love the person and ask, "How can I help this person? How can I pray? What can I do to help him learn to get his needs met in the right way?" We can avoid fear with two responses: humility and love. Humility says, "I can't handle this situation, but you can, Lord. What do you want to do for this person?" And love says to the person, "I understand that you have needs in your life that you should learn how to fulfill righteously. How can I help you learn to get your needs met in the proper fashion through Jesus?"

Homophobia will, I hope, one day be a thing of the past. Until then, three principles will help keep us on an even keel: trusting other people's motives (love believes all things), honestly confronting those who may be sharing affection with impure motives, and humbly admitting fault on either side (that is, the fault of having impure motives or of having falsely assumed that another's motives were impure). Having God's heart attitude and accurate information about the problem of homosexuality may eventually eliminate the suspicion so prevalent in the body of Christ and free us to share affection openly without fear of criticism.

WHERE DOES IT ALL END?

"Christ is OK; it's Christians I can't stand." This outlook, phrased in many different ways, is expressed frequently by members of the gay community. Usually a result of hurt, this attitude poses one of the most formidable roadblocks to effective witness. Until this hurdle is crossed and a homosexual feels confident in our love for him, we will encounter nothing but walls in our efforts to tell him of the good news of Jesus Christ. Our inability to reach gays with the Gospel is a result, in large part, of bad attitudes stemming from misinformation. It is hard to hide a bad attitude. It is better to change the attitude from the inside out, acquiring accurate information about the subject and allowing God to change our hearts through a revelation of His love.

Jesus said, "Out of the abundance of the heart, the mouth speaks." With our hearts full of compassion, and free from fear, guilt, and shame, we should be able to use our words to edify others, to work on our speech patterns, changing them to speak love to homosexuals rather than condemnation.

Many terms are used to describe or identify members of the gay community that should not be part of the vocabulary of the

Church. Words like "queer," "faggot," "fruit," "fairy," or "pervert" are not helpful in communication about or with homosexuals. These words have come out of the rebellious, proud, hateful hearts of unbelievers and are used to reject the homosexual. Even though some members of the gay community may use these terms to describe themselves, the Church does not need these deprecating labels. On the contrary, believers can take the opportunity afforded by the use of such words to speak God's truth into the situation.

"Why would you want to come here to talk to a queer like me?" someone might ask. We can use such an occasion to tell the person the truth about himself: "I would appreciate it if you would not refer to yourself by the term 'queer.' To describe your behavior as homosexual is adequate. Besides, you are made in the image of God, a little lower than God, and you are worth more than the whole world. You are too valuable to speak of yourself in such deprecating terms." It may come as a shock to the person that you consider the term "queer" deprecating and that you treat the person as more valuable than the whole world, but if you persist in evaluating the person according to the truth of God's Word, you will find that most will eventually appreciate your loving attitude. They may even thank you for the uplifting conversation.

With our words we can kill or bring life. As the body of Jesus, we need to determine to bring nothing but life with our words, and drop all of the unnecessary "disdain" words from our vocabulary. When our hearts and attitudes have been changed, and we are communicating truth, acceptance, and love in speech and actions, then the gay community will pay attention to our message of God and His gift of eternal life.

Feeling misunderstood and rejected is never easy, but to feel that you will have to deal with misunderstanding the rest of your life is a prospect most people simply refuse to endure. This expectation may explain why numbers of those who have come into the Church from homosexual lifestyles have exited after only a short period of involvement with Christianity. Constantly battling against temptation, the Devil, fleshly impulses and worldly thoughts is tough enough, but to have to battle with "brothers and sisters" can make the task almost impossible. In light of this rejection, it is not surprising that "gay" churches form. Final responsibility for the formation of "gay" churches does not rest with the body of Christ, of course, but if Christians had more fully displayed the love of Christ, perhaps no one would have ever felt a need for a "gay" church.

Many men and women sit in our churches, hurting yet hesitant to express their great need because they fear misunderstanding and rejection. Every now and then they poke their heads out of their shells of self-protection, looking for love. But they withdraw when the only message they receive is that they should not feel the way they do. Their hearts cry for someone to love them without criticism or condemnation, but their cries go unheard because so few people are free enough in themselves to bear the burdens of others. Sometimes they manage to endure, persisting in their Christian walk through sheer willpower: but what a shame that they should have to live in isolation from the very family that could give them the comfort and support they desperately need! They are searching for unconditional love, and if they do not find it in God with the help of the body of Christ, where will they?

CHAPTER TWO

AN IMPORTANT
DISTINCTION

N ow, what was that word again?" John asked.
English was John's second language, and although he spoke it
almost fluently, this new word was not registering quickly. Grap-
pling with a new concept that related intimately to his personal
struggles was making it more difficult to remember the word
itself.

"Ori-en-ta-tion," I said slowly, separating the syllables.

"Orientation," he repeated softly. An expression of deep con-
templation played on his face.

As I continued to explain the difference between orientation
and behavior, I saw a spark of hope in John's eyes. He was feeling
a hope that God really did love him, hope that he could live for
God just like anyone else, and hope that he could be changed.
He also understood that evening that God demanded repentance
but did not expect instant healing. As John discovered the difference between his homosexual orientation and his homosexual
lifestyle, repentance began to make sense, and healing began to
appear possible.

In the past few years there has been much debate over just
how one should define homosexual preference, homosexual behavior, and the difference between the two. Because the material
under discussion is so subjective in nature, there are a variety of
opinions and definitions to consider. As a zoologist friend of
mine once said, "Where the theories abound, the facts are few."
This wide gamut of interpretations requires not only a careful
reading of the available material, but also an openness of mind
to new information.

It is fairly simple to record the specific behavior of individuals and to then attempt to draw some conclusions from the observations. But when we try to record the feelings or desires of a person, it is much more difficult to know just how to interpret the information we have collected. Beyond this, though, is the mammoth task of attempting to locate and describe the possible motivations associated with the desires of the person, and then the almost impossible job of discovering the factors that could have contributed to the development of those motivations and desires. The subjective, elusive nature of this last aspect of the problem makes it difficult both to define and to treat the homosexual condition. Proper, effective treatment is predicated on proper diagnosis.

Accurate diagnosis is a major step in the solution of any problem. The *differentiation* and *identification* of the various aspects of a problem are necessary parts of the process of diagnosis. Without differentiation, the problem will seem so overwhelming to the counselee that motivating initiative for problem-solving may be inhibited. Without identification, both counselor and counselee could take "stabs in the dark" forever without making concrete progress. Sorting out the unique aspects of the counselee's problem and proposing biblical solutions for each aspect are absolutely basic to Christian counseling.

Yet, when dealing with the problem of homosexuality, the Christian Church seems to see only one side of the problem. Sin appears to be the only part of the problem in the Church's field of vision. Once the person has repented, many Christians have nothing more to say to the new brother or sister. If the person experiences struggles or temptations subsequent to his conversion, other Christians may lead him to believe: (1) that he should not be having these difficulties, so he must be doing something wrong, or (2) that he needs to be delivered from a demon, or (3) that he never fully repented, and so did not actually become a Christian. In any case, the body of Christ generally treats only the *moral* aspect of the problem.

But there is both a moral and a psychological aspect to the problem of homosexuality. The moral aspect consists of deliberate choices, whether these be lustful thoughts or genital acts. This is, simply put, the behavior of homosexuality. The psychological aspect is much more complex. During early childhood development, the person's mind was affected in such a way as to influence him to try to meet his need for love through relationships with the same sex. To refer to this psychological side of the problem, I will be using the terms orientation, condition, tendency, or sexual preference.

In order to teach a person a balanced view of his responsibilities as a moral agent, it is necessary to teach him not only those things for which he is responsible, but also those things for which he is *not* responsible. Unless a man can distinguish between what is under the direct control of his will and what is not, he will have difficulty knowing the difference between temptation and sin, and is likely to carry around a load of condemnation over things for which he is not responsible. Christians are often very noble in their efforts to be responsible for everything in their lives, but to carry around a sense of false guilt is simply not healthful. On the other hand, it is not good for a person to excuse sinful behavior by saying that he is not responsible for his actions. It is necessary to recognize and maintain a balance between these two extremes.

It is at precisely this point in understanding that many homosexuals experience an enlightening revelation about themselves and God. Consider, for instance, Dave's story.

The team house was buzzing with activity, but Dave and I were alone in the living room. We had had many conversations about the intricacies of the homosexual condition. As it turned out, this was to be our last time together.

"Thanks so much," Dave said as he slouched in the tattered, greenish-gray armchair.

"Thanks for what?" I asked.

"For telling me the difference between the way I think and the way I act. Just knowing the difference between my homosexual sexual preference and my homosexual behavior has changed my life. I can finally believe that God really loves me. That is, He may be displeased with some of my actions because they are sinful, but He loves *me* as a person nonetheless. And knowing that God loves me makes it easier to come to Him. So thanks."

Dave's story is not an isolated case. Many men who have come to realize the difference between their sexual preference and their behavior have at the same time been released to believe that God could really love them. Understanding often *is* healing.

Many gay men have come to believe something like this:
God hates homosexuality.
I am a homosexual.

Therefore, God hates me.

This kind of misunderstanding stems from the mistaken idea that there is no distinction between preference and behavior. Thus the person is responsible for both the way his mind works (i.e., being attracted to the same rather than the opposite sex), and his response to his preference, a response which may or may not be sinful.

To illustrate: A man sees a woman walking down the street. The man is attracted to the woman sexually. The man then has to make a decision. "Will I go on with this thought and lust after the woman, or will it stop right here?" The man makes the decision to turn his mind to other things. Has the man sinned? No. He was *tempted* to sin by the presentation of the thought to his mind, but he chose to avoid sinning by turning his thoughts away before he committed himself to lust in his heart. He was tempted, but he did not sin.

Second case: Man "A" sees man "B" walking down the street. Man "A" is attracted to man "B" sexually. Man "A" chooses to turn his mind to something else and away from the other man. Did man "A" sin? No. He was tempted by the presentation of the thought to his mind, but his decision to change his thoughts to something else kept him from breaking the law of God that forbids lusting.

The dilemma here is that many people (including Christian men who have a homosexual orientation) may *assume* that a man is sinning just because he is attracted to another man. But to assume this is to hold the person responsible not only for the choice to lust, which would be a sin, but also for being tempted, which is not a sin. "But it seems as if something is terribly wrong here," someone might say. Indeed, there is something wrong, but it is not something for which the person is morally culpable. As one gay man once told me, "Nobody in his right mind would choose to be homosexually oriented if he had a choice in the matter."

Before a counselor has comprehended and accepted the involuntary nature of the homosexual sexual preference he may speak tremendous condemnation into the life of a counselee. Constant, subtle insinuation that a person is responsible for his sexual attractions can be a terrible psychological pressure. This pressure may not be intentional on the part of the counselor, but the counselee may still sustain substantial hurt and discouragement. The counselee may receive the message that he is guilty not only for his unbiblical behavior but also for his desires and attractions. He may ultimately be led to believe that just *existing* places him in a culpable position. Losing hope, he may turn away from Christ who is his only hope for change. All the while, the counselor may be oblivious to his own role in the counselee's discouragement.

This depressing situation can be avoided if the Christian counselor learns to differentiate between the moral and psychological aspects of the homosexual problem. The fallacy "I have to do this because this is the way I am" does not have to lead us to conclude illogically "You are that way because you chose to be that way." While there are many members of the gay community who will try to use their preferences to excuse their sin, this is no reason for the Christian community to hold people responsible for something they did not choose.

Homosexuals themselves often fail to recognize the distinction between their sexual preferences and behavior. For this reason the Christian counselor must be familiar with the difference between orientation and action and must keep this difference in mind in all his witnessing and counseling. On the one hand you will hear, "I can't help feeling like this. Why does God say I shouldn't have these desires? Why does He condemn me for having these attractions?" In this case the person is assuming that he is responsible for something which is not his fault, that is, his homosexual preference. On the other hand you will hear, "Well, I just couldn't help getting into bed with the man. After all, this is the way I am." Here the person feels he is not responsible for something which *is* his fault, namely his homosexual behavior. Both mistaken ideas arise from the homosexual's failure to keep preference and behavior separate in his mind. If the Christian counselor does not make this distinction in his thinking, he will not recognize such fallacies when he hears them, and will lack the necessary clarity to point the homosexual toward viable solutions for his problems.

Some Christians refuse to recognize the homosexual sexual preference as a psychological reality. "Deep down inside," they think, "homosexuals really are attracted to those of the opposite sex, but they are denying it. That is why God condemns them. They really are deliberately perverted." While some homosexuals do have some attraction to the opposite sex, it is quite common for homosexuals to have no interest in the opposite sex or they might even experience a sense of revulsion at the thought of relating sexually to the opposite sex.

To the heterosexually oriented person, as a part of the statistically "normal" segment of society, it can be difficult to imagine that a homosexually oriented person could find it just as difficult to relate to the opposite sex as the heterosexually oriented person would find it to relate to the same sex. As one female homosexual once told me, "Now, why would I ever want to relate sexually to a man? It's so unnatural for me." To the person with a homosexual preference an attraction to the same sex feels perfectly natural. This attraction is not chosen by the person, but is simply "there" in the person's mind, often being recognized at the dawn of the person's awareness of himself as a sexual being.

Christians who fail to recognize and grapple with the psychological fact of a person's homosexual preference are prone to communicate rejection to the person because they do not clearly understand the person's inner struggles. Those who struggle with homosexuality often face a 24-hour-a-day battle with their feelings. This constant internal turmoil is really only fully understood by those who have experienced the same problems. Christian counselors who do not work through the ramifications of the homosexual condition tend to be impatient with their counselees because they cannot understand the immensity of the counselee's problem, and thus cannot comprehend why the person is not recovering faster.

Because the problem of homosexuality is twofold, healing for the homosexual must proceed along a twofold path. Both the behavior and the preference of homosexuality require healing, but the solutions for each will be different because the problems are different.

CHAPTER THREE

THEORIES, THEORIES . . .

B ut why me?" Mark whined, interrupting the counseling session. "Why did I have to be the one to end up with homosexual feelings?"

This anguished cry rises again and again from the hearts and minds of those who feel saddled by their homosexual orientation. Feeling guilty about something they have deliberately chosen to do is bad enough, but to feel unjustly burdened by something they received as a passive, innocent party is almost unbearable. How the homosexual condition develops thus becomes an unavoidable question demanding a reasonable and compassionate answer.

The complexities of the human personality and the influence of environment on human development make absolute statements about the source of the homosexual condition virtually impossible. Factors such as parenting, social and economic status, home environment, religious training, race, nationality, and temperament make the collection of data very difficult. The subjective nature of the topic also makes the interpretation of the data a very delicate task. Nonetheless there are some general observations that can be of significant value in the treatment of the homosexual condition.

Of the many theories used to explain the development of the homosexual sexual preference, the possible explanations fall into several major categories. Since case histories form the basis of these theories, it is reasonable to assume that counselors will interview at least *some* counselees whose stories fit one or more of these theories (with the exception of the genetic theory). The crucial question is whether or not evidence supports the idea that *one* of these theories will explain the *majority* of cases. Exceptions

39

should not keep us from recognizing general principles.

The theory of rebellion (i.e., the person is in deliberate rebellion against the standards of God, parents, or society) and the theory of boredom (i.e., the person became bored with heterosexual encounters and turned to homosexual experiences out of curiosity or inordinate desire) do not apply to the discussion of how homosexual orientation develops. These theories describe possible reasons for some homosexual behavior, but do not explain the psychology of homosexuality. Most homosexuals report that they experienced homosexual desires long before the commission of any homosexual act. If preference exists prior to behavior, then theories concerning behavior cannot be used to explain the origin of preference.

The major theories fall into three main categories and subdivide from there. First, there are the *physical* explanations, including the *genetic* and the *hormonal* possibilities. Second, there are the *internal* theories, encompassing various forms of fear and confusion. Third, there are *interpersonal* explanations, including traumatic sexual experiences, the domineering mother, and the "weak" or "passive" father.

PHYSICAL THEORIES

The genetic and hormonal explanations for the homosexual condition are two variations on the same theme. Behind both of these theories lies the basic idea that a person's physical body predisposes him to homosexual tendencies. The practical outworking of this idea is that the affected person must live out what he is physically, and so must live a homosexual lifestyle. Some adherents to the theory claim that the person maintains no responsibility whatever for his actions, while others claim that the person can control how he expresses his homosexuality, but he must behave in a homosexual fashion. After all, they say, that is what he is.

It was very popular in the recent past to propose the physical theories as a conclusive, scientific explanation for homosexual orientation. But as the theories crumbled under more extensive scientific scrutiny, the proponents of these ideas had to look elsewhere for viable explanations. The literature of psychology abounds with scientific evidence and counter-evidence; even a brief investigation will reveal the discrepancies and confusion over the subject.

One of the practical problems with the scientific proposals and their subsequent debunking is that the denial of the proposals did not filter down into the gay community to the same extent that the original theories did. Thus one can still meet many individuals in the gay community who are firmly convinced that they are genetically or hormonally predisposed to homosexuality, and thus bear no responsibility for their actions.

Failure to distinguish between what we are (our metaphysics) and what we do (our morals) can become a convenient excuse for bad behavior. If what I do proceeds from what I am, then it follows that if I am physically predisposed to be homosexual, then I must behave in a homosexual fashion. Although many members of the gay community do not use this line of reasoning, some homosexuals still cling tenaciously to this explanation for their behavior.

Mixing what we are with what we do may give us an excuse for our behavior, but it also causes a very grave problem. If I have to be homosexual because of a physical condition, then I also have no hope of change unless I can find some way to change my physical being. To date, there exists no evidence that such a change can be accomplished, so the homosexual is left without any hope if he believes he must be changed physically in order to change his behavior.

From the standpoint of biblical revelation, we cannot conclude that there is absolutely no possibility of physical predisposition to homosexuality. Since the Bible is silent on this subject, the only method of discovery open to us is that of honest, inductive scientific investigation. Up to now there appears to be no conclusive evidence that a person's genetic or hormonal makeup is a factor in the development of a homosexual sexual preference. But we do not fully comprehend the effects of the fall of man. Should we discover in the future that there is some connection between a person's genetic makeup and his sexual orientation, this should not surprise or upset the Christian. The question at that point would still be whether or not a physical disposition is a *cause* for behavior or only an *influence* upon it. If the latter is true, then the treatment of the homosexual condition would remain the same despite the presence of physical influences.

Some homosexuals ardently insist that they must have been born homosexual because they were attracted to the same sex at such an early age. It is common to hear men say that they were attracted to other men at the ages of ten or eleven. Others may even claim that they knew of their attraction to the same sex by the age of six or even four. There are two pertinent questions we must ask about these observations. First, are these memories of early childhood accurate—that is, did they actually occur? Second, are the men interpreting these experiences accurately? That is, were these experiences actually sexual attractions or perhaps only a need for male affection that is being interpreted as sexual in the light of subsequent sexual experiences? Even if the experiences are being correctly interpreted, this does not necessarily lead us to conclude that the person must have been born with a homosexual predisposition. The only conclusion we can draw from such reports is that the person's mind was affected at a very early age. We are still left with the question of exactly *how* the person was affected.

Until there is conclusive scientific evidence that the person was born with a genetic or hormonal tendency toward homosexuality, we will have to look for other explanations for the development of the homosexual condition.[1]

"INTERNAL" THEORIES

"Internal" theories are those theories that try to explain psychological disturbances on the basis of the inner workings of the person's mind with very little or no recourse to environmental factors. Psychologists who hold these theories tend to treat these phenomena as occurrences within the boundaries of the person's mind and lay little emphasis upon the environmental influences that may have brought them about. The major internal theories dealing with the development of the homosexual condition include factors of fear and confusion.

The terms *paranoia, fear, anxiety*, and *inhibition* appear frequently in the literature that addresses the question of how the homosexual preference develops. The three categories of fear most often cited are inhibition about asserting oneself, anxiety over general social contact, and fear of the opposite sex.

Fear of retaliation is often the underlying cause related to an inhibition about asserting oneself. Some counselors see the fear of retaliation as originating during childhood experiences of an-

---

[1]Some of the best information available concerning the lack of evidence to support the genetic or hormonal theories is found in the book *Homosexuals in the Christian Fellowship*, by David Atkinson (Grand Rapids, Mich.: Eerdmans, 1981).

gering the father or some authority figure by an effort to accomplish a task. Other counselors consider the fear as originating strictly from within and treat it as such. But regardless of its origin, an inhibition about asserting oneself can result in lack of discipline, passivity, laziness, and withdrawal from social contacts. Assertiveness is required to establish relationships with the opposite sex, so if a person is afraid of some real or supposed retaliation for his efforts, he is less likely to express assertiveness in social situations.

My friend John is a good example of this problem. John found it difficult to please his father. Whatever John did seemed to irritate his dad. After a while John gave up trying to impress his father with his accomplishments. John withdrew to a lonely world of solitude and fantasy through reading books. When we discussed John's laziness, passivity, and general lack of discipline, we traced these symptoms back to John's fear of retaliation. He lived with a constant foreboding that any effort to assert himself would result in punishment either from God or the people around him. Because John refused to exert the effort it takes to make and maintain friendships, he lived a very lonely life.

While many homosexuals do exhibit an inhibition about asserting themselves, certain questions arise about the relationship of this fear to the development of the homosexual preference. First, is this inhibition a symptom or a cause? That is, does the homosexual condition develop out of this inhibition, or is it the other way around? Second, since many heterosexually oriented people exhibit strong aversions to asserting themselves, is there any connection at all between this fear and the development of a sexual preference? Third, what is the exact nature of the origin of the inhibition? The answer to this last question will determine which course the counselor will take in the attempt to help the counselee overcome this fear.

The fear of asserting themselves is a factor in the lives of many homosexuals, but there does not seem to be enough evidence to support the idea that this inhibition can completely explain the development of a homosexual sexual preference.

Psychologists sometimes attribute a general anxiety over social contact to a lack of social skills or graces. The homosexual, they say, is a person who has not learned how to relate to other people within the context of his own cultural norms. Consequently, the person has trouble developing proper relationships with members of the opposite sex, and then turns to his own sex out of convenience. Again we must ask, is this a symptom or a cause? And what about the numerous heterosexuals who lack social skills? Why did they develop a heterosexual orientation? Although the counselor encounters many homosexuals who are deficient in social skills, this does not seem to explain fully the homosexual's attraction to the same sex.

Fear of the opposite sex ranks highest in the list of fears suggested as possible root causes of the homosexual condition. Some psychologists suggest that the affected person has somehow become afraid of the opposite sex and seeks sexual relationships with the same sex because he finds them less threatening. Although this may explain why a person does *not* want to relate to the opposite sex, it does not account for a positive attraction to the same sex. Again, some counselees do exhibit a strong aversion to the opposite sex, but this appears to be an exception rather than a rule. As with the other fears, we have to ask, is this a symptom or a cause? Also, what about men who are afraid of women but do not manifest a desire to relate sexually with men? Why did these men not develop homosexual tendencies? While some homosexuals report a fear of women, most speak in terms of lack of interest or absence of desire. Many male homosexuals will prefer a female counselor over a male and at the same time express little or no desire to relate to women sexually. So, while fear of the opposite sex is a problem in the lives of some homosexuals, it by no means explains the complexities of the homosexual condition.

These three fears—inhibition about asserting oneself, anxiety over general social contact, and fear of the opposite sex—are present in the lives of many counselees who have homosexual tendencies. As counselors, we should not underestimate the importance of these fears to the people who suffer from them. On the other hand, since many struggle with these fears who do not experience temptations toward homosexual involvement, we must question whether we are dealing with true causes or only symptoms. Practically speaking, it is important to keep these fears in mind as possible problems in the lives of those we seek to help, but we are forced to look elsewhere for explanation of the root causes of the development of the homosexual sexual preference.

Psychologists sometimes propose various forms of confusion as the possible origin of homosexual tendencies. Some speculate that the person becomes confused as to his or her role in society.

This is called gender-role confusion. Others think that the affected persons are actually confused as to their identity as male or female human beings. This is referred to as *gender-identity confusion.*

If the parents of a male child had wanted a female, they may be tempted to treat their boy as if he were a girl. They may dress him as a girl, buy him girls' toys, and involve him in activities appropriate for a little girl. Such child-rearing may create a confusion in the child's mind as to just how he is expected to behave in his society. Because he was treated as a female, he may respond as one and so want to relate to men sexually rather than women. Cases of gender-role confusion like this are sometimes uncovered during counseling, but they are definitely an exception rather than a rule. Other influences in the person's life may be applicable to the development of a homosexual orientation. While the possibility of gender-role confusion must be kept in mind during counseling, it does not explain the majority of cases of homosexuality.

"Gender-identity confusion" is more a description of the problem itself than an explanation of the source of the homosexual condition. If we define gender-identity confusion as a preference for a member of the same sex as the object of sexual desire, then this designation can be helpful. But if by gender-identity confusion we mean that the person is confused as to which sex he or she is, the clinical accuracy of the term is questionable. Although homosexuals readily admit a desire to relate affectionally or sexually to members of their own sex, very few seem to experience feelings of confusion as to exactly which sex they are. Counselees more often exhibit a general sense of identity confusion or "personal identity confusion" during counseling. Gender-identity confusion is a small sub-category of this general loss of identity. This would more accurately be a description of the problem known as transsexualism. In any case, the term "gender-identity confusion" only describes the problem—it does not explain the problem.

INTERPERSONAL THEORIES

The most profound influences in our lives come from the people around us. The relationships we have during early childhood often set the course for our entire lives. Because so much of our welfare is dependent upon our experiences with others, the area of interpersonal relationships is one of the most obvious places to investigate for the sources of psychological problems. I would like to take a brief look at three theories: traumatic sexual experiences, the "smother mother" or "mother fixation" theory, and the "weak" or "passive" father theory.

Traumatic sexual experiences are sometimes given as a reason for the beginning of homosexual tendencies in a person's life. These experiences could be heterosexual or homosexual in nature, voluntary or coerced.

Voluntary homosexual encounters are most often prompted by curiosity or a desire for affection. If the motivating factor is desire for affection, then it is evident that the person's mind has already been influenced toward a homosexual orientation. The sexual experience is then a result rather than a cause. If curiosity motivates the encounter, the experience will likely have very little effect on the development of the person's sexual orientation. Experimentation out of curiosity is a common childhood phenomenon that usually leaves very little lasting effect on the child's mind. If physical or emotional trauma accompanies the experience, this may affect the person's relational development but is still unlikely to have much bearing on the direction of sexual orientation.

When performance failure or rejection attend a voluntary heterosexual experience, an aversion toward future heterosexual encounters could develop. Many psychologists would call this a "heterophobic" response, that is, a fear of the opposite sex. While the influence of a negative sexual experience must not be overlooked during counseling, we still have to ask, "Are failure and rejection during voluntary heterosexual experience strong enough to mold sexual preference or only to influence future sexual behavior?" In most cases of this nature it appears as if sexual orientation was already well established before commission of the act, and the encounter had no effect on the person's sexual preference.

Since coerced sexual encounters tend to be more traumatic than voluntary experiences, the effect on the coerced party is usually more drastic. Molestation is always ugly. It would appear, however, that parental response to the event carries more weight for the child than the molestation itself. If the parents support the child, encourage the child to discuss his feelings about the event, and help the child to understand that he is not guilty for being victimized, then the child may come through the trauma relatively unscathed. Children tend to take their emotional cues from the parents' responses. During floods, for instance, the children of calm parents often treat the whole disaster as an adventure, while the children of fearful parents often become hysterical. It seems to work the same way with molestation. The parents' response will probably determine the child's outcome.

Homosexual molestation (which constitutes the *minority* of child-molestation cases) appears to have little effect upon determining the sexual tendencies of the child. If anything, one would expect that the child would develop a fear of the same sex rather than a homosexual attraction. In counseling homosexuals who were molested in childhood, I have found very little if any connection between these events and the origin of a homosexual preference. There are other factors which are much more common and more relevant to the person's sexual identity.

Another theory that has received much attention (especially from students of Freud) is the "smother mother," or the domineering mother. Psychologists call this "mother fixation" when the problem is viewed from the perspective of the child. The idea is that an abnormally strong attachment has developed between the mother and the male child. This unnatural attachment then affects the development of the child, pushing him toward feminine attitudes and actions. The final result of this unbalanced role-modeling is that the male child thinks of himself in feminine terms and is therefore attracted to men as objects of desire.

The difficulty with this theory is similar to some others we have reviewed. The question is, is this a symptom or a cause? Does "mother fixation" exist on its own and generate homosexual orientation, or is "mother fixation" a result of other factors in the child's life? I tend to agree with Elizabeth Moberly at this point. She suggests in her excellent book, *Homosexuality: A New Christian Ethic*, that an abnormal attachment to the mother is most likely the result of an abnormal detachment from the father (p. 8). The resultant "mother fixation" is then a symptom which may, in itself, have adverse side-effects, but is not the root cause of the homosexual condition.

One theory comes closest to answering the question of how the homosexual orientation develops. This theory is often designated as the "weak father" theory, or the "passive father" theory. In this theory the main characters of the homosexual drama are finally unveiled—the father and the son. The theory states that because the father is weak or passive, the son loses his appropriate role model and relates to the mother for modeling, thus developing feminine traits. The weakness I see in this idea is that having a weak or passive father will not, in itself, produce in the male child the elements necessary for the origin of a homosexual sexual preference. Many men who are thoroughly heterosexual have had weak fathers. Conversely, many men who have a homosexual condition have had very strong, aggressive fathers. So it is not the element of weakness in itself that explains the beginning of the homosexual condition, but weakness may be one of the factors related to the entire problem. It seems that a constellation of contributing factors comes together to form the environment for the development of a homosexual sexual preference.

CHAPTER FOUR

WHAT WENT WRONG?

The darkness in the bar enfolded us, giving me the impression that ours was the only conversation in the world as we stood close together to hear each other over the blare of the driving rock music. The depth of intimacy in our conversation amazed me, considering our surroundings. As we leaned on the bar we spoke of our lives, our dreams, and our families.

"Tell me about your father," I ventured.

"I never really knew my father," he said. "He left our family when I was very young."

It's the same old story, I thought. *The same old story.*

"My dad was never around."

"Our father never spoke to us unless he was angry."

"Dad was so aggressive that he scared me out of talking with him."

"My father never touched me except to beat me."

"My mom and dad were divorced when I was two."

Again and again I hear the same old story. Even when the preliminary account sounds fairly good, a close check into the situation usually reveals that the homosexual man has had some kind of relationship problem with his father. Sometimes the father was gone entirely. Sometimes he was present but was uncommunicative with the children. In some cases the father was so volatile that the sensitive male child withdrew to protect himself. But always, always there was some kind of breakdown in the father-son relationship.

Family relationships are very complex, and many problems can develop. Some people would have us think the problems are so intricate that they are impossible to solve. But counseling is possible because amid all the problems are traceable patterns

49

useful for diagnosing and treating the related problems. One of the most prevalent patterns in the life of the male homosexual is the disturbed father-son relationship.

God strongly emphasizes the importance of good family relations—God's Word is filled with instruction about how a family should operate. He clearly describes the responsibilities of fathers, mothers, and children, showing His obvious concern that we know how to have good families.

This abundance of material also teaches us another important lesson: When the family breaks down, the consequences can be devastating. Our family background affects what we think about ourselves, other people, and even God himself. And since our behavior proceeds from our thoughts, our entire lives can be influenced by our family relations. The development of a person's sexual orientation, for instance, is directly linked to his relationship with his parents—particularly with his same-sex parent. Because of the important role-modeling that the same-sex parent will perform for the child, any disturbance in this parent-child relationship may affect the child's idea of his own identity.

A "constellation" of factors converges to produce an atmosphere that aids the development of the homosexual orientation. Those factors, along with the process of the development of a homosexual lifestyle, provide two foundations for helping the homosexual: first, an understanding of the basic needs of the person with a homosexual orientation; and second, a strategy of counseling to direct the person along the road to healing.

THE BASIC ELEMENTS

In any developmental problem of human personality we always find the factors of people, places, and events. In this discussion we will concentrate on the *people* and the *events*. (The physical environment surrounding the development of a homosexual preference is usually a minor factor.) The major characters in the story are the child and his same-sex parent, including other family members as they become relevant to the story. The events of the drama consist of the interactions between the child and the same-sex parent as we observe the history of the development of a homosexual condition. This history can be summed up in one word: rejection.

THE PROCESS

In the complex process of human personality development, many factors contribute to the building of one personality. Sifting through case histories thus can pose a real challenge. In the midst of the investigation, however, patterns do emerge, revealing an interesting and useful process.

The five-step process of rejection outlined below is not an iron-clad explanation of the development of homosexual tendencies. The elements will vary with each person's case, so the application must vary to fit the counselee. The explanation, however, provides a framework that helps to explain a majority of cases of homosexuality, thus providing a strategy for counseling.

1. *Rejection by the father.* The first step toward homosexuality is that the male child is rejected in some way by the father. Whether it is passive or aggressive, real or supposed, the rejection nevertheless *feels* real to the child.

Rejection can be communicated to a child in many different ways. Perhaps the father neglected the family by remaining away from home for long periods of time. Maybe he worked out of town, only returning home for weekends. In other cases the father could have been home consistently, but was distant or uncommunicative with the child. Again, maybe the father was killed in an accident when the child was very young. The father may be culpable or innocent for his absence (in body or attitude), but the child can still interpret the absence as rejection by the father. These are illustrations of *passive rejection.*

Aggressive rejection occurs when the father responds in anger to the child, who then withdraws emotionally, and sometimes physically, in order to protect himself. Many homosexuals say fear of their fathers drove them to hide in their bedrooms to avoid angry confrontations. But whether the father's actions are passive or aggressive, the result can be the same. The child feels rejected by the father.

Many of the hurts we experience are unintentional. That is, the other person did not intend to hurt us by what he did or said. But the person who supposes the hurt to be real feels the hurt as if it were intentional, so, whether the father purposes to hurt the child or not, the child may still feel hurt. As mentioned in the previous chapter, weakness or passivity in a father will not, in itself, cause problems for the child. The real problem is the child's interpretation of the weakness or passivity of the father.

2. *Rejection of the father.* The child responds to the real or supposed fatherly rejection by rejecting his father in return. This rejection also may be passive or aggressive.

Children often withdraw emotionally from their parents when they feel rejected because they cannot (or will not) effectively deal with their anger. Since parents often interpret such "coldness" as sulking, they either ignore the response or become angry with the child, thus increasing the child's sense of rejection, beginning a cycle of responses which aggravates the sense of separation between the parents and the child. In extreme cases of this kind, the child may even cease to communicate with the outside world.

If a child has an aggressive temperament, he may respond to rejection with bitterness and resentment or outright hostility, which often will be met with greater rejection from the father, thus compounding the situation. Again, a cycle of responses starts that drives the father and son further from each other. But whether the child's rejection of the father is passive or aggressive, the result is still a relational breakdown between father and son.

3. *Rejection of the male image.* The child rejects the image of "maleness" for himself.

Identification with the father is a necessary step in the development of a proper male image in the male child. If this identification process has been aborted by rejection and hurt, the male child may refuse the "male image" for himself. Children think concretely. Consequently, when a child is hurt by someone, he fails to analyze and categorize different painful events. Thus, if a man hurts him, a child may generalize and conclude that all men are dangerous. The child may even go one step further and think, *If men are that way, then I don't want to be like them,* thus rejecting the image of maleness for himself and refusing to be identified with it. Of course, the small child will not do this consciously, but as a "gut-level" emotional reaction. In Christian terms, the child is responding intuitively from his spirit and not from his natural mind.

C. S. Lewis once observed that hatred blurs all distinctions. For the man who hates black people, there are no good blacks and bad blacks. They are all bad. For the person who hates country-western music, there is no good country-western music. It is all bad. In the same way, for the child who hates his father there are no good and bad traits in his father. His father is simply bad.

So when the child rejects the father out of hurt, he rejects the male image along with the father.

At this point the notion of "mother fixation" enters the picture. Because the child has refused to align himself with the male image, he is left with his mother as the only other parent with whom to identify himself. Mother fixation, therefore, is more symptomatic than causative. The child who has disassociated himself from his father naturally attempts a closer relationship with the mother, though she may not reciprocate.

4. *Rejection of self.* The child adopts a view of personal worthlessness.

When a person is rejected, he receives many negative messages from the person who rejects him. The messages may refer to the sender: I don't love you, I don't appreciate you, I don't want to be around you. Or, the messages may be interpreted by the rejected person as referring to himself: You are not acceptable, you are not lovable, you are worthless. If a person hears this often enough, he may begin to believe these evaluations are true. His perception of himself is then determined by the lies communicated to him by the people who rejected him. This untrue estimation of the person's value is what constitutes a bad self-image.

If a child believes he is worthless, his emotions will respond to his thoughts about himself, and the child will feel badly about himself. In a sense, he rejects himself.

Homosexuals commonly manifest very poor self-images. They frequently think, speak, and act in accordance with the false ideas they have about their own value. Once as I spoke with a homosexual man about his value, he began to weep. Amid sobs he said, "I don't know how anybody could love me. I'm so awful." He was not referring to his lifestyle, but to his concept of his value as a human being. If, as this man, a person *thinks* he is worthless, he will *feel* worthless, and will *treat himself* as worthless.

Such lies about who a man is and what he is worth could also be called an identity crisis. For instance, the son feels rejected by the father, so the son rejects the father. He also rejects the male image for himself. By refusing to be identified with his father, the son has an identity crisis. Because of rejection by the father, the son thinks and feels he is worthless. Thus the son rejects himself.

This self-rejection leaves the child in a position of great personal need. All human beings have basic personal needs; besides our physical needs, there are psychological needs. We all need to know who we are. We need to feel important. We need a sense of power and competence as a person. We need to know what our value is, our self-worth. Some of our other personal needs are the need to be loved, to feel secure, to be needed by someone else, to receive affection from others. God created us with these needs, and there is nothing wrong with our having them.

But God did not only create us with needs. He also gave us desires corresponding to these needs so that we would work on getting our needs fulfilled. We have a need for love. We also have a desire for love. Both the need and the desire are valid. It is also legitimate for us to work on getting our needs met. But how and why we try to meet our needs can either bring us fulfillment or cause us great sorrow.

A child needs the affection of both parents. The male child requires both male and female affection. When a breakdown occurs in the relationship with one of his parents, the child misses the affection of that parent. The need for this gender-specific affection goes unmet, and the child may grow into adulthood with a love deficiency. Thus, when a male child has lost the affection of his father, he may grow up with an unusually strong, valid, but unmet need for male affection. His need is valid, and trying to get this need met is also valid. But how can he fulfill this need in a valid, constructive fashion?

5. *Rejection of others.* As a result of his hurt, the child begins to reject other people. The child has been rejected by his father. Rejecting the father and the male image, the child begins to have an identity crisis. Based on his erroneous self-image, the child will begin to reject both men and women, although for different reasons.

An unmet need for male affection places the male child in an awkward position. Though he has rejected the male image and disassociated himself from it, he still misses the affection he did not receive from his father. At the same time he both dislikes the male image and desires male affection. This dilemma begins early in the boy's life and continues with him through puberty and into adulthood.

The man's rejection of women is perhaps harder to understand. Refusal to embrace the male image for himself makes it difficult for him to relate to women as *heteros*—as "other." Lack of association with "maleness" makes it difficult for him to relate to women as "opposite" and as objects of desire. In the course of normal development, a man comes to completion in his sense of maleness and then turns to the qualities in the female to complete him as a person. In the case of the male homosexual, it appears as if the sense of completion as a man is arrested by the rejection process. Thus the man is still looking for male qualities to make him feel complete. Female qualities are not attractive to him since he still needs to incorporate male qualities to finish the development of the male image in his life.

Passive rejection of women—a lack of interest—seems to result when the man has had a fairly good relationship with his mother. Aggressive rejection of women—sometimes exhibited as open hostility—seems to be related to a background of bitterness and resentment toward the mother. In either case the man does not relate to women as objects of desire because of his failure to embrace "maleness" for himself.

This leaves the man in the position of wanting and needing male affection, while at the same time not desiring women. Therefore the man may try to fulfill his need for love in the only way that makes sense to him—by entering into a homosexual lifestyle.

A MATTER OF CONFUSION

"What were you looking for when you had your first homosexual experience?" I have asked many gay men this question and have received many and varied responses. But there is one answer I have never heard: "sex." Each was seeking affection, companionship, communication, identity, or security—but never sex. This curious silence made me wonder about the relationship of sex to human needs in the homosexual's life.

There is a false idea that runs rampant in our society—the notion that sex is the most intimate expression of affection: If you love someone, and want to show the person affection, you have sex with him or her. During their moments of objective reflection, most people will admit that sex does not equal affection. Ask any prostitute if affection always accompanies sex. Yet, because sex *can* be an expression of affection, it is understandable how this false equation can result. As a consequence of this incorrect idea, many people enter into sexual experiences hoping to receive or to communicate affection.

People often attempt to fulfill their basic human needs through a relationship with another person. When sex is a part of the relationship, a kind of psychological confusion may set in. If sex is associated long enough with the meeting of basic needs, the person may begin to assume falsely that sex itself can meet his needs. This kind of confusion can project the person into a lifestyle of promiscuity as he tries desperately to meet his basic human needs through sex. Thinking that his needs for self-worth, love, identity, or security can be met by having sex with someone is called sexualizing or eroticizing his needs.

Most homosexually oriented men do not enter into relationships with other men just to have sex. Rather, they are trying to fulfill their needs for unconditional love and a sense of identity. But sex often plays a part in these relationships, and after a while confusion may occur. The man may begin to think sex will meet his basic needs, so he attempts to satisfy his needs in that way. Since sex is such a powerful, pleasurable experience, it can quickly reinforce any behavior associated with it. This is how the habit patterns of thinking (sexualization) and behavior (promiscuity) can so quickly become entrenched in the homosexual's life.

The man who has endured the rejection process as a child has a strong desire for male affection. A homosexual lifestyle thus appears to offer a source of warmth, affection, and love, so in an effort to have his needs met, he may enter the "gay community," establishing friendships with homosexual men. Since sex is considered the most intimate form of affection, sex soon becomes a regular part of the friendships. As he associates sex with the fulfillment of his basic needs, the man sexualizes his needs, thinking sex will give him identity, security, or love. Eventually he is thoroughly entangled in the homosexual lifestyle.

Sexualization of needs is a powerful influence toward committing sexual sin. As long as a man thinks he needs to do a particular thing to meet his needs, he will participate in that behavior. If a person can learn to separate his real needs from the sexualization of those needs and then meet the needs in the right manner, he can learn to be free from that false method of fulfillment.

"BUT MY BROTHER'S NOT GAY"

People often wonder why one male child in a family may develop a homosexual orientation while a male sibling of nearly the same age will not. If two brothers, they ask, are raised by the same father in the same environment, then why is one gay and the other not? This good question is relevant to the "constellation" of factors contributing to the homosexual condition.

The reason actually seems quite simple. A comparison of the general temperament of the homosexually and heterosexually oriented brothers usually reveals that the homosexually oriented man has a sensitive temperament and tends toward passivity. The heterosexually oriented brother, on the other hand, is usually more aggressive and less sensitive. The more sensitive the child, the more easily and deeply he can be hurt, so rejection by the father is more likely to adversely affect the sensitive son than his aggressive counterpart.

Another related factor is preferential treatment by the father. It is possible for a parent to treat one child quite differently from another (e.g. Jacob's favoritism toward Joseph and Benjamin). So, while it appears that the brothers have the same father, in actuality each may have a different relationship with him.

One more relevant factor is the introduction of an appropriate father-figure at a crucial time in the child's development. If, after the father's rejection, the boy finds a suitable father-figure, his father's rejection may not result in the development of a homosexual orientation in the child.

THE FEMALE HOMOSEXUAL

The development of the homosexual condition in the female child largely parallels that in the male child. The same-sex parent is crucial to the process, so the mother-daughter relationship is the most important in this case, and the process of rejection is essentially the same. There are, however, a few major differences.

First, the female homosexual's sense of rejection is more often related to actual acts of rejection, whereas the male homosexual complains more frequently of the absence of the father.

Second, female homosexuals usually exhibit more heterophobia (fear of the opposite sex) than do male homosexuals. This is almost always related to some very traumatic events in the woman's life. Often the girl was beaten or sexually molested by her father or some other male relative. In some cases the girl felt rejected by the mother because the mother would not believe the girl when she claimed to have been molested by the father. The very person the girl expected to protect her would not help her.

Third, I have found more female homosexuals who hate men than I have found male homosexuals who hate women. Many male homosexuals have had good relationships with their mothers, whereas most female homosexuals complain of mistreatment by their fathers.

Female homosexuals seem to have an easier time receiving emotional healing than their male counterparts. Perhaps it is easier to deal with overt acts of rejection that caused hurt than to completely rebuild an image which was absent from the person's life. Repenting of bitterness and resentment over concrete acts is easier than trying to relate to a "vacuum" in the mind that is supposed to be filled with the image of one's father. Repentance and forgiveness come more readily than re-education.

IS IT ALL THAT SIMPLE?

Human development is very complex, making it virtually impossible to explain all the intricacies of the homosexual orientation. The rejection process described above, the comments about the sensitive male child, and the remarks about the female homosexual are intended only to provide a general view of the problem. With the complexities of life there will always be exceptions. But exceptions should not hinder us from recognizing general principles that can stir compassion to aid hurting people and encourage believers to guide others along the road to stable Christian living.

CHAPTER FIVE

WHAT DOES THE BIBLE SAY?

I f God loves me so much, why does He say I can't be gay? All I'm trying to do is meet my need for love just like anybody else. So why can't I do it with a man instead of a woman?"

"Being gay is completely natural for me. Why does God demand that I act in an unnatural fashion? It's being heterosexual that would feel unnatural to me."

"The Bible was written by a bunch of straight, bigoted Jews who were out to preserve a bloodline."

"You say the Bible says I shouldn't be gay. The Bible also says you shouldn't eat oysters, or pork, or rare steak. So, why pick on homosexuality as something I shouldn't do when you do those other things yourself? Aren't you being a hypocrite?"

Gays frequently express sentiments like these when they are brought face-to-face with what God says about homosexuality. While it is true that they are usually responding to what they think God has said rather than what God really said, it still appears to them that God is against them. If they are loving others and not hurting anyone, they say, shouldn't they be free to find love any way they please? These are tough and important questions that deserve sensitive answers. We are dealing with the feelings, aspirations, even the very lives of real people and need to handle the issues with a delicate seriousness.

WHY GOD SAYS "NO"

The cold, wet weather had kept the patronage at the bar minimal. I stood in the outdoor patio shivering from the cold.

The lack of clientele made it easier to converse with the bartender. Since he had no one to serve, he had plenty of time to talk.

A customer approached the bar and ordered a drink. He introduced himself to the bartender and me. "Name's Fred," he said, shaking our hands.

We chatted informally about the weather and other trivial subjects. Fred seemed to be thoughtful and observant as we spoke. When the bartender walked into the other section of the bar to do some work, Fred focused his attention on me.

"He's from the East Coast, isn't he?" Fred said, referring to the bartender.

"Yes, he is," I said, noting that Fred was very perceptive of accents and mannerisms. What Fred said next, though, indicated that his perceptions were more than normal.

"And you're very religious, and the bartender is not."

All I could do was stare at him. We had not discussed or even mentioned religion, God, or any related subject. Yet Fred could perceive the spiritual status of both the bartender and me.

As the conversation progressed I discovered that Fred was a hospital administrator with responsibilities involving the work of over three hundred people. He was intelligent, mature, and spiritually perceptive. He was also a committed relativist.

When the subject changed to moral absolutes, I could feel that Fred was becoming tense and agitated. He could not see why anyone, including God, should insist that there were moral absolutes. It seemed arbitrary, bigoted, and harsh to him. I decided it would be best to place the subject in a less religious framework.

"Ask any psychologist or psychiatrist if stealing, lying, murder, and adultery are beneficial activities for a human being. Except for a few professionals on the fringes, almost every psychologist will tell you that a person harms himself when he does these things. It is simply not healthful for a person to do whatever he wants."

Fred nodded agreement.

"Because God loves us," I continued, "He has told us which behavior will benefit us and which will hurt us. God is not arbitrary in His commands. He only forbids our doing what will destroy us."

"Yes, I understand," Fred said. "It sounds reasonable."

"And so if God has forbidden any kind of sexual activity, it is because He loves us and knows that behavior will harm us."

To this Fred made no response. He stared at me for a moment, turned, and walked away. He understood the truth, but was not willing to face it.

God knows what He is doing. As the infinite, personal, loving governor of the universe, He knows exactly how things should run. In His vast wisdom and love for us, God established laws in the universe. He gave us these laws, both physical and moral, for our well-being. If we try to live in opposition to these laws, we will only harm ourselves. If we try to deny the law of gravity, we will pay the consequences. Breaking the moral law of God also has its consequences. In order to protect us, God commanded us not to break these laws. Thus, His commands are not arbitrary; He is not being a killjoy. He has only commanded us not to do what will destroy us. Whatever He commands is for our good (Deut. 10:12, 13). This is why God says "No."

We finite humans often try to second-guess God. We somehow think we can figure out a better way to live than God has already shown. God says, "Love your neighbor as yourself," and we think we can determine what is loving and what is not. But God has already declared what love is and is not by the commands He has given. Love is the fulfillment of the law (Rom. 13:10), so any breaking of the law of God is an unloving act. Now, a man may think that he is doing something loving if he comforts a grieving, married woman by having sex with her. But God has declared that adultery is not loving. So, no matter how loving the person thinks he is, God has declared him unloving. There is no loving way to commit adultery.

We humans also want to know the reason for everything. Though God knows perfectly what the consequences of any choice will be, he does not always tell us the reason that something is good or bad for us. It is not unreasonable to obey a command without a stated reason when the command has come from an all-knowing, all-wise, all-loving Creator and Ruler. In some cases, we can figure out for ourselves why a particular activity is detrimental for us. In other cases we must simply trust God's wisdom and love. In His wisdom and love toward us, God has spoken to us about the importance of proper sexual conduct. Along with this instruction He included some significant statements about the subject of homosexuality.

There are only seven major passages in the Bible that deal directly with homosexuality. These passages fall into three categories. First, there are the historical references. Second, there are legal references. Third, there are instructions in the New

Testament epistles. Besides these direct references, there is some mention of male cult prostitution in a few Old Testament scriptures.[1]

The interpretation of the Bible texts generates many questions, and people who are attempting to mix the homosexual and Christian lifestyles often ask the most pertinent questions. Since other Christian authors have given rebuttals to the "gay Christian" interpretations of these texts,[2] I will only mention some major objections to the "gay hermeneutic" for these passages. My purpose in investigating these Scriptures is to discover what God's Word says about helping the homosexual. I am not intending to give a complete theological discourse on the interpretation of these texts.

THE HISTORICAL PASSAGES

Probably no other scripture passage about homosexuality is as well known as the story of Sodom and Gomorrah. Because of this event, words like "sodomy" and "sodomize" are a part of the English language. Until recent years there was little controversy over the meaning of this text. With the advent of the "gay Christian" movement, serious disputes arose about how we should understand this bit of Bible history. Let's take a look at the text itself.

> Before they lay down, the men of the city, the men of Sodom, surrounded the house, both young and old, all the people from every quarter; and they called to Lot and said to him, "Where are the men who came to you tonight? Bring them out to us that we may have relations with them."
>
> But Lot went out to them at the doorway, and shut the door behind him, and said, "Please, my brothers, do not act wickedly. Now behold, I have two daughters who have not had relations with man; please let me bring them out to you, and do to them whatever you like; only do nothing to these men, inasmuch as they have come under the shelter of my roof."
>
> But they said, "Stand aside." Furthermore, they said, "This one came in as an alien, and already he is acting like a judge; now we will treat you worse than them." So they pressed hard

---

[1]Deut. 23:17; 1 Kings 14:24; 15:12; 22:46; 2 Kings 23:7; Job 36:14.
[2]Kent Philpott, *The Gay Theology* (Plainfield, N.J.: Logos International, 1977).
   Ronald M. Enroth and Gerald E. Jamison, *The Gay Church* (Grand Rapids, Mich.: Eerdmans, 1974), Chapter 3.
   Richard Lovelace, *Homosexuality: What Should Christians Do about It?* (Old Tappan, N.J.: Fleming H. Revell Company, 1984).

against Lot and came near to break the door.

But the men reached out their hands and brought Lot into the house with them, and shut the door. And they struck the men who were at the doorway of the house with blindness, both small and great, so that they wearied themselves trying to find the doorway. (Gen. 19:4–11)

The orthodox interpretation of this passage has remained the same for centuries. Scholars and laymen alike have understood this scripture in a straightforward manner. It appears that these verses are referring to attempted homosexual assault on two angels who appeared in human form. Since the emergence of the "homosexual Christian" movement, gay theologians have suggested alternative interpretations of this ancient text.

One of the recent alternative explanations is that this story has nothing to do with normal homosexual relationships. Rather, it is an account of homosexual gang rape. Some theologians then argue that God is not condemning normal homosexual relationships, but rather the gang rape. But Lot understood the attempted assault to be wicked, not only on account of its violence, but also its homosexual nature. Would heterosexual gang rape be better than homosexual gang rape? Lot seemed to think so. One could argue over whether Lot's assessment of the situation was proper, but Lot's offer of his daughters tells us that he was applying the word "wicked" to the homosexual aspect of the act, not just to the gang rape.[3] To equate homosexual gang rape with what happens between two consenting male adults would be unfair. These acts are not the same. But the implication of the Genesis passage is clear. Not only was the attempted rape evil, but the homosexual nature of the act was also deemed wicked. It is true that God is not commenting on normal homosexual relationships in this text, but He is referring to homosexual acts.

Some people argue that the story of Sodom is only a culturally prejudiced example to discourage Hebrews from homosexuality. Others might think that the story is only a fanciful myth. These opinions reveal much more about the person's attitude toward the Scriptures than his position on homosexuality. It is clear from

---

[3]God makes no comment in His Word about the morality of Lot's offer of his daughters. The Bible simply records the history as it happened. On the basis of other principles, it is clear that the offer was improper, if not evil, because people are not allowed to do evil that good may result (Rom. 3:8). But whether Lot's actions were right or wrong, they tell us that he thought the homosexual aspect of the assault was evil.

such statements that the person views the Bible as the work of man rather than the inspired Word of God. The response to these arguments would have to be a validation of the Bible as God's Word rather than a discussion about homosexuality.

Another rebuttal to the usual interpretation contends that the word "to know," which is often translated as "to have (sexual) relations with," could be referring to the extension of hospitality. In other words, the residents of Sodom were guilty of a lack of hospitality. In order to rectify this they came to Lot late at night to make up to the men for their discourtesy. This may seem a fanciful interpretation, but it is espoused by some gay scholars. In the light of the passage itself, it is easy to see the problems with this reasoning. First, who ever heard of vicarious hospitality? How could the men of the city make up for their lack of hospitality by showing hospitality to Lot's daughters? Second, why did Lot call their offer of hospitality "wicked"? Third, why did Lot offer his daughters to them? Fourth, what difference did it make to the men that Lot's daughters were virgins? Fifth, why did the men try to mistreat Lot? It seems obvious from the words of the text that this is no story about hospitality.

There is good reason for the traditional interpretation of the Sodom story. A simple reading of the text warrants that conclusion. The application of good hermeneutical principles upholds the traditional view. The recent haggling over the fine points of this passage has come mostly from those who have a vested interest in the outcome of the interpretation. But it is hard to ignore the obvious implications of the scripture. Homosexuality may have been only one of many sins committed by the residents of Sodom, but immorality is given as an example of their wickedness and a as reason for their destruction.[4]

The next relevant historical passage is Judges, chapter nineteen. This text records the attempted homosexual assault of a Levite and the actual sexual assault on his concubine.

> While they were making merry, behold, the men of the city, certain worthless fellows, surrounded the house, pounding the door; and they spoke to the owner of the house, the old man, saying; "Bring out the man who came into your house that we may have relations with him."
> Then the man, the owner of the house, went out to them and said to them, "No, my fellows, please do not act so wickedly; since this man has come into my house, do not commit this act

---

[4]C.f. Gen. 13:13; 18:20–21; 19:1–11; Jer. 23:14; 2 Pet. 2:4–11; Jude 1:7–8.

of folly. Here is my virgin daughter and his concubine. Please
let me bring them out that you may ravish them and do to them
whatever you wish. But do not commit such an act of folly
against this man."

But the men would not listen to him, so the man seized his
concubine and brought her out to them. And they raped her
and abused her all night until morning, then let her go at the
approach of dawn.

As the day began to dawn, the woman came and fell down
at the doorway of the man's house where her master was, until
full daylight. (verses 22–26)

The next morning the woman's master found her dead at
the doorway. He put her body on his donkey, went home, carved
her body into twelve pieces, and sent one piece to each of the
tribes of Israel. Civil war followed, and one of the tribes of Israel
was nearly annihilated.

The details of this gruesome and tragic story are strikingly
similar to the Sodom account. A man was a guest in another
man's home. The men of the city surrounded the house. The
purpose of the men was to homosexually assault the guest. Ech-
oing the words of Lot, the old man said, "Do not act so wickedly."
To this he added, "Do not commit this act of folly." The man
considered the acts of the men of the city to be both wicked and
foolish. As in the Genesis story, the men offered women to the
would-be attackers. In this case, though, there were no angels to
help the men, and one of the women was abused to the point of
death.

One major difference between this account and the Genesis
story is that God gives no assessment of the situation from His
viewpoint. Here we have only the opinion of man. God does
make a general statement about the entire history of the Book
of Judges. He says that every man was doing what was right in
his own eyes. In other words, the people did what they wanted
and refused to follow the law of God. In this way God does make
a comment on the story of the Levite and his concubine. Other
than that, though, we have only the record of how people felt
about the event.

There is another difference between the accounts. In Genesis, the story of Sodom is a pre-Decalogue event—that is, the story
occurred before the giving of the Law at Sinai. The Judges account is post-Decalogue history. This is significant because it indicates that the people involved in the accounts were possibly
responding to different elements of moral law. In Sodom, Lot

could only be responding to an innate or intuitive sense of right and wrong, since the written law did not exist at that time. In Gibeah, the old man could have been reacting to both intuitive and written moral law, since the Law had been given before his time. So, whether the sense of morality originated in intuitive or written moral law, the conclusion was the same. They both regarded homosexual acts as wicked.

The lesson of the historical passages is simple. Whether from God's or man's perspective, homosexual acts were seen in these cases as acts of wickedness. This conclusion should not be interpreted to mean that God is against homosexuals as people. God loves everybody and wants every person to have abundant life through Jesus. But when an activity is contrary to that abundant life, God prohibits the detrimental behavior for our well-being. If God's disagreement with destructive activities meant that He did not love us, then He would love no one, for we are all sinners.

What these passages do *not* say is also worth noting. It is interesting that these texts never mention the homosexual orientation, homosexual desires, or anything related to the psychological aspect of homosexuality. Only the act or behavior of homosexuality is presented. This is important because by not referring to sexual orientation, the idea of "wickedness" is limited strictly to the behavior of homosexuality. If a person with a homosexual orientation reads these scriptures without noting what God does *not* say, he may be left with a feeling of condemnation over his thoughts and desires. These stories only discuss sexual behavior, and the texts cannot and should not be used to condemn those who have a homosexual condition.

THE LEGAL REFERENCES

Being introduced to someone as a missionary has its advantages and its disadvantages. It can be helpful in that you don't have to figure out how to bring Christianity into the conversation. One of the drawbacks is that the other person's preconceived ideas about what a missionary is and what missionaries think are projected on you before you even start talking. Jeff had introduced me to Mike as a missionary, and the conversation was difficult from the start.

"I suppose that as an evangelical you think homosexuality is a sin," Mike said. His tone wasn't accusative, but I knew I needed to answer carefully.

"That depends on what you mean by 'homosexuality,' " I replied, trying to keep the conversation open.

"By that I mean sexual activity, not tendency."

Good, I thought. *At least we don't have to define the difference between orientation and behavior.*

"Well," Mike continued, "I consider myself to be an evangelical Christian also, but I find nothing in the Bible that says I shouldn't be involved in homosexual relationships."

" 'You shall not lie with a man as one lies with a woman' seems pretty clear to me," I said, trying not to sound harsh or condescending.

"But I bet you don't keep all those other laws in the Old Testament. What about not eating oysters, or pork, or rare steak? Do you keep those laws?" A valid point, but Mike's tone indicated that he was more interested in winning an argument than in discovering truth. Since further discussion would be fruitless, I turned the conversation to more personal matters. The exchange ended well, yet I felt frustrated that his attitude prevented our considering God's Word in greater detail.

The reference I quoted is one of the two Levitical codes against homosexual acts. These two texts state almost the same thing, and appear in nearly the same context:

> You shall not lie with a male as one lies with a female; it is an abomination. (Lev. 18:22)
> If there is a man who lies with a male as those who lie with a woman, both of them have committed a detestable act; they shall surely be put to death. Their bloodguiltiness is upon them. (Lev. 20:13)

These commandments are found in a series of laws that God commanded the Israelites to observe in the land of Canaan. Capital punishment was the penalty assigned to violation of the commands (concerning the first reference, see verse 29 of the same chapter). God's appointment of the death penalty to the breaking of these laws indicates two very significant principles: First, the law was not only a moral precept, but also a civil law. The Israelites observed this as a law of their nation. Second, the severity of the penalty was an indication of the importance of the moral precept behind the commands.

Great misunderstanding takes place in people's minds when they do not distinguish between the different kinds of law in the Old Testament. There are at least five major kinds of law described in the Old Testament, but many people lump them all together into "the Law." It is this kind of confusion that makes some of the most common objections to the Bible possible. For instance, some unbelievers ask why the Old Testament says "an eye for an eye, and a tooth for a tooth," while the New Testament teaches us to love our enemies and turn the other cheek. The point is that these are two different kinds of law. "An eye for an eye" is a civil injunction limiting the amount of punishment for certain crimes. In other words, if someone pokes out your eye, you might want to kill him. The law allows you only to take out the other person's eye. Remember, though, that this is *civil* law.

The Old Testament *moral* law which applies to the situation is "You shall not take vengeance, nor bear any grudge against the sons of your people, but you shall love your neighbor as yourself; I am the Lord" (Lev. 19:18). Another precept that applies is Prov. 25:21, which states: "If your enemy is hungry, give him food to eat; and if he is thirsty, give him water to drink." So the moral precepts of the Old and New Testaments are the same. You should love your enemy. The problems come in when people compare the *moral* precepts of the New Testament with the *civil* laws of the Old. The civil law stated what you *could* do; the moral precepts stated what you *should* do. You could take out one eye for one eye. You should love your enemy and forgive him.

The five kinds of law mentioned above entail: (1) physical law, (2) moral law, (3) civil law, (4) ceremonial law, and (5) what I will call "circumstantial law."

Physical laws are the cause-and-effect-forces that God created into the universe to keep the non-living material in order. The law of gravity and the laws of chemistry would be examples. Inasmuch as instincts are laws of force, they would also be classified as physical laws since given the proper stimulus you get the appropriate response.

Moral laws are those principles related to absolute right and wrong. They constitute the sense of "oughtness" perceived by moral (free-will) beings. "Thou shalt not steal" is the verbal expression of a moral precept. These laws, by definition, cannot change since they are based on the nature of God and man.

Civil laws are the laws used for the temporal government of a body of people. These laws relate to moral precepts, but may or may not correctly embody absolute right and wrong. This would account for the difference between righteous and unrighteous laws. In the case of the Israelites, the civil laws would have been righteous, since the laws were being instituted by the Moral Governor of the human race.

The *ceremonial laws* that concern us are the regulations related to the religious life of the Israelites. These laws governed the activities of the priests and the worshipers. These laws were pictures, or symbols, of spiritual realities: once the realities were fulfilled in the life of the worshiper, the symbols were no longer necessary. Thus, the ceremonial laws were superseded by a spiritual reality, and the ceremonial laws became obsolete and unnecessary. It is not that the law was abolished, but that it was fulfilled in another manner.

A good example of this is the prohibition against eating blood. Although eating blood is not, in itself, an evil practice, the Israelites were forbidden to eat it. This restriction was imposed because the ceremonial shedding of blood symbolized the future death of the Son of God. This foreshadowing was so important that God assigned capital punishment as the penalty for eating blood, thus making a civil law out of the ceremonial. After the death of Christ, the prohibition was no longer necessary. The death of Christ fulfilled the ceremonial symbol, and the symbol became obsolete.

Animal sacrifices are another good example of the same principle. God instituted the sacrifice of animals to "cover" people's sin until the death of Christ, through which sin could be "taken away" or completely cleansed. Once Jesus died, the animal sacrifices were no longer necessary since the spiritual reality had come, as recorded in Heb. 10:1–18, the marvelous description of how Christ's death supersedes animal sacrifice.

Circumstantial laws are those laws related to special circumstances and thus would apply only as long as the circumstances existed. The regulations governing the handling of manna would be one example. As long as the people had manna to eat, they were responsible to follow the injunctions concerning when to collect it, how much to collect per person, how to cook it, and how long to keep it. When the Israelites entered the land of Canaan, the manna stopped, and so did the necessary requirements for handling manna. Another example is the body of laws relating to the "camp" of the Israelites. Once the Israelites lived in villages instead of a camp, the regulations relating to the camp were obsolete and therefore no longer applied to the people.

Mixing these five aspects of Old Testament law causes the confusion illustrated in my conversation with Mike. Mike's failure to distinguish between the ceremonial, civil, and moral laws of the Old Testament kept him from seeing that some laws (i.e., the ceremonial and civil) would become obsolete in the New Testament, while others (i.e., moral laws) would continue due to the nature of moral laws. Thus the ceremonial law concerning eating oysters could become obsolete—and did,[5] whereas the moral law relating to homosexual activity would remain the same under the New Covenant. The Old Testament injunction against homosexual acts was a civil law based on a moral law. (While the civil laws regarding homosexuality might change from country to country, the moral law will not change since it is rooted in the nature of man. Homosexual activity always disrupts personal relationships and will therefore always be wrong, regardless of the civil laws of any country.)

The second principle concerning the law is that the severity of the penalty was an indication of the importance of the precept behind the command. Some commands carried stricter punishments because the precept behind them was more important. God evidently thought that homosexual activity was different from eating oysters. Under the Old Covenant, if you ate oysters and were caught, you were to remain ceremonially unclean until the evening. If you were involved in homosexuality and were caught, you were dead by evening. The severity of the penalty tells us something about what God thought of the act.

Thus there are two important lessons for us from the legal texts on homosexuality. First, the laws are civil laws that embody moral law, which is indicated by the inclusion of a moral injunction against homosexual acts in the New Testament. Second, the severity of the penalty assigned to the commission of homosexual acts indicates the importance of the precept that has been violated.

As in the case of the historical texts, only the behavior of homosexuality is discussed. Sexual orientation is not even mentioned. In our interpretation and counseling, it is important to maintain a clear distinction between behavior and tendency, lest we produce undue condemnation in those we seek to help.

NEW TESTAMENT REFERENCES

The New Testament contains only three brief references to the subject of homosexuality. All the references are from Paul's

---

[5]"And He said to them, 'Are you too so uncomprehending? Do you not see that whatever goes into the man from outside cannot defile him; because it does not go into his heart, but into his stomach, and is eliminated?' (Thus He declared all foods clean.)" (Mark 7:18, 19).

epistles. These passages of Scripture (Rom. 1:26–27; 1 Tim. 1:8–11; 1 Cor. 6:9–11) provide some interesting and valuable information not found in the Old Testament texts. In these appear the only reference to female homosexuality, the "unnaturalness" of homosexual acts, the augmentation of desire through persistence in unnatural behavior, the personal penalty for participation in homosexual activity, the passive and aggressive aspects of homosexual behavior, and the good news of deliverance and cleansing from the homosexual lifestyle through the Lord Jesus Christ.

The first reference appears in the Epistle of Paul to the Romans:

> For this reason God gave them over to degrading passions; for their women exchanged the natural function for that which is unnatural, and in the same way also the men abandoned the natural function of the woman and burned in their desire toward one another, men with men committing indecent acts and receiving in their own persons the due penalty of their error (Rom. 1:26, 27).

These verses, which constitute the longest New Testament passage on homosexuality, contain five major points worth noting.

First, this is the only passage in the Bible that mentions female homosexuality. It is a brief reference, and only states that certain women turned from the "natural function" or "natural relations" to that which is "against nature." From the parallels between verses 26 and 27, it is clear that the "natural function" mentioned here is heterosexual sexual relations, and that the "unnatural" function to which the women turned is "women with women."

A second interesting point arising from these verses revolves around the use of the words "natural" and "unnatural." These words came up one time in a conversation I was having in a gay bar as I was talking with Mark, who claimed to be both an evangelical Christian and a practicing homosexual.

Mark, who had first mentioned the text, said, "Well, when I was reading this chapter one day, I realized that heterosexuality never was 'natural' for me. What is natural for me is homosexuality. So, I am not doing something unnatural for me by being homosexual. But I would be doing something unnatural if I were heterosexual."

At first glance, Mark's reasoning may seem plausible, but the words of the passage do not warrant this conclusion. The scripture does not speak of natural or unnatural *feelings*, but natural and unnatural *function*. Mark was referring to how he felt and not his behavior, but the scripture is referring to what the men and women *did*, not how they felt. In other words, this passage discusses homosexual behavior but not orientation.

"But," someone might say, "doesn't it say that the men burned in their desire toward one another? Isn't that talking about orientation?"

Yes, these verses do refer to desires, and that brings up the third major point. A careful reading of the words shows that the desires originated at the same time as, or subsequent to, the abandonment of the natural function of the woman. So, it appears as if the men were involved in "indecent acts" and stirred up unnatural desires as a result. It is possible that the men were already predisposed to homosexuality due to a broken family pattern, but the desires described here were the direct result of involvement in homosexual acts.

The fourth point is directly related to the third. When the scripture states that the men were involved in unnatural relations and then burned in their desire toward one another, it then goes on with a parallel statement that the men committed indecent acts and received in their own persons the penalty of their error. Note that the verses start off with a statement that God gave them over to degrading passions. It may be that the judgment of God on the "indecent acts" was the "giving over" to degrading passions. Again, this would be a result of their activities, and not a reference to a psychological predisposition to homosexuality. In other words, the "degrading passions" to which God gave them up would be those desires that were stirred up by the unnatural acts, and not the normal human desires for male affection and love that result from the rejection process.

Though verse 24 states that "God gave them over *in the lusts of their hearts* to impurity," this still does not speak about homosexual orientation. This verse starts with the word "therefore," indicating that God's judgment was a result of the activities described in the previous verses (18–23). In other words, lusting in their hearts was part of the sin that prompted the judgment of God. The following verse begins with the word "for," indicating that the sins outlined in that verse are also a part of the reason for God's judgment. The people were lusting in their hearts and the judgment of God was to abandon them to the impurity that they so desired.

Lusting in one's heart is something quite distinct from sexual orientation. An attraction to the same or opposite sex is non-moral, that is, it is just the way the person's mind happens to work. The commitment of the heart to lust, however, is a choice the person can avoid, and if the person chooses to lust, he has sinned. Jesus made this same distinction when He taught that "every one who looks on a woman to lust for her has committed adultery with her already in his heart" (Matt. 5:28). The sin, Jesus said, was committed in the heart prior to the looking.

So, when verse 24 states that they were given over to impurtiy "in the lust of their hearts," it is referring to the sin that produced the judgment of God, not to a preexistent orientation stemming from a broken family pattern.

The fifth point revolves around the interpretation of the phrases "God gave them up" and "God gave them over." Some Christians believe that once a person has been "given over" to something by God, there is no hope for salvation. The difficulty with this interpretation of Romans, chapter one, is that God describes the person who has been "given up." In verses 28–32 we can read a list of the activities of a person who has been given over to a depraved mind (a mind void of judgment). If the list of sins mentioned in these verses is an indication of total abandonment by God, then no one will be saved. Besides this, Paul goes on in chapter two to accuse anyone who judges another person (particularly the people described in chapter one) as practicing the same things. The judgment of God will fall, Paul says, on the person who practices homosexual acts and on the person who judges the homosexual in his heart. And again, how could Paul be stating here that the homosexual is beyond hope when he writes to the Corinthians that some of them had been homosexual but had been washed, sanctified, and justified, just like any other Christian (1 Cor. 6:9ff.)? Paul is declaring that judgment falls on people who do ungodly things, but he is not saying that the homosexual cannot be saved.

The very plain teaching of these verses from Romans is that people who are involved in homosexual acts are doing things that are "indecent" and "unnatural," will stir up desires considered "degrading passions," and will receive their penalty in their own persons. Note again, as with other scriptures, that the homosexual orientation is not mentioned. Homosexual acts are outlined, but not the psychological condition of the people.

The second New Testament passage is found in Paul's letter

to Timothy. I will give the entire passage, even though the reference to homosexuality is brief.

> But we know that the Law is good, if one uses it lawfully, realizing the fact that law is not made for a righteous man, but for those who are lawless and rebellious, for the ungodly and sinners, for the unholy and profane, for those who kill their fathers or mothers, for murderers and immoral men and homosexuals and kidnappers and liars and perjurers, and whatever else is contrary to sound teaching, according to the glorious gospel of the blessed God, with which I have been entrusted. (1 Tim. 1:8–11)

Though the words "and homosexuals" constitute the briefest reference to homosexuality in the Bible, still these two words, in their context, reveal some valuable information about the subject.

The first, and probably most obvious thing about the words is that they present homosexuality as a sin. Homosexuals are included with a list of people involved in activities defined as sinful, lawless, rebellious, and contrary to sound teaching. The point is clear that homosexual acts are sinful.

Second, all of the examples Paul presents are choices people make contrary to the law of God. There is no mention of any kind of nature or psychological state in the list. Though many people might find it difficult to keep the distinction between behavior and tendency clearly in their minds when they read the word "homosexuals," still, the word is describing what some people do, not their psychology. Just as a kidnapper is recognized by what he does and not what he is, so the homosexual is responsible for his activities, not his psychological condition. Thus, one can separate the behavior from the person and accept the person while rejecting the behavior.[6]

A third and interesting thing to note is that homosexuals are not singled out as worse sinners than other people. Paul includes homosexuals in a straightforward manner along with other sinners, and makes no comparison between different kinds or degrees of sin. God deems homosexual activity "sinful," but does not even hint at any special disdain for those committing the sin.

---

[6]For those who have difficulty with the "accept the sinner, reject the sin" idea, consider Jesus' command to love our enemies. If there is no distinction between the sinner and his sin, then Jesus has commanded us to love the sin of our enemies. This would surely be a strange command from Him who "loved righteousness and hated lawlessness."

In this, God demonstrates His complete impartiality toward all men.

Although these two words in 1 Timothy teach us three important lessons, still, there is one question they do not answer: How can the homosexual be free from the sin of homosexuality? God's Word gives a clear, simple answer to this question.

In Paul's letter to the Corinthian church, Paul mentions homosexuality along with a number of other sins that bar people from the kingdom of God. Of the other six major passages, all six declare homosexual acts to be sinful, and five of the six texts state that punishment awaits the homosexual offender. (Punishment is implied in the 1 Timothy passage, though not directly stated.) If we had only the other six texts, the outlook for the homosexual would be grim. But in 1 Cor. 6:9–11 we can read the glorious good news that homosexuals can be delivered from their lifestyle to live in the freedom that Jesus Christ gives.

> Or do you not know that the unrighteous shall not inherit the kingdom of God? Do not be deceived; neither fornicators, nor idolaters, nor adulterers, nor effeminate, nor homosexuals, nor thieves, nor the covetous, nor drunkards, nor revilers, nor swindlers, shall inherit the kingdom of God. And such were some of you; but you were washed, but you were sanctified, but you were justified in the name of the Lord Jesus Christ, and in the Spirit of our God.

There are three negative and three positive facets to this portion of Scripture.

The first negative aspect is that the people listed are classified as "unrighteous." That is, because they are participating in unrighteous activities, they are called unrighteous people. Second, the kingdom of God is "off limits" to these people. They cannot be under the loving rulership of God and practice their unrighteousness at the same time, so they miss the privileges of being under God's government, and fail to experience the righteousness, peace, and joy that characterize God's kingdom (Rom. 14:17). Third, Paul indicates that it is possible to be deceived into thinking that an unrighteous person can still inherit the kingdom of God. The first recorded deception concerned the consequences of sin ("You surely shall not die!" Gen. 3:4), and the enemy who deceived Eve is still deceiving the whole world today (Rev. 12:9). The nature of deception is primarily moral; that is, if a person is deceived, he mistakenly believes that there are no consequences for his sinful choices.[7] So Paul cautions the Corinthians against thinking that someone can continue in unrighteous behavior and yet escape punishment.

These three negative aspects are true of all the sins listed, thus they are also true of the sin of homosexuality. The specific words used to describe these homosexual acts are interesting and instructive. The first word, μαλακοί, translated as "effeminate," actually means "men and boys who allow themselves to be misused homosexually."[8] The second Greek word, ἀρσενοκοῖται, translated as "homosexuals," more precisely means "a male homosexual, pederast, sodomite."[9] The first person gives himself to be used by the second, and the second person takes advantage of the first sexually. Thus the two words actually describe two different aspects of the same homosexual act, much as the words whore and whoremonger describe the two sides of the act of prostitution. This explains why some translators of the Bible combine the two words into one phrase or word in their versions.

Between the negative and positive aspects of this text, there is a short, beautiful, powerful phrase that reveals the hope of the Corinthian Christians. In just six words, this phrase encapsulates the glorious good news of the transforming power of Jesus Christ: *"and such were some of you."* Paul says that some of the Corinthians had been drunkards, some had been thieves, some idolaters, some adulterers, and some homosexuals—but no longer! They were no longer drunkards, thieves, or homosexuals, but children of God, new creations in Christ, and their old lives had passed away. And what had brought this change? They had been washed, sanctified, and justified in the name of Jesus and in the Spirit of God. God made the difference.

The Corinthian Christians had been *justified.* To be justified means to be put morally and legally right with God. It means to have our sins forgiven, our relationship with God restored, to be treated by God as if we are righteous even though we have broken the law of God. The Corinthians had been *sanctified.* To be sanctified means to be set apart and made holy, set apart from

---

[7]Some verses that show the relationship between morality and deception include: Prov. 12:20; 14:8; 1 Cor. 6:9–10; 15:33; Gal. 6:7, 8; Eph. 4:22; 5:5–6; James 1:22, 26; 1 John 1:8; 3:7–8.

[8]William R. Arndt and F. Wilbur Gingrich, *A Greek-English Lexicon of the New Testament and Other Early Christian Literature* (Chicago: University of Chicago Press, 1957), p. 489.

[9]Ibid. 109.

sin and to God. They were set apart from their old lives of un-righteousness to new lives of holiness before God. And they were separated from their former lives of uselessness to God unto fruitful service in the kingdom of God. Finally, they had been *washed*. They had been made clean inside. The guilt and shame of their former sinful lives had been removed and a new sense of purity, freedom, life, and joy had come into their hearts. And in the midst of this washed, sanctified, justified group of believers were people who had used others and been used by others in homosexual relationships. So then, God extends real, exciting hope for change to those whose lives are bound by the sin of homosexuality.

CONCLUSION

In light of the historical, legal, and epistle texts referring to homosexuality, one might still ask, What does all this mean? First, all of the texts speak only of the behavior (or acts) of homosex-uality. None of the passages mentions homosexual orientation, tendency, or condition. The Scriptures do not directly refer to the psychological aspect of homosexuality. Second, God's Word declares these acts are sinful. God does not hold up homosexual behavior to special ridicule, but calls it, along with all other sins, a transgression of His law (1 John 3:4). And third, the Bible says that these acts can be forgiven and cleansed just as any other sinful acts.

Thus, God's Word maintains an admirable balance. On the one hand, God gives man no excuse for his sin, while on the other hand, God does not condemn someone for something that is not his fault (i.e., his sexual orientation). If a person trans-gresses the law of God, he is guilty and deserves to be punished, yet God extends to him His mercy, forgiveness, and cleansing. If a person has a homosexual orientation, God does not condemn him, but offers him avenues of healing.

PART TWO

COUNSELING THE HOMOSEXUAL

CHAPTER SIX

COMING OUT OF THE LIFESTYLE

The attrition rate among newly converted homosexuals is extremely high. One of the reasons for this falling away is that some of these converts were never really converted. Because someone feels remorse over his sin and prays some kind of prayer of confession does not mean the person has had a true change of heart. In this day of "instant" everything, Christians often want to see others "instantly" converted, and this urgency swells the church with unconverted people who think they are right with God because they have "prayed the prayer." Just because a person says that he wants to give his life to Christ does not mean that he is ready to do so. Witnessing Christians need to be more like the Lord Jesus who told people to "count the cost" before they followed Him, and not to make the decision until they could do so wholeheartedly.

Preachers and teachers of the Gospel have explained the elements of true conversion many different ways on many different occasions. The conditions of regeneration that follow are nothing new, but the Church seems to have forgotten how to insist on their application to the life of the unbeliever. Until Christians learn to prepare the unbeliever fully for his conversion, the departure of young "Christians" from the Church will continue.

When John called me to arrange a counseling appointment, my first question was, "Do you remember a time when you consciously committed your life to the lordship of Jesus?"

"Well, I was raised in a good Christian church," John replied.

"That's good," I said, "but when did you give your life to Jesus as your Lord?"

"I've tried to live a Christian life since I was a child."

"That's good too, John, but I will ask you for the third time—when did you consciously submit yourself to the control of Jesus, allowing Him to be master of every area of your life?"

"Well," John said with a sigh, "if you put it that way, I guess I never have made that kind of commitment."

"Good," I said, "then the first thing we will discuss when we get together is how you can become a Christian."

Now, some Christians would view this kind of questioning as "being too picky." Some might even consider this approach as an improper judgment of the other person's life. But I have found it necessary to be sure that a counselee is soundly converted before I attempt to counsel him as a fellow Christian.

The process of helping the newly converted homosexual to attain stability in his Christian life is sometimes lengthy and difficult. If the new "convert" is not really a Christian, then he will not have the strength of commitment necessary to follow Jesus and live the Christian life. When things become difficult, the true believer buckles down to the task of obeying God, and changes as a result. The person who is not quite sure about his salvation will usually give up, and thus another "young convert" is lost to the pull of the world.

The three conditions outlined below are simple and well known to most Christians, but they are crucial in aiding the homosexual to be free from his lifestyle. Without the proper foundations in the counselee's life, the process of change is bound to be retarded, or even aborted, when the going gets rough.

REPENTANCE

The kind of "godly sorrow" described by Paul in his letter to the Corinthians seems to be a rare occurrence in the Church today. Paul says that this sorrow produces a repentance "without regret" that leads to salvation (2 Cor. 7:10). Paul then goes on in verse 11 to describe the fruit this "godly sorrow" produced in the Corinthians:

> For behold what earnestness this very thing, this godly sorrow, has produced in you: what vindication of yourselves, what indignation, what fear, what longing, what zeal, what avenging of wrong! In everything you demonstrated yourselves to be innocent in the matter.

This godly sorrow moved the Corinthians to show that they

wanted to be holy in every way, to stand aggressively against all sin, to show reverence to God, to earnestly desire righteousness in their lives, to energetically live for God, and to correct anything not in line with the will of God. In other words, a godly sorrow produces the love of righteousness and hatred of evil that characterized the life of the Lord Jesus. How different the Church would be if each believer experienced this sorrow as a part of his conversion!

The process of repentance involves several essential elements. Though this process can happen quickly in someone's life, if the person is truly repentant the essential elements should all be present.

1. *Conviction of sin.* The person needs to see sin as God sees it and understand its consequences.

The word "conviction" is a legal word referring to the presentation of evidence to a person's mind until he is persuaded of his error. The means to conviction of sin is always *truth*, though the agents presenting the truth may be varied (e.g., the Word of God, the Spirit of God, the life of an obedient Christian, the creation, circumstances, etc.). Many Christians confuse conviction with a sense of remorse, but feelings of remorse do not always attend conviction of sin. Then again, sometimes a person feels remorse, but for the wrong reasons (e.g., he is sorry he was caught, or does not savor the prospect of being punished for his sin, or fears the social disgrace associated with the public admission of guilt). But a person is convicted of sin when he has been brought to the place where he understands that he has broken the law of God and deserves to be punished for it.

Many people in the Church today have come to Christ without a thorough conviction of sin. This explains the lax attitude toward sin in these peoples' lives. They have never had a revelation of how their sin has grieved the heart of God, hurt other people, and damaged their own lives. As a result, they do not war aggressively against all sin, and thus live lifestyles of ungodliness.

Paul the Apostle said "through the Law comes the knowledge of sin" (Rom. 3:20). If we apply the law of God to a person's life while we are witnessing to him about Christ, God will then use His law to bring conviction of sin, and the person will have made his first step toward salvation. Lack of conviction of sin in the beginning will only lead to weakness of commitment in the end, so it is important to apply the law of God right from the start.

Only the person who has been deeply convicted of his sin recognizes the good news of God's mercy and forgiveness. The deeply convicted person tends to repent more fully and resist temptation more aggressively. Thus, the homosexual who is strongly convicted is more likely to live a godly lifestyle than the one who receives little conviction of sin.

2. *Brokenness over sin.* The person needs to hate sin in response to his conviction of sin.

A sense of self-loathing for sin is not very common in our *me*-oriented society. Many of us have trouble understanding the publican who beat his breast as an indication of his feeling of unworthiness (Luke 18:9–14). He felt so terrible about his sin that he would not even lift his eyes to heaven when he asked God for mercy. But this kind of radical response to our sin is necessary if we want to see radical change in our lives. We will only shun what we really hate, so a brokenness over sin, a hatred of evil, is essential to true conversion. Just as God brings conviction of sin, so God can bring brokenness over sin if a person will cry out to God for this revelation.

A friend of mine once told me that he had felt sorry for his sins many times before his conversion. He felt sorry, but he really felt sorry for himself. One night, as he was reading a Christian book, he began to feel sorry, but this time it was quite different. This time, as he put it, he felt "sorry for God." What he meant is that he felt sorry for the right reason. Before, his motivations had been selfish—he felt sorry because of what his sin had done to him. This time he was sorry for how his sin had affected God, how his actions had brought grief to the heart of God. And this time he was truly converted from his selfish lifestyle.

As a rule, people who have had a revelation of the awfulness of their sin, and have been broken before God, will hate sin and do everything they can to avoid it in their Christian lives. On the other hand, those who have never been broken over their sin tend to allow sinful habit patterns to continue in their lives unchecked. The person leaving a homosexual lifestyle needs to be broken over his sin. If he does not experience this essential aspect of conversion, he will probably struggle with selfish habits in his Christian life. Even if he does struggle, if he is broken, he will at least have the necessary motivation, desire, and commitment to change to work through his problems.

3. *Humility.* The person must be willing to admit his sin.

As strange as it may seem, some people are convicted of their sin, are broken by God over their sin, and then refuse to admit that they have done anything wrong. This is a reaction stemming from pride. The person is simply too proud to admit that he is a sinner and deserves to be punished for his sin. If the person is not willing to humble himself and agree with God that he is a sinner, then he will remain in his unconverted state. God has said, "He who conceals his transgressions will not prosper, but he who confesses and forsakes them will find compassion" (Prov. 28:13). Mercy can be justly extended only to the person who acknowledges that he is guilty.

"I'm so awful," Jim sobbed. "What can I do about my life? I'm so messed up." The alcoholic with whom I was speaking put his head down on the table and wept. As I watched Jim cry, I felt completely unmoved. I was concerned that perhaps I was lacking in compassion.

God, is there something wrong with my heart? I asked. *I don't feel moved for this man.*

"No," God said, " there is nothing wrong with your heart. The problem is that this man is ready to do everything but the right thing. He will cry over his sin, but refuses to admit his guilt and get his life straightened out with Me and with his family." I reached across the table, grabbed the man's arms and shook him. "Stop that," I said. "You need to stop crying and start doing what is right. You need to confess your sin to God, forsake your selfish lifestyle, and make things right with your wife and children."

The man straightened up, dried his eyes, and asked me to explain what I meant. As I described the process of confession and repentance to him, he seemed less and less interested in becoming a Christian. Finally he collected his things, said good-bye, and left the coffee shop. He felt sorry, but was not willing to admit his sin and change his behavior.

Homosexuals often regret their lifestyles and feel sorry for the way they are living, but this will not bring conversion. The homosexual must be ready to admit that his sexual lifestyle is wrong and be willing to forsake it before he can receive the forgiveness of God for his sin. This is a necessary step in the conversion of any sinner, regardless of his particular form of selfishness.

4. *Renunciation.* The person must forsake his former lifestyle of selfish gratification and be willing to learn another way of life.

After a person has been convicted of his sin, been broken over it, and humbly admitted that he has sinned before God, he must actually stop his sinful behavior. Some Christian churches teach that a person can be saved "in" his sin, but God's Word states that Jesus came to save His people "from," literally, "out of," their sin. God does not intend that we should continue in our sin after we come to Christ. If we are truly converted, then we must be converted from sin and to righteous living. Homosexuals are only deceiving themselves if they think they can have all the benefits of the Christian life without fulfilling this essential condition of salvation.

Chris and I listened intently as the vicar intoned the Anglican liturgy. We were attending a "gay" church at the invitation of one of the parishioners. While I am not familiar with Anglican liturgy, Chris had memorized and taught the liturgy in two languages, and was therefore able to follow the service word for word.

"That's very interesting," Chris said, musing.

"What?" I asked.

"Well," he said, "they have left out two very important words from this sentence—the words 'and repentance.' "

Before the service ended, Chris had pointed out several more places where the liturgy had been altered to omit references to repentance as a condition of salvation. The liturgy left us with the feeling that we could live any way we wanted and still be a Christian. But Christianity without repentance is powerless and insipid—a hollow imitation of the abundant life Jesus offers to all those who truly turn from their sin. True conversion involves true repentance, and true repentance includes ceasing sinful activities.

5. *Continuation.* The person must continue in a holy lifestyle, replacing ungodly habit patterns with righteous living.

After a person has turned away from a life of selfish gratification, it is imperative that he replace his old habit patterns with habit patterns of righteousness. That is, the person cannot live in a vacuum. His life must be filled with something; he cannot just turn away from sin and expect that any manner of living is acceptable to God. The person must go on to develop a loving lifestyle (as God defines loving), or he is likely to go back to his old way of living.

For homosexuals, leaving the old "lifestyle" is very important. Homosexuals often come to the point of renouncing their sin and then wonder what they will do with the rest of their lives. The negative must be replaced with the positive, that is, they must learn a new way of living that puts God and others first and their own interests last. If they do not go on to learn to live God's way, their lives will be empty, and they will eventually succumb to temptation, turning back to the world for a sense of experiential fulfillment.

The counselor must communicate these five essential aspects of repentance to the homosexual. Conviction of sin, brokenness, humility, renunciation, and continuation are necessary parts of the conversion process. If the Christian counselor hopes to see the homosexual truly converted, he must take care that none of the conditions of salvation is omitted.

RECONCILIATION

While the five aspects of repentance are well known to most believers, another element of conversion often escapes the notice of Christian counselors. That element is reconciliation: the reconciliation of man to God and to other men.

Reconciliation is the process of restoring two parties to friendship when they were once enemies. When man lives selfishly, he is living in opposition to God and thus becomes an enemy of God (Rom. 5:10; James 4:4). What Christ has done on the cross can bring man to the place of laying down his weapons and ceasing his warfare against the loving Ruler of mankind.

If a person has met the five conditions of true repentance mentioned above, he should have had an experience of reconciliation to God as part of that process. There are times, however, when a person makes the right choices to repent, and there still seems to be something lacking in his relationship with God. It seems as if he has cleared the way to have a relationship with God, but has not yet started to relate to God as a friend. In cases like this, only a simple step of faith is required to start the process.

At a Christian coffee shop in Germany, one of our Christian workers confronted a man named Steve with his need of salvation. At first, Steve rebelled at the thought of giving his life to Christ and ran from the shop. About half an hour later, though, he returned, greatly humbled, and submitted his life to God. Steve made the choices to be right with God, but somehow the connection between him and his Father was not obvious, at least not to Steve.

As we talked to another young Christian, Steve observed us

as we prayed. Later, on the way home, Steve's curiosity about our relationship with God erupted in a question.

"How do you talk to God?" Steve asked with a note of urgency in his voice.

"You just have to start talking," I said. "God will hear you."

"But how do I start?" he asked again.

"How about starting with something like 'Lord,' or 'God,' or 'Father'? Anything will do as long as you mean it from your heart and believe that God loves you and will hear you."

There was a short pause, and then Steve said his first words of prayer to God.

"Lord?" Steve said. The tone in his voice indicated that this was a question rather than a statement. With one word Steve was asking, "Are you really there? Are you really listening?"

There was another short pause. Evidently something happened between Steve and God in those moments, because Steve's next words were alive with realization. "OH! LORD!" Steve almost shouted. His reaction clearly announced that he had made contact with God. The three of us wept as Steve continued to pour out his heart to his Father in heaven. As he prayed, I had the impression I was watching a little bird flapping its wings to fly for the very first time. Steve had come to his reconciliation to God.

Reconciliation to God should be the natural result of a person's meeting the conditions of repentance. If this next step does not happen automatically, the counselor should encourage the counselee to speak to God, in faith, trusting that God will both hear and answer. This step of calling upon God appears necessary for salvation, since God has said, "Whoever will call upon the name of the Lord will be saved" (Rom. 10:13). *Believing* and *calling* are given in this passage (v. 14) as two different aspects of one "event" of salvation. So, if a person has met the conditions of repentance, but has had no contact with God, it would be good to encourage the person to call upon God, thus establishing experiential verification of his reconciliation to God.

Reconciliation to man is probably less understood and more often neglected than reconciliation to God. Many Christian counselors or evangelists encourage others to be reconciled to God, seldom mentioning our responsibility to make our relationships right with other human beings. But being right with God should always affect the way we relate to other people. If we love God, we should show it by loving other people; if we serve God, we should show it by serving others. Jesus placed right relationships with others as a priority over worshiping and serving God (Matt. 5:23–24), so we need to treat reconciliation with others with the same seriousness.

Being reconciled to others is a profound experience, but requires only three simple steps for its accomplishment. First, the person must have a change of heart about what he has been doing. Second, the person needs to go to the offended party to seek reconciliation. Third, the person needs to confess his wrongdoing and seek forgiveness for his offense.

These three steps can be clearly seen in the parable of the prodigal son. When the son "came to himself," he said to himself, "I will get up" (indicating a change of heart about what he was doing), and "I will go to my father" (determination to go to the offended party to seek reconciliation), and "I will say to my father . . ." (rehearsal of what he would say in confession to his father). These same three elements are found in Matthew 5:23–24, which was mentioned above. Jesus said that if you are offering a gift at the altar and there remember that your brother has something against you, "leave your gift before the altar" (a change of action indicating a willingness to deal with the broken relationship), "go your way" (approaching the person to seek reconciliation), and "be reconciled to your brother" (confession and forgiveness). Though these steps are amazingly clear in Scripture, it is surprising how many counselors do not encourage their counselees to be reconciled to other people.

Wherever it is possible and wise, a person should seek to be reconciled to everyone with whom he has had a broken relationship. If the counselor breaks "everyone" into smaller categories for the counselee, the task will appear more attainable. Working with concrete categories such as immediate family members, relatives, friends, teachers, and other authority figures (such as the police and employers) can help simplify the counselee's work. Though the effort may at first seem impossible to the counselee, he will soon find that it was only his generalization of the task that made it appear so formidable.

For the former homosexual, relationships with former partners may well be the most crucial aspect of reconciliation. Fornication always results in broken relationships, thus, the counselee should seek to restore all the relationships he has broken through involvement in sexual sin. If possible, the former homosexual should ask forgiveness of others for involving them in sexual sin. Since it is not always wise to come face-to-face with former partners, a brief telephone call or a brief note to ask forgiveness may be better than personal contact. If there should be any danger of blackmail or other retaliation, the phone call would be best, as a note leaves behind tangible evidence of the communication. If the offended party should refuse to forgive, the counselee has still fulfilled his responsibility to seek reconciliation. Normally, an effort at reconciliation restores a relationship without causing further trouble, but if the effort *could* cause a greater rift in the relationship, or possible harm to the counselee, then the counselee will have to be content to ask God's forgiveness and let it go at that.

Since being reconciled to God and man are essential steps in the process of true conversion, it is important for the counselor to aid the counselee in restoring broken relationships with both God and man. The counselee needs to repent, go to the offended party, confess his sin, and ask forgiveness.

RESTITUTION

In order to live successfully in the present, and to look forward to the future with hope, it is necessary to clear up the past completely. Restitution is sometimes sensitive, and often costly, but since it has been commanded by God, it is always necessary.

Introducing the subject of restitution in a conversation always seems to cause little "flutters" of disagreement. Even many conservative, evangelical Christians balk at the thought of making restitution for past offenses. "The past is over and done," they say, "and you don't have to do anything about it. You don't bring up what God has forgiven." With these and other catchy phrases, they easily sweep a person's entire past life under the carpet and act as if the person has no responsibility to others because God has forgiven him.

The handsome, intelligent young man sitting before me was one of the "guests" in a house of refuge where I had been invited to speak. Knowing that restitution can be a very sensitive topic to people who have lived on the street, I tried to present the subject in the light of the love of God for us. Still, when John heard that he was responsible to make the past right with other people, the idea provoked an agitated response.

"But if God has forgiven my past," John snapped, "then I am

only responsible to make restitution for the things I have done since I became a Christian."

I could tell from the way John phrased his remark that he was under the influence of the teaching of some preachers on a local Christian television station. Thus, John was only responding according to what he believed was the truth of the Christian position. I knew I had to be both sensitive to John, and loyal to my brothers and sisters on television. As John spoke, I prayed for wisdom.

"Well, John," I asked, "how much are you supposed to sin after you become a Christian?"

"None," John said.

"That's right," I said. "Then the only things you should have to make restitution for would be from *before* you were a Christian."

But whether from before conversion or after, the idea of making restitution still seems improper to some people. This stance is both understandable and unbiblical. It is understandable in light of the totality of the forgiveness of God. Once God has forgiven someone, it would appear to be unnecessary, even disrespectful, to dredge up the past. With respect to *forgiveness* this is true, though God will sometimes bring up the past in order to heal the individual. God does completely forgive, but this does not automatically make things right with other people. To be righteous means to be right with God *and* man, so restitution to other people becomes necessary if a person is going to live an upright life. Since God commands that restitution be made,[1] it is unbiblical to treat restitution as unnecessary or wrong.

The direct references to restitution in the Bible relate to our relationships with other humans. Though it is only indirectly stated, there is a sense in which one can make restitution to God. When someone sins against God, he brings great grief to the heart of God. When God commands the repentant sinner to "bring forth fruit suitable to repentance," He is demanding a change that will bring delight to God's heart. Thus, when a person repents and changes his way of living from lawlessness to loving obedience to God, God is pleased, and the person performs an act of restitution to God.

---

[1] In Num. 5:5–8 we read that a person is responsible to make restitution, in full, for *any sin* that he commits. In the New Testament, Jesus interpreted Zaccheus' willingness to make restitution as an indication of his salvation (Luke 19:1–10). See also, Ex. 21:34; 22:1–15; Lev. 5:14–16; 6:1–7; 2 Sam. 12:1–6.

Material restitution usually involves three steps. First, the person making restitution needs to contact the offended party to ask forgiveness for the offense. Second, the person should offer to make material restitution for any goods or money that he stole or damaged. Third, if the offended party demands it, the restitution should be made according to terms acceptable to both parties. This process could take place by letter, over the telephone, or in person, depending on the circumstances of the two parties and the level of intimacy between them.

Legal restitution is often a very sticky matter. The expectation that a person make restitution is absolute. *When* and *how* the person makes restitution are not absolute, but must be governed by other principles applicable to the particular case. Douglas, for example, was led to faith in Christ through one of the members of our mission organization. Douglas was an accomplice to a murder, and from the time of his conversion he knew he would eventually have to turn himself over to the police. But Douglas gave himself time to become spiritually strong enough to handle prison, and then gave himself up. *That* he would make restitution was never in question; *when* and *how* were determined by the specific circumstances of the case.[2] There may be times that homosexuals leaving their lifestyle may need to make legal restitution. If so, they should be taught the difference between the what, when, and how of restitution so they can make an intelligent decision as to how and when they will make things right.

Relational restitution will probably be the most common form of restitution for the converted homosexual. Because the sin of homosexuality occurs in the context of relationship, the restitution must agree in nature with the offense.

The method of relational restitution is the same as for reconciliation to other people, with one exception. In reconciliation, the final goal is usually the restoration and deepening of relationship as the two parties live responsibly toward each other. In restitution, especially with former homosexuals, the goal is usu-

---

[2]The reader should note that the material concerning legal restitution is taken from the viewpoint of the guilty party only. The responsibilities of others who know about the legal offense may differ from state to state, country to country, and case to case, making a definitive statement of the responsibilities impossible. Also, the balance between the spirit and letter of the law and how it will be treated by the conscience of the individual will differ from person to person. The number of factors involved in this angle of legal restitution puts that discussion beyond the scope of this book. The counselor should seek legal advice if he has questions concerning his responsibilities in any particular case.

ally the restoration, then severing of relationship in order to protect the new Christian from temptation. This does not mean that the new Christian does not have unbelieving friends, but that these friends will probably not be people with whom he previously had improper relationships. It also does not imply that the new convert is to harbor bad feelings toward his former partners. The young Christian should love his former friends and pray for them, but his contact with them will need to be minimal or eliminated, depending on the amount of temptation these contacts could produce.

"You will have to break off your contact with your former partners," I told Les. "It is simply too dangerous for you spiritually and morally to keep up your relationships with them. Sooner or later you will face temptation because of them."

"You mean I need to burn all my bridges behind me?" Les asked.

"Exactly," I replied. "Until you take this step you will probably struggle with your Christian life."

Les did not take my advice at that time and subsequently went back into a sinful lifestyle. But the story has a happy ending. Eventually, Les did see the wisdom in cutting himself off from his former partners. He contacted them one last time, asked their forgiveness for involving them in sinful behavior, and then informed them that he would not be maintaining any continuing relationship with them. Later, he became a member of an active Christian ministry and his Christian life stabilized.

God says that the person who thinks he can have close relationships with immoral people and remain unaffected is only deceiving himself. "Do not be deceived: 'Bad company corrupts good morals' " (1 Cor. 15:33). Unless the converted homosexual makes relational restitution and establishes new friendships with a close circle of Christian friends, he is deceiving himself and will probably not survive as a believer.

SUMMARY

Repentance, reconciliation, and restitution constitute the moral healing that lays the groundwork for psychological healing. The Christian counselor has the responsibility to impress on the counselee the importance of thoroughly repenting, being reconciled to God and man, and making restitution where necessary. These three steps will prepare the new convert to live a stable Christian life. If he has properly dealt with the past, he will be better equipped to resist temptation in the present, and then look forward to the future with hope as he lives a responsible, godly life. Without this preparation, the young Christian will probably struggle, falter, and then return to his former lifestyle in defeat. The road to healing can sometimes be long and hard, but it is possible and definitely worthwhile.

CHAPTER SEVEN

KNOWING GOD

Spiritual "tunnel vision" plagues many Christian counselors and ministries when they deal with the problem of homosexuality. Some counselors treat only the moral aspect of the problem. Some think that everything will be fine if the homosexual is delivered from demons. Others attempt to change the homosexual's behavior through conditioning, while completely ignoring his spiritual condition. And some, unfortunately, accept the world's view that the homosexual cannot and need not change, so they try to help him "adjust" to a homosexual lifestyle. The first three methods are lopsided, the fourth is tragic, and all four are insufficient. If the homosexual is to receive psychological healing, therefore, it must come through a multi-faceted approach.

The homosexual is very complex. He has many needs, desires, aspirations, dreams, problems, faults, failures, and sometimes, sins. In other words, he is a human being just like everyone else. To try to reduce the problem of homosexuality to a single aspect of the homosexual's life, and then apply one methodology to the problem, will not affect sufficient change. What the homosexual needs is a complete restructuring of his life, and to accomplish this, the counselor will have to treat the counselee as a complete person, applying different solutions to different aspects of the problem.

SETTING GOALS

Psychological healing is a very interesting phenomenon, similar to happiness or having fun. All three are by-products of other activities—none can be directly chosen. Someone can choose to go to the beach, swim, have a picnic, and play volleyball in the sand, but he cannot choose to have fun. He may have fun while he is engaged in these activities, but the fun is a by-product, and the person cannot directly choose it. The same is true of happiness. A person can choose to be involved in those activities that may produce happiness—loving other people, being a responsible person, serving God obediently—but he cannot directly choose to be happy. And while psychological healing is more than just an emotion (as opposed to happiness and fun), it is still a by-product. Someone can choose to be involved in activities that produce healing indirectly, but he cannot directly choose to be healed.

Establishing healing as a goal is the source of all kinds of frustration, impatience, confusion, and condemnation. If a counselee thinks that his goal in life is to be healed, he will constantly look for the by-products in his life rather than applying himself to those activities that produce the changes he desires. Questions like, "Why is it taking me so long to be well?" are very revealing. Note that the goal in the person's mind is to be well. It would be more beneficial if the person asked, "How can I bring my choices more in line with God's Word?" or "How can I learn to love people more?" Concentrating on healing as a goal causes the counselee to look for changes that he cannot directly control, and he will tend to feel disappointed when his objectives are not reached within his self-appointed time frame.

"It has been a full five years now, and that's enough. If God were going to heal me, it should have happened by now." Ron's face disguised the anger he felt, but his voice clearly revealed his disappointment.

"Did God tell you that you would be healed in five years?" I asked.

"Well, no, but I figured that would be enough time. If He hasn't healed me by now, He probably never will. He probably doesn't care about me anyway. What's the use?"

Counselees often come for help with the goal of healing already fixed in their thinking. Unfortunately, many counselors only reinforce this improper objective by assuming that it is true, or they unwittingly communicate the idea because they have never thought the issue through. Often, both counselor and counselee are striving for change that cannot be directly realized, and both parties eventually become discouraged with the seeming lack of progress. Sometimes the counselee feels he is disappointing the counselor because he is not changing quickly enough, and this only adds anxiety to an already pressured situation. Even with the frustration, impatience, discouragement, or confusion that may result from a healing orientation, the biggest problem, for the homosexual, will likely be condemnation.

Condemnation is probably the biggest enemy of the person with a homosexual orientation. He already thinks of himself as different, or even abnormal, and feeling that God disapproves of his thoughts and desires can become a weight almost impossible to bear. If changing from a homosexual to a heterosexual orientation is the person's major goal, he will feel guilty as long as he faces homosexual desires and temptations.

"I always feel as if God is breathing down my neck," Mark said. "I feel as if I can never please Him no matter what I do. It's as if He will only be happy with me when all my thoughts and desires change, and I finally become heterosexually oriented."

Mark imagined that he could not please God, so he felt God was against him. God is actually *for* him, but Mark will not feel that way if he thinks God is impatiently waiting for him to become heterosexually oriented.

God does not demand that a person be healed, heterosexually oriented, or happy—God demands *holiness*. The person cannot choose to be healed, but he can choose to be holy. Adopting goals other than those commanded by God will ultimately produce frustration and condemnation in the counselee's life, making it more difficult to live in harmony with God, himself, and other people. The counselee may receive healing and move toward heterosexual orientation as a result of his holiness, but setting up by-products as goals will only hinder the counseling process.

Therefore, I take a fourfold, obedience-oriented approach to the problem of homosexuality. The troubled person needs to (1) know God, (2) understand himself, (3) resist the enemy (i.e., evil spiritual beings), and (4) relate properly to other members of the Body of Christ. To the Christian counselor, this approach will not appear novel, but the application of these principles to the homosexually oriented person will differ significantly from general Christian counseling. The final goal of this process is that the counselee should come to stability and obedience in his Christian life. God offers freedom to everyone who is willing to follow Jesus Christ wholeheartedly, and the homosexual is no exception.

THE FEAR OF GOD

"How can I stay away from homosexual sin? Is there anything that can break the power of this thing in my life? I've tried everything I know, but I just can't seem to stop disobeying God." Tom was close to tears as he poured out his plea before me.

"Yes, Tom, there is a solution to your problem," I said, "and it's called the fear of God. God says in the book of Proverbs that it is by the fear of God that a man stays away from evil.[1] If you want to stay away from sin, you will have to learn to fear the Lord."

The terms "the fear of God" and "the fear of the Lord" are used over two hundred times in the Bible. To "fear" God means to worshipfully revere and to stand in awe of God. One of the automatic results of this reverence of God is the hatred of evil. If you love God, who is holy, then you learn to hate evil because He hates evil. This result is so consistent that the Bible defines the fear of the Lord in these terms: "The fear of the Lord is to hate evil" (Prov. 8:13a). So if a person fears the Lord, he hates evil; and since people don't do what they hate, the person stays away from evil because he hates it.

The person forsaking a homosexual lifestyle seldom has a hatred for the sin of homosexuality. If the person has spent years of his life sinning against his conscience, his thoughts and feelings about that sin will be distorted. In addition to having a seared conscience (1 Tim. 4:2), the person is often deceived by the sin into thinking that there is nothing wrong with it (1 Cor. 6:9; Heb. 3:13). Unless the person can get a clear picture of the sin and learn to hate it, he will continue to struggle.

God uses different methods to teach us to reverence Him. First, as we read and study God's Word, we gain His perspective on sin. We learn to see all sin for what it is—the ultimate horror of the universe. With this new understanding will come a different attitude toward sin and a resulting freedom to resist temptation. Second, as we pray and worship, the Holy Spirit reveals the character of God to us, and in contrast to His holiness we begin to comprehend the awful impurity of sin. Again, the result is the hatred of evil and a turning away from sin. Third, we can learn the fear of God from others who have learned to hate evil. David said, "Come, you children, listen to me; I will teach you the fear of the Lord." So, we can *learn* the fear of God from

---

[1]Prov. 16:6.

others. This could be part of the "training in righteousness" Paul mentions in 2 Tim. 3:16. Fourth, God can teach us to hate evil through daily circumstances. Sometimes He will allow us to see the terrible, destructive nature of sin by observing the consequences of sin in our own life or the lives of others. And finally, every time we choose to shun evil, we are making the choice to fear the Lord. Thus, Proverbs speaks of those who "hated knowledge, and did not choose the fear of the Lord" (Prov. 1:29). Evidently, we can choose to hate evil, too, and by so doing, fear the Lord.

Since the counselee's holiness is one of the main goals of the Christian counselor, the counselor must teach the counselee about the fear of God. This should be done in the counseling session, but the counselor can also assign helpful homework to aid the counselee in his efforts to obtain the fear of the Lord. The counselee can do Bible studies centered on the topic of the fear of God, or he can meditate on passages of Scripture related to the subject. Again, the counselor can assign prayer/worship assignments or the reading of good Christian literature related to the topic.[2]

As the counselee learns the fear of God, he will be developing his relationship with God. Some of our most basic psychological and emotional needs are met in our relationship with God. Without the development of a strong devotional life, the counselee's basic needs will go unmet, and he will be tempted to meet those needs in the only way with which he is familiar. Thus, the on-going adventure of coming to know God is part of the healing of the homosexually oriented person.

DEVOTIONAL LIFE

"Hi, Mike!" Richard's cheery voice came over the telephone. Richard and I had met at a Christian camp where I had been invited to speak. As we talked at the camp, Richard shared with me about his previous involvement in a homosexual lifestyle. We had met a few times after that for counseling.

"Hello, Richard. How are things going for you?" I replied.

---

[2]Two excellent tools that deal directly with the subject of the fear of God are (1) a tape series entitled *A Series of Messages on the Fear of the Lord* by Joy Dawson, and (2) the book entitled *Intimate Friendship With God*, also by Joy Dawson. Both are available from Pilgrim Tapes, P.O. Box 296, Sunland, CA 91040–0296. The book is also available from Chosen Books, Fleming H. Revell Company, Old Tappan, New Jersey.

"Well, Mike, I just had to call you before you left to tell you what the Lord taught me this morning. It was wonderful! Remember what you told me about learning to get my needs met in my relationship with Jesus and not from other people? Well . . ." Richard's excitement was obvious as he related the events of the morning.

Evidently, Richard had been quite lonely that Sunday morning, and thought he would get his need for companionship met at his local church. But when he arrived at church, no one greeted him. During the service no one greeted him. And again, as he left the church, not one person acknowledged him. Richard speculated that perhaps God had arranged the events that way so he could learn a valuable lesson.

Still lonely, Richard got into his car and started the drive home. Along the road he thought about what had happened at church and what I had taught him about his needs. I had tried to impress on him that his needs for unconditional love, identity, security, affection, and self-worth would not be met fully in relationships with other people. Rather, he should look to God for the fulfillment of those needs.

As he drove along, he decided he would try what I had suggested. He began to worship and praise God from his heart. As he did, the presence of God, through the Holy Spirit, became very evident to him. As he continued to worship, he could, as he put it, "feel God meeting his need for companionship."

"It was wonderful, Mike," Richard continued on the phone. "It was as if God filled up a big vacuum in my soul, and the loneliness and emptiness just vanished."

Richard had learned a lesson that many Christians never seem to learn. God can meet our needs, God wants to meet our needs, and turning to human beings to try to have these needs met will only end in frustration and emptiness.

All of us, as human beings, have personal needs.[3] Different psychologists and counselors describe these needs in different ways, but they often group them under general headings: unconditional love, a sense of identity, a feeling of self-worth, a sense of security, a need for affection, a sense of value, or a sense of competence as a person. God created us with these needs, and the corresponding desires that urge us to fulfill these needs.

---

[3]I am referring here to psychological needs, assuming that the physical needs (air, water, sleep, food, shelter, etc.) have been met.

There is nothing wrong with having the needs or trying to meet these needs. The point is, there are appropriate, healthful ways to meet these needs, and many ungodly, destructive ways to try to meet them. The troubles in a person's life begin when he attempts to meet his needs in ineffective, harmful ways.

Men coming from a homosexual background have learned all kinds of inappropriate ways to try to meet their needs, but the ideas behind this behavior boil down to essentially one lie: *A relationship with a man will meet my basic personal needs.* It is understandable that a person who has suffered the loss of relationship with his father would be left with an unmet need for love, especially for male affection. It is also reasonable that the person would try to bolster his sense of self-esteem through relationship with another man, since this should have happened with his father.[4] But a relationship with another man will not vicariously satisfy those desires that only God was intended to fulfill. That happens only in a daily relationship with God.

Many of the aspects of personal need are in the "sense" or "feeling" realm. It is important that we feel loved, that we feel secure, that we feel valuable, important, a sense of self-worth, or competence. Our feelings are reactions to what we think, what we do, and the circumstances around us, but most often our feelings are the results of our thoughts. At any particular moment, we are responding either to truth or lies in our thoughts. If our thoughts are centered around the truth of God's unconditional love for us, we will feel secure. If we know the truth of who we are, from God's Word, then we will feel valuable, or have a sense of identity and competence. In other words, we need to *know* in order to *feel.* And where do we obtain this truth that directs our feelings and meets our needs? We hear this truth from God in our communication with Him.

The objective aspects of a relationship include different forms of communication. In a relationship with God, the objective forms of communication are summed up in the acts of prayer, worship, and the study of the Scriptures. Generally speaking, when we pray, we are talking to God; when we read the Bible, God is talking to us; and when we worship, some of

---

[4]In counseling, one sometimes sees the love-related needs (love, affection, security, dependency, etc.) and the power-related needs (identity, self-worth, value, competence, etc.) associated with the passive and aggressive expressions of homosexuality, respectively. This could be helpful when trying to establish motivation for particular forms of behavior.

each is happening. In daily communication with God we obtain the truth that we need to have our basic needs met. This principle is one of the foundations of life essential to the process of healing.

"I don't quite understand why, but I've been dry for a month now, and I seem to have no desire whatever to drink," Jim said thoughtfully. Jim had been referred to me by one of his relatives. As he sat in my living room, puzzling over his recent victory over alcohol, a question began forming in my mind.

"What have you been doing differently for the last month?" I asked.

"Well, nothing much," Jim said. "I prayed with someone about my problem, and then the person told me I needed to start reading my Bible and praying every day. I made a commitment to spend fifteen minutes a day with God, and have been doing it since then. But what could that have to do with losing my desire to drink?"

"Everything," I said, "just everything."

Jim did not realize that he had begun doing the very thing that would ultimately deliver him from a problem with alcohol. He did not understand the process, but he knew that it worked. As we spent time together in counsel, Jim learned why his daily devotional time brought such power into his life. Eventually Jim learned how to help himself in other ways, and a wonderful change took place in his life. I probably saw more change in Jim's life in a shorter period of time than with anyone else I have counseled, and the "secret" to Jim's success was daily communication with God.

Three vital areas of prayer, worship, and Bible study are not just "good Christian things to do," but are avenues of healing for the homosexually oriented person.

PRAYER

The prayer life of the counselee needs to be consistent and concrete. Sporadic prayer teaches the person to be undisciplined, and the contact with God is not frequent enough to meet the person's psychological needs. Through a consistent prayer life the person learns to spend time with his Father, to assert himself before his Father, to see that the Father does seriously consider his needs, and to be dependent on the Father, all of which the person probably did *not* experience with his earthly father.

Along with daily times of prayer, the person needs to learn

to pray in crisis situations. Jesus commanded His disciples to "keep watching and praying" (Matt. 26:41) so that they would not be overcome by temptation. The counselee will need to watch out for situations of temptation, too, and pray for strength and help in that time of need.

Counselees need specific directions in how to pray; I encourage them to have some subjects concretely in mind (if not written down) before they pray. This helps the person to concentrate while he prays, and gives the person a sense of accomplishment when he has finished his prayer time. I suggest a length of, perhaps, fifteen minutes, and increase the length as the counselee is able to handle it. Other details of how to pray should be familiar material to the Christian counselor who is used to discipling others.

WORSHIP

Worship is commonly overlooked as a means of healing in the Christian life. In times of worship, however, a person really comes to know God for who He is, and that knowledge both changes the person and makes it easier for the person to relate to God. Just as Richard did, people find that their personal emotional, spiritual, and psychological needs are met as they spend time with God in worship. In worship, we give to God and God speaks to us. Thus, we receive the satisfaction of bringing pleasure to the heart of God, and God speaks the truth to us about His love for us and who we are. Out of this knowledge of God's love and our identity we obtain a sense of security and value.

"I usually have trouble hearing God's voice clearly," Tim said, "but this time was completely different. Even though I was a little scared, I asked God what He thought of me. The answer was so clear and unexpected, I knew it wasn't from my own mind."

"What did God say?" I asked, realizing that this was a very significant experience for Tim.

"God said, 'The world would seem to be a very empty place to Me if you weren't there.' "

No wonder Tim came in the room with such a peaceful look of security on his face! This communication from God had given Tim a sense of his own significance as a person. It is one thing to have a human being tell you that you are important, but when the God of the universe says He would miss you if you weren't there, the sense of importance is unmistakable.

If the homosexually oriented person does not spend adequate time in worship, he will miss this vital communication from God that meets the needs of the human heart. If his basic needs go unmet, he may turn to homosexuality as a method of meeting those needs. Thus, times of worship are a crucial element in the healing process.

BIBLE STUDY

Most Christian counselors know the importance of Bible study; a person learns the truth from God's Word, and that truth helps fulfill the person's basic needs. Also, consistent Bible study helps renew the person's mind as he starts to think the way God thinks, enabling the counselee to control his thoughts, resist temptation, and live in obedience, thus establishing a stable Christian lifestyle.

Five major facets of contact with God's Word are (1) reading, (2) meditating, (3) memorizing, (4) studying, and (5) obedience. If the counselor can assign homework to involve the counselee in these five areas, it should be sufficient to train the person to have daily contact with the Bible. As in the case with prayer, it is not so important how much time is spent, but that it is consistent and specific.

With the promulgation of many humanistic, behavioristic methods of counseling, it is vital for the Christian counselor to maintain the basics of biblical truth. Some Christian ministries to homosexuals have changed their methods of counseling from a biblically oriented approach to more of a "condition-response" system. This assumes that the person is only an animal, rather than a moral being made in the image of God. It is sad to see this change, and in light of this, it is even more important to stress the value of the devotional life to the healing of the homosexually oriented person.

One of the major hindrances in a person's relationship with God is his *God concept*. A person's image of God often determines how the person will respond to God. Two principles become increasingly important as the counselee develops his relationship with God. First, the person needs to come to know God as He truly is, not as the person conceives Him to be. Second, the person needs to come to know God as his perfect heavenly Father. Correction in these two areas of his thinking will aid the counselee in his progress toward psychological change.

CHANGING THE GOD CONCEPT

No one worships God as He truly is, because no one knows God as He truly is. With our finite minds, it is impossible to comprehend God completely. God reveals His nature and character in the Scriptures, but He has not revealed all that He is or knows. Whatever the Scriptures say about God is absolutely true, but the Scriptures do not reveal everything there is to know about God (Deut. 29:29). God has revealed to us all things pertaining to life and godliness (2 Pet. 1:3), but that does not mean He has revealed absolutely all things. Thus, what we know about God from the Bible is absolutely true, but there is much more to God than even He himself has disclosed. So, we worship what we know of God, not what He perfectly is.

When man sins, he subordinates God in his mind, and as a result distorts the image of God. First, man refuses to glorify God and give Him thanks (Rom. 1:21). Next, he begins to imagine that God is like a man (Ps. 50:21). Finally, man begins to liken God to animals (Rom. 1:21–23). This descent from theism, through humanism, and into pantheism is outlined by Paul the Apostle in the first chapter of Romans. The starting point, Paul says, is the suppression of truth through unrighteousness (v. 18).

The practical outworking of this principle is simple. When someone comes to Christ, his mental image of God is distorted by sin. God must then begin the task of reeducating the person as to what He is really like. As long as the person thinks God is something He is not, the person will find it difficult to relate to God. If the person thinks God is untrustworthy, he will find it difficult to trust God. If the person imagines that God does not really love him, as many homosexuals do, it will be hard for the person to feel secure in God's love. Prayer may be difficult for the person who pictures God as continually angry with him. Consequently, God must work with the person to straighten out this corrupted "God-image" so that the person will find it easier to relate to Him.

Kevin couldn't pray. Whenever he would try to talk to God, he would choke up with fear, grow silent, and succumb to his sense of hopelessness. After a long, heavy counseling session, it became evident to both Kevin and me that his problem was his concept of God. We talked about the true character of God revealed in the Scriptures, and then Kevin tried to pray again.

"Dear Lord," Kevin ventured haltingly.

"Try saying 'Father,' " I said.

"No! I can't say that!" Kevin snapped.

"Kevin, God is not your earthly father, so stop imagining that God will treat you the way your father did. Your heavenly Father is slow to anger, gracious, and abounding in lovingkindness. He wants to hear your prayer. Now try again."

Kevin eventually learned to pray, but not until he had diligently worked on changing his concept of God.

Though there are many *resources* for correcting one's mental image of God, there are basically two *agents*: God, and the person. Outside of prayer it is difficult to engage God directly in the process of changing someone's "God-concept." The value and power of prayer should not be underestimated, but since there is no guarantee that God will respond in any particular fashion, the most immediate way to effect change in a counselee is to encourage the counselee to help himself. Out of His love and wisdom, God will help the person; but in counseling, one must work with the agents and resources at his immediate disposal— in this case, the counselee and the Word of God.

The basic difficulty with having a distorted mental picture of God is that the person thinks that this false image is true. Homosexuals often think that God hates them, and that this concept of God is accurate. In the light of this improper *thinking*, the person makes incorrect choices, which result in negative responses from the person's emotions. The root of the problem, therefore, is the person's thinking; and if the person's thoughts about God can be changed, then the person's responses to God can be altered, and the person's emotions will stop bothering him.

The process of changing a thought pattern is actually quite simple. But there is a big difference between what is simple and what is easy. Many projects in life, like the process of digging a ditch, are very simple, but not at all easy. "Love one another" is a simple concept, but in a fallen world it may not be easy to perform. The same is true of the renewal of the mind, changing thought patterns—the process is simple, but can require a great deal of work on the part of the counselee. It may take some time for the counselee to establish the habit patterns necessary to exchange his false ideas for true ones. The process will have to continue indefinitely if the person hopes to change. But changing one's "God concept" is possible, and extremely important to the counselee's spiritual life, so the result is definitely worth the effort.

The three major steps to correcting one's concept of God (or any false idea) are (1) learning the truth, (2) establishing the truth, and (3) practicing the truth.

LEARNING THE TRUTH

Learning the truth is a twofold mental process. On the one hand, the person must learn what the truth *is*, that is, what God says about himself in His Word. On the other hand, the person must learn what the truth is *not*, that is, what lies he is accepting in his mind as the truth. These steps are a process of gathering information.

Since the basis for absolute truth is revelation from the mind of God, the Bible is the best resource for concepts that line up with reality. The clearest description of the nature and character of God lies in the Word of God, so it is extremely important that the counselee regularly read and study the Bible. In addition to the Bible, the person can learn the truth about God in daily experiences with God, by studying nature, through the Holy Spirit's speaking to his heart, and through instruction from other Christians. The last category may include teaching or preaching, Christian books, teaching tapes, fellowship, or counseling. This gathering of "raw material" provides the basis for changing the person's false ideas about God.

The "flip-side" of this process of information gathering is to uncover the false ideas the person has about God. Once the person has collected some true concepts concerning the nature and character of God, he should more easily be able to see where his present thoughts differ from God's revelation of himself. It is very important to be specific with these ideas. The counselee may think that his God concept is vague, but this is only because he has held a false picture in his mind for so long that he responds out of habit rather than consciously. Actually, the counselee's incorrect thoughts about God are very specific, but it may take some thoughtful digging to uncover this in the counselee's mind.

One of the easier methods of identifying false God-concepts is to start with the emotions arising from these untrue notions. Emotions respond to our *thoughts*, our *choices*, and the *circumstances* around us. If we think lies, our emotions will make the appropriate negative response. If we sin, we will feel guilty and depressed (providing we have not seared our consciences). If we listen to music with a negative message, our emotions will respond correctly by making us feel down or hopeless. But most often, our emotions respond to what we are thinking; thus, if we can identify and change the thinking, we can indirectly change the emotions.[5]

A bright red helium balloon on a string could illustrate this point. The balloon represents the person's emotions (e.g., anxiety, anger, or guilt), while the string attaches the balloon (emotions) to a thought. The most glaring reality to the hurting person is the balloon, but actually, the object to which the string is attached keeps the balloon down. If the person can find the negative or false ideas producing the emotions, and change the ideas, then the string will be "cut" and the emotions will change (the balloon will float away).

"Whenever I think about doing something for God, I get this knot in the pit of my stomach." Robert's distress was evident in his posture.

"Can you identify the emotion you're having?" I asked.

"I guess I'm afraid," Robert said. Uncertainty tainted his voice.

"Afraid of what?"

"I feel like there's this big, invisible father standing over me ready to clobber me if I try to do something. Anything I do might bring his displeasure, so I don't do anything."

Robert had just learned how to identify his false ideas about God by tracing his negative emotions to the thoughts that produced them. As Robert worked with his mind, making his concept of God conform to the Bible, his fear of assertion diminished and he experienced a new freedom to serve God.

Another interesting example of negative emotion is the anxiety that the homosexually oriented person often feels when he is tempted by homosexual thoughts or desires. A brief excursion into the person's thoughts usually reveals his concept of God: "God thinks I'm abnormal and is just waiting for me to change. God would accept me if I stopped having these thoughts and desires. God is angry with me just for feeling like this. God is

---

[5]This and some related points of therapeutic methodology are common to cognitive behavior therapy and rational emotive therapy. Dr. William Backus has done a brilliant presentation of some of these ideas, from a Christian perspective, in his works *Telling Yourself the Truth* (Bethany House, 1980), *Why Do I Do What I Don't Want to Do?* (Bethany House, 1984), *Telling the Truth to Troubled People* (Bethany House, 1985), *Telling Each Other the Truth* (Bethany House, 1985), and *Finding the Freedom of Self-Control* (Bethany House, 1987). I am indebted to Dr. Backus for many of the thoughts in this portion of the chapter.

against me. God hates me." This kind of thinking is bound to produce anxiety, and the only way to stop the anxiety is to change the thinking.

So then, if the person can learn to pay attention to his negative emotions and uncover the negative thoughts that produce them, he can work on changing the thoughts, and his emotions will change to match his thinking.

A second way to uncover the lies in a person's mind is to listen to his negative speech patterns. Jesus said that whatever is in a person's heart will come out of his mouth, so it is important that both counselor and counselee listen to the counselee's words to discover what is in his heart. Negative comments about one's value, one's position in life, one's relationships, or one's future proceed from the untrue ideas that the person has adopted as the truth. Thus, if the person can be trained to listen to himself speak, he can be trained to recognize the false notions that generate negative speech patterns.

"My life is such a mess," Carl moaned as he tipped out some tranquilizers into his hand.

"Didn't we just talk about that?" I asked. "Your life is not a mess. That is an inaccurate, untrue generalization that will cause you a lot of trouble."

"Oh, but I wasn't serious," Carl responded, trying to make light of the situation.

"You were dead serious," I said, "and your speech patterns are a good illustration of what we were just discussing. You think negative thoughts about yourself, your present circumstances, and your future, and you become depressed. You need to learn to listen to yourself."

Carl's incorrect thinking could be traced by investigating his negative speech patterns. I encouraged Carl to be more accurate in his statements about himself and his condition, but beyond that, to correct the false thoughts that produced the negative speech patterns. In that way he could indirectly control his depressed emotions.

A third way to locate falsehood in a person's thoughts is to watch the person's actions. Negative reactions toward oneself is an indication of what the person thinks about himself. If a person does not attend to his personal hygiene, does not care for his body when injured, does not keep his environment clean and tidy, or deliberately injures himself, he obviously thinks many false ideas about himself, and possibly about God and other people, too.

One of my counselees refused to care for his injured wrist. It was highly possible that he had broken a bone, but he would not go to the doctor to have the wrist x-rayed. A brief investigation into his thoughts revealed that he harbored many negative concepts concerning himself and God. He thought he was worthless (both spiritually and physically) and so saw no reason to care for himself. He also believed that God did not think him valuable, and concluded that his negligence did not affect God. Thus, he acted out of his false ideas and responded negatively to his physical well-being. Once he determined to start thinking the truth about himself and God, he realized that it was proper to care for himself, and went to the doctor.

Thus, a person's emotions, speech patterns, and actions are indicators of his thoughtlife. By collecting information we can aid the homosexual in the selection of truthful concepts to counter his false ideas. The counselee must develop two lists of concepts. The first set consists of the negative, untrue ideas that he has about God, himself, and his relationship to others. The second set is those portions of God's Word that directly contradict the person's false ideas. These two lists comprise the "raw material" essential to changing someone's false concepts.

ESTABLISHING THE TRUTH

Once the counselee has collected the information necessary for changing his thinking, he must then begin the process of fixing this truth firmly in his mind. It is good to know the truth in our conscious minds, but unless the Word of God becomes part of the "spirit of our minds" (Eph. 4:22–24), we will find it difficult to "put off the old man" and "put on the new man" as Paul admonishes.

Probably the best way to describe the process of combatting the lies in someone's mind is the way Jesus dealt with the thoughts of the devil who confronted Him in the wilderness. The devil is not stupid, so he probably did not appear to Jesus in visible form in the first temptation. The thought to change stones into bread was probably just that—a thought. The lie involved in the temptation was to think that if He turned the stones to bread, He would prove that He was the Son of God, thus doubting His Father's word: "This is my beloved Son, in whom I am well-pleased."

Jesus handled the situation by first recognizing that He was being confronted with a lie. Unless a person knows that he has a lie in his mind, he will not deal with it. Second, He resisted the lie by resisting the "father of lies," the devil. He said, "Get behind me, Satan!" Third, he replaced the lie in His mind with the Word of God. He said, "It is written" or "God has said," and then quoted the Word of God to replace the lie in His mind. These are three simple steps—recognize the lie, resist the lie, replace the lie with the truth. They are simple, but not necessarily easy.

The first step is probably the hardest—recognizing the lie. When a person has thought lies for years, it is often difficult for him to recognize these thoughts as lies. He will think that these ideas are true. For instance, it is quite common for the homosexual to think that God hates him, or that he cannot please God until he is heterosexually oriented. He has thought these lies for so long, he really believes they are the truth. So, the first step is to recognize these thoughts for what they really are—lies.

The Bible says that the whole world is under the power of the great liar, the devil (1 John 5:19). Consequently, most of the thoughts we receive from the world around us are lies. When confronting these lies, it is appropriate to recognize that these thoughts originated in the "father of lies," the devil. Resisting the liar and his lies constitutes the second step in establishing the truth in our minds.

Once the counselee recognizes the lies in his thinking and is actively resisting them, he can then replace these false ideas with the truth from God's Word. This is where the information he has collected about God's nature and character becomes useful. As he replaces the untrue thoughts with the truth about God, a correct impression of God will form in his mind, thus making it easier for him to relate to God in his emotions and actions.

PRACTICING THE TRUTH

After the counselee has learned to establish the truth in his mind, it is important that he learns one last step in correcting his distorted "God-image." In order for the truth about God to become a part of the counselee's life, he must practice the truth in his thoughts, speech, and actions, with respect to God, the devil, himself, and other people. A simple way to do this is to apply the truth to his life through his worship, his warfare, and his witness (both to himself and others).

Since the counselee should be worshiping God every day,

worship is a convenient avenue for immediate application of the truth to his life. As the counselee worships, he can learn to speak the Word of God back to his Father. For example, he should have learned and established in his mind the truth about God's faithfulness. In worship he can say, "Thank you, God, that you are so faithful to me. You said, 'Faithful is He who calls you.' " Or, he could respond to God's kindness by saying, "Thank you, God, for your kindness to me. You said that you are just in all your ways and kind in all your deeds. Thank you that I can trust you that everything you do in my life will be kind." In this way, in worship, the counselee can practice the Word of God in his everyday life.

The counselee can also practice God's Word in warfare. Sometimes wicked spirits will try to inject lies into a person's mind. This attack affords the counselee another opportunity to practice the truth by using the Word of God as a weapon against his enemy. As the counselee speaks the truth from the Bible against the lies of the enemy, he further establishes that truth in his own mind and life. This kind of attack may not happen every day, but as often as it does, the counselee can use the situation to get to know God better.

"My mind just went blank, and all I could think of was that God didn't love me anymore," Don said. Don was a young Christian, not yet accustomed to recognizing the voice of the enemy in his mind. His confusion was understandable, since the attack on his mind had been so severe.

"What did you do when that happened?" I asked.

"I couldn't think of anything to do," Don said, "I just felt more and more depressed when I thought that God had left me."

I explained to Don that this was a spiritual attack and that he could respond by saying something like, "I rebuke you, you unclean spirit, in the name of Jesus. I command you to leave me alone! God's Word says that He will never leave me or forsake me, and whoever believes in Him has eternal life. Now go from me, and don't speak to me again!"

The next time this kind of attack came, Don knew what to do, and he immediately performed the spiritual warfare necessary to clear the enemy's lies from his mind.

Finally, the counselee can apply God's Word to his life by "witnessing" the truth to himself and others. It is good for him to talk to himself, as long as he is speaking the truth. Talking to others about the truth of God also helps secure the truth in his mind.

"I'm sure glad I learned the difference between my 'wants' and my 'needs,' " Greg said. "I used to tell myself all the time that I really *needed* to have sex to feel fulfilled. When I learned to tell myself that this was a 'want' rather than a 'need' and that I wouldn't die if I didn't have sex, life became a whole lot simpler. Now I tell myself this same truth about many other things in my life, and I've learned that I can live without many of the things I used to think were absolutely essential. What a relief!"

Greg had learned that knowing the truth and speaking that truth to himself could direct his choices and emotions. In this way he was counseling himself using God's Word, and was, as a consequence, practicing the truth in his life.

So, whether it is through worship, warfare, or witnessing to himself, the counselee can practice the truth daily, thus establishing his life on the foundation of God's Word. This stability of thought will ultimately produce a stability of choice and emotion that will help the person live a consistent, victorious Christian lifestyle.

In the homosexually oriented man, one specific application of the thought-renewal process is extremely important. Since the person has suffered from the rejection syndrome described in Chapter 4, the person's image of God as heavenly Father is very likely distorted. To promote the counselee's psychological healing, it will be necessary to deal aggressively with this corrupted "father-image." Without correction of this improper image of God, the counselee's relationship with God will be more difficult, and the identification with an appropriate father image will be lacking, thus hindering the psychological development of the counselee.

KNOWING GOD AS FATHER

In the very young child, it would appear that the knowledge of God comes almost entirely through his parents. There may be some intuitive or mental comprehension, but this would be very difficult to verify, so it is safest to deal with what is objectively observable.

When we watch a child's responses to his parents, we find that the child seems to assume that the parents have the same qualities as God. For a long time the child treats the parents as omnipresent—that is, the child truly believes that the parents can be everywhere, and therefore are always present with the child. The child also assumes that the parents know everything that the child does. Thus, the parents are omniscient to the child. And to the small child, the parents can apparently do anything, thus taking on the quality of omnipotence in the child's eyes. So the parents are omnipresent, omniscient, and omnipotent as far as the child is concerned, and in this respect, the parents represent the *nature* of God to the child. Inasmuch as the parents truly love and care for the child, they will also represent the *character* of God in the child's life.

Perhaps, in an unfallen world, this scenario would be most desirable. But since the fall of man, parents have not truly represented the character of God to their children. Even the most godly parents still have times of occasional selfishness, and to the extent that the parents are selfish, the child sees a distorted display of God's character. No parents are perfect, so no child has been raised with a completely unblemished impression of God's character.

There is an interesting phenomenon which some psychologists call "focus." People focus their attention upon different objects of "worship." Some people focus their attention on people, some on activities, and others focus on objects. The fascinating result of this "worship" is that the person actually becomes like the thing to which he is attracted. Young people dress, act, and talk like the rock stars they idolize. They have become like the things they worship. The Bible clearly acknowledges this process when it declares that the people who make idols and worship them will become like them (Ps. 115:8; 135:18), and that those who focus their attention on the true God will become like Him (2 Cor. 3:18).

It is both natural and appropriate that the child should focus his attention on his parents to learn about the character of God. But there are two ways that the child can do this: out of love, or out of hatred. Once a child has been hurt, it is difficult for him to maintain a loving attitude toward the parents, so children commonly become bitter or resentful. C. S. Lewis noted astutely that "hatred blurs all distinctions" and when someone hates someone or something, he finds it difficult to distinguish between individual members of the group that he hates. To the person who hates black people, there are no good and bad black people; there are only bad blacks. And to the bitter child, there are no good and bad actions of the parents; there are only bad actions. Thus, the child lumps all of the actions of the parent(s) together in his mind and rejects them as a unit.

The problem with this kind of focus is that the child becomes "locked into" a negative focus on only the selfish qualities in the parents' lives. As the child hates the parents and focuses his attention on them through his bitterness, he will become like them, but he will adopt only those qualities that he dislikes. How often the counselor encounters an alcoholic who is the son of an alcoholic, the child abuser who was abused, the wife beater whose mother was beaten by his father! This pattern is recognized in the Bible when it speaks of God's "visiting the iniquity of the fathers on the children, on the third and the fourth generations of those who hate Me" (Ex. 20:5). The condition for the perpetuation of the consequences of sin from generation to generation is hatred.[6]

If the child loves the parents, he can see both the good and bad aspects of the parents' lives, then acknowledge and reject the bad qualities, while recognizing and focusing on the good qualities. This is the focus of love. But in our fallen world, this perfect state of affairs seldom, if ever, occurs. The general pattern is one of bitterness and resentment with the resultant perpetuation of the negative character qualities.

One of the spiritual ramifications of this process is the projection of the negative character qualities of the earthly father onto the heavenly Father. It is natural for the child to assume that his heavenly Father has the same characteristics as his earthly father. The problem with this is that some, if not many, of the qualities of the earthly father are not representative of the character of God. Thus, the child projects a corrupted "father image" onto God and assumes that God, his heavenly Father, really has that character. Even if the person became a Christian as an adult, this projection can still present serious problems.

Assuming that one's heavenly Father has the same character as his earthly father can produce many negative fruits in a person's life. This distortion can affect the counselee who is coming out of a homosexual background in a number of ways:

1. *The presence of God.* The counselee who has experienced

---

[6]The term "visiting the iniquity" refers, throughout the Old Testament, to the consequences of sin, either natural or governmental, and not the guilt of sin. The Scriptures very clearly teach that one person will not be held accountable for the sin of another person (cf. Ezek. 18). The consequences of the sin of one generation can affect the next generation, though, if the necessary condition of hatred is fulfilled.

the rejection process described in Chapter 4 will probably have difficulty with the idea that God will never leave him or forsake him. Since the counselee missed the presence of his earthly father, either through withdrawal of the child or absence of the father, it may be difficult for him to believe that God will be faithful to remain with him forever. Anxiety results from the nagging thought that God may leave him, often a direct result of separation from the earthly father due to work schedule, lack of communication, death, or divorce. So, it is important for the counselee to learn that God will never leave him.

"This strange feeling would come over me that somehow God had left me, that He didn't care about me anymore," Jim said. "At first I didn't know what to do, but when I learned from the Bible that God promised never to leave me or forsake me, I had some truth to apply to my life. When the thought would come that God might have left me, I would speak out God's Word in response. After a while, the thoughts became less frequent, and less intense. Now I know that God is with me, whether I feel like it or not, and I'm seldom bothered by those untrue thoughts."

By carefully confronting his untrue thoughts about God, Jim gained control over his thought patterns and eventually changed his concept of God. When his idea of God was corrected, his emotional reactions changed, and he found it easier to relate to God as he really is.

2. *God's faithfulness.* Some fathers deliberately deceive their children in order to teach them not to trust others. Some fathers make promises to their children and then knowingly break their word. The majority, however, simply make promises and then seem to forget, whether through busyness or oversight. For example, the father may promise his child that on Saturday the family will go to the park to play, visit their favorite ice cream shop, and then spend the evening together. Saturday comes, Saturday goes, and the child is left wondering what happened to the father's promise. Though this kind of lapse is understandable, it still produces the same thought in the child—fathers are unfaithful.

"It's hard for me to believe that God is going to keep His word to me and send me out as a missionary." Bill's discouragement was evident in his voice as he related his struggle to trust God.

"Do you think this might be related to your relationship with your earthly father?" I asked.

"Probably," Bill said. "My dad was always promising things and never kept his word. Do you think that's why I think God will let me down?"

"It's likely," I said, "but let's dig a little further into the situation."

As we continued with Bill's counseling, it became obvious that Bill was projecting his image of his unfaithful earthly father on God, his heavenly Father, and thus found it difficult to believe that God would keep His promises. When Bill used the Scriptures to confront those false ideas, his concept of God gradually changed, making it easier for him to trust that God would be faithful.

3. *God's goodness.* The person whose father lavished time, attention, and goods upon him is a fortunate person indeed. This person learned, as a child, that "fathers are generous." This communication of goodness in the earthly father will be projected on God later in the Christian's life. If, however, a person's father was stingy with his time, attention, or goods, the opposite impression will be made on the child. The child will get the message that fathers don't really care for the needs of the child, whether those needs are relational or physical.

With this kind of father-image patterning, the person will likely view God as unconcerned about his needs. The person may actually think that God does not have the person's best interest at heart, and could think that God is out to "mess up his life." It is no surprise, then, that people affected with this view of God find it hard to yield their lives entirely to Him. The internal thought is that God is malevolent, and the outward behavior ranges from suspicion over God's motives to outright rebellion against God. Without the proper father-image correction, one can only expect that this person will continue to struggle in his relationship with his heavenly Father. The mind of the homosexually oriented man has been severely affected by his broken relationship with his earthly father. Thus, if the person wishes to stop rejecting himself and others as a result of his past experiences, father-image correction is imperative.

4. *God's authority.* Answers to the question, "What was your father's discipline like?" range from "nonexistent" to "brutal." It is little wonder, then, that men who have experienced these kinds of authority have problems accepting the loving, gentle discipline of their heavenly Father. Those who have had brutal fathers tend to fear the authority and discipline of God. Others cannot even

comprehend what loving discipline is.

One man reported, "What do I think of God's discipline? I don't know. I can't even tell when I'm being disciplined. My father didn't care enough to discipline me." He simply drew a blank.

Whether the reaction is fear due to brutal treatment, confusion due to inconsistent discipline, or "drawing a blank" due to lack of discipline, the cure is the same. As the person comes to know what God is really like, he can learn that God's discipline is always offered in love, for the person's well-being. As this image of fatherly authority changes, the person's reaction to God's authority in his life can change accordingly.

5. *The justice of God.* The Bible clearly states that God is "righteous [just] in all His ways, and kind in all His deeds" (Ps. 145:17). God's righteousness, or justice, means that God is completely fair with every being. He will treat every being according to His law, and will never be partial or arbitrary in His judgments. Unfortunately, many homosexual men did not have fathers with this moral quality. Many men remember their fathers as unfair, tyrannical despots who demanded strict adherence to a set of arbitrary rules, but who never followed those rules themselves. Having had unfair fathers, the men may assume that God is also unfair in His dealings with men.

One of the major ramifications of this view of God is that the person with a homosexual orientation can feel that God is ultimately responsible for the person's psychological condition. The assumption here is that God is unfair because He gave the man homosexual desires, and then commanded the man to never fulfill those desires. Mark, one of my younger counselees, had this mistaken idea.

"It's just not fair!" Mark barked angrily. "Why should God allow me to be homosexually oriented, and then command me never to fulfill those desires? If He's loving and kind, then He shouldn't have allowed me to have homosexual desires in the first place, or He should allow me to fulfill them. It's just not fair!"

Mark and I worked through his concept of the justice of God, the development of the homosexual condition, and the issue of why the innocent can suffer. Eventually, Mark began to accept that God was *not* responsible for his sexual orientation, and with this revelation came a new freedom to relate to God.

As long as a man thinks that God is responsible for his sexual preference, he will find it difficult to relate openly with God. For this reason, then, it is important for the counselor and counselee to work through the issue of the justice of God with reference to the existence of the person's homosexual tendencies. The person's sexual preference is not God's fault; it has come about as a result of the fallenness of the human race. But until the person is convinced that God is not responsible for his struggles, he may find it difficult to trust God.

6. *The affection of God.* It is difficult for many men who are leaving a homosexual background to understand the affection of God. The men commonly had fathers who did not communicate affection to their sons, or the fathers were so aggressive that they scared their sons into withdrawal. With this idea of what fathers are like, homosexually oriented men will find it difficult to give and receive affection with God.

The love, affection, and concern of God are essential elements in the emotional healing of a rejected person. If the person never comes to understand and experience the love of God for him, it is most likely that he will continue to try to meet his basic emotional needs through insufficient, ungodly means. For the homosexually oriented man this means that he will attempt to meet his needs for love, security, protection, identity, etc., through another man. Since another human cannot fully meet these needs, the person will run a treadmill of need, relationship, unfulfilled need until he learns to have his needs met in his relationship with God. Knowing that God is loving and affectionate is a prerequisite to an experience of the love of God. So, the person must learn what God is truly like, and apply this knowledge in his daily relationship with God.

7. *The truthfulness of God.* Complete honesty and truthfulness in communication are a vital part of God's character. God is love, and to be completely loving, God must be totally honest and truthful in all His communications with man. Unless a person knows and accepts this as the truth about God, it will be difficult for the person to trust the communications of God, especially what God says in His Word.

For example, God says in the Bible that everything He has commanded us is for our good (Deut. 10:12–13). God also commands men to abstain from any form of homosexual activity (cf. references in Chap. 5). One could logically infer from these two facts that involvement in homosexual activity is detrimental to one's well-being. But the counselee who distrusts God's Word does not necessarily reach this conclusion. Counselees often feel that God does not have their best interests at heart, and He is not communicating with them 100 percent truthfully. They somehow feel that God does not understand their needs and desires, that His commands are unreasonable and harsh, or that He actually intends pain for them. These feelings result from a lack of understanding of the love and truthfulness of God.

As the homosexual works on establishing the true concept of the character of God in his mind, he will find it easier to trust that whatever God commands is for his good. When the counselee's feelings start to respond to these new thoughts about God, he will find temptation easier to resist and begin to see obedience as a reasonable response to the commands of God. Finally, experiencing the fruit of his daily choices to trust and obey God will further establish in his mind that God is loving and truthful in all He says and does.

In light of how a person's father-image is formed, how it can be corrupted, the necessity of father-image correction, and some specific aspects of God's character that need to become part of a person's concept of God the Father, three simple, effective steps can be employed to apply these truths in the counselee's life.

1. *Repentance.* David sobbed on my shoulder for over half an hour. We had been dealing with David's disturbed relationship with God when we discovered that David was still focusing on his earthly father. The bitterness and resentment David had toward his father was keeping him from knowing God. As David repented, asking God's forgiveness for his sin, he realized that he had to make things right with his earthly father, too.

Over a year later, David visited us again in our home. His report was very encouraging. David had gone to his father asking his forgiveness. As a result, their relationship was restored, David was released from the unnatural focus on his father, and David's relationship with God was improving steadily. We rejoiced with David as we witnessed the changes true repentance had produced.

The unnatural "focus" on the negative qualities of the earthly father produces a corrupted father-image in the child's mind. This focus occurs because of the bitterness, resentment, or hatred of the child toward the father. In order to break the focus, the person needs to repent of the bitterness that holds his attention on his earthly father. This will allow the person to focus his attention on something else, thus producing a different father-image and different qualities in his own life.

This repentance needs to be twofold. First, the person must ask God's forgiveness for his bitterness (cf. Chap. 6 for details on true repentance). Second, he should then ask his earthly father's forgiveness, if this is possible and wise. If the person's father is dead, the person is free from this responsibility, since it is impossible to rectify the situation.[7] In some cases, to ask the counselee to contact his father could jeopardize the counselee's spiritual or physical well-being. In these cases the person will have to wait for the right time to make restitution to the father. It is not a case of whether or not the person will do it, but when, and under what circumstances. Repentance toward God and his earthly father is the first step.

2. *Revelation*. Most people do not deal very concretely with their lives. Instead, they muddle along through life, paying no attention to who they are or what they are doing. As a result, they live fitful lives, full of questions, constantly wondering why they are the way they are, and why they do the things they do. Very few people, including Christians, realize the impact that their earthly fathers have had on their concept of God. Consequently, people need revelation from God, through His Word and His Spirit, to comprehend just which aspects of their father-image require correction.

The Bible contains the clearest revelation of God's character. As the counselee spends time with the Word of God, he will discover what God is like and how He differs from the counselee's earthly father. Thus the counselee will uncover the areas of distortion in his father-image. With these differences in mind, the counselee can go on to read the Word of God more conscientiously, looking for specific aspects of God's character to help balance out the distortions learned from the earthly father. A list of the affected areas and related scriptures will be essential to the counselee as he proceeds to apply the truth about God's character to his daily life.

Another source of information open to the counselee is revelation from the Spirit of God. God speaks to us in His Word, the Bible, but He also speaks to us in our spirits as we spend time

---

[7] I find "forgiveness by proxy" both unrealistic and unbiblical. Speaking to an empty chair or another person as if that were your father is out of touch with reality (neither the other person nor the chair is your father), and a violation of the biblical injunctions against attempting to contact the dead. Deep repentance and acceptance of the forgiveness of God will suffice in such cases.

with Him in prayer and worship. So, in a time of prayer, the counselee can thoughtfully and prayerfully consider his father-image, asking God to reveal the areas of distortion. God, in His faithfulness, will give the person revelation in his mind and spirit. This information, together with the information from God's Word, should help the counselee know which areas of his father-image need correction, and exactly how God differs from his earthly father. The counselee then has the raw material necessary for application to his daily life.

3. *Renewal.* God tells us that our lives will be transformed by the renewing of our minds (Rom. 12:2), and that the functional step for "putting off the old man" and "putting on the new man" is to be renewed in the spirit of our mind (Eph. 4:22–24). In other words, if our minds are changed, then our lives will be transformed—if we think differently, we will act and feel differently. The final step toward father-image correction is renewal of the mind through daily application of the Word of God.

The first step of the renewal (learning the truth) is accomplished through the acquisition of "revelation" mentioned above. This effort should bring the counselee to an understanding of both the negative and positive sides of his father-image problem. That is, the person should know the lies that he is accepting as the truth, and the truth about God from His Word. The second step (establishing the truth) is to recognize these lies in his thinking, to resist the lies, and to replace them with the truth. The counselee's third step (rehearsing or practicing the truth) is to use the truth about God's character in his daily worship of God, warfare against the enemy, and his witness to others and to himself.

CHAPTER EIGHT

SELF-UNDERSTANDING

I'm amazed at how much freedom I feel after talking with you these few hours!" Larry's voice bubbled with excitement. "I thought I'd have to live with that heavy feeling of condemnation the rest of my life. It sure is good to know what God thinks of me and how I should think about myself. Thanks a lot!"

As Larry sat across the dinner table from me, I couldn't help but be impressed with his gentleness, his intelligence, and his sincere desire to serve the Lord. I also contemplated what a privilege it was to be a small link in the chain of events the Lord was using to bring healing into Larry's life. It reminded me once again that God uses me to bless others because He loves the other people, not because I deserve to be used. My little part in Larry's life was to bring understanding.

A good friend once said to me, "Mike, in many cases, *understanding is healing.*" He did not mean that understanding *brings* healing, but that understanding the truth of a situation often *is* healing itself. Sometimes, when a person learns the truth about himself, God, relationships, or reality, the problem the person was having normalizes, and his behavior and emotions change. Thus, the power of truth alone can liberate people. God's Word is truth (John 17:17), and that truth is alive and powerful (Heb. 4:12).

The person leaving a homosexual lifestyle can be very confused. He may not understand many of his feelings, thoughts, desires, or actions. It is the job of the counselor to help the counselee understand himself so the counselee can proceed, unhindered by confusion, toward a stable Christian lifestyle. Failure to communicate this understanding is the reason underlying much

123

of the ongoing struggle experienced by the homosexually oriented counselee. Final responsibility for change rests on the counselee because he must practice the truth he knows; but if he never receives the information necessary to understand himself, how can he apply this unknown truth to his life?

For the Christian counselor to be equipped to understand some of the "inner workings" of the homosexual, he must understand how the counselee can overcome problems with rejection, think of himself biblically (self-image correction), and overcome condemnation. The person's basic attitudes need to be carefully watched, and his questions about the justice of God answered. In addition to the practical "how-to's," sometimes just the knowledge of these truths can be enough to bring new freedom to the troubled person.

DEALING WITH REJECTION

Chapter 4 outlines the five-step rejection process that lies at the root of the homosexual condition. Some of these steps are applicable only to the development of the homosexual preference (such as rejection of the male image), whereas some of the steps can apply to the rejection that almost everyone experiences at some time in his life: (1) rejection *by* others, (2) rejection of self, and (3) rejection *of* others. A person can, however, engage in biblical responses to overcome the "rejection syndrome."

One way to look at this is in a vertical fashion, like the growth of a tree. *Rejection by others* is a root cause. *Rejection of self* is a problem arising from the root, much like the trunk of the tree. And *rejection of others* is a symptom stemming from the problem (rejection of self), just as the branches spring from the trunk of the tree. Thus, we could diagram the process with rejection by others at the bottom, rejection of self in the middle, and rejection of others at the top. In other words, rejection by others produces rejection of self, which produces rejection of others.

People's problems are usually rooted in hurt and/or sin. Most often both hurt *and* sin are involved. If someone is rejected by other people, he feels hurt, and this is understandable. But then he must make a response to that hurt. His basic options are to love the person, returning good for evil, or to become bitter and resentful. The usual response is to become bitter, thus making the root consist of both hurt and sin.

There is not much a person can do about being hurt. Hurt

is a matter of history. But it is not necessary for a person's history to be different in order for the person to cope with his problems. What troubles a person most is not the hurt itself, but the improper responses he has learned. The world is fallen, and people will get hurt; what matters most is how people respond. People can learn not only to make the correct response to hurt presently, but can also unlearn the old, sinful responses they learned in the past. Thus, it is not necessary for a person's past to change, either in reality or memory, in order for the person to gain freedom in his present habit patterns.[1] In looking at the root of rejection, therefore, it is best to concentrate on the aspects that can be handled—namely, sin and its consequences.

When someone is rejected and responds by becoming bitter, there are two things to deal with. First, the sin itself is a transgression of the law of God. God says it is a sin to hate others, so if a person hates another he is guilty of breaking God's law, and deserves to be punished. This part can be handled by repentance, reconciliation, and restitution as outlined in Chapter 6. Second, there are the consequences of sin, in this case, the internal, intangible damage in the offending person's spirit. It is this latter aspect that usually troubles counselees the most, since relationships can often be rectified without too much difficulty. All sin produces death (Rom. 6:23), and the sin of bitterness has its effect on a person's spirit, too.

The following passage of scripture is interesting because, although it is quite familiar to most Christians, the scope of the text seems very limited in most Christians' minds: "If you confess with your mouth Jesus as Lord, and believe in your heart that God raised Him from the dead, you shall be saved; for with the heart man believes, resulting in righteousness, and with the mouth he confesses, resulting in salvation" (Rom. 10:9–10). The phrase "with the heart man believes, resulting in righteousness" covers the aspect of getting things right with God, namely the forgiveness of sin. The next phrase, however, loses some of its impact when Christians limit the meaning of "salvation" to the forgiveness of sins. To be saved is a simple word with a broad

---

[1]After watching the "inner healing movement" in the church for about ten years, I have wondered whether people who have received prayer for "healing of memories" really changed very much. I have nothing against the laying on of hands, or biblical prayer for healing of a "wounded spirit," but I have noticed that people change most radically, not by the laying on of hands, but by the diligent, daily application of the Word of God to their lives.

meaning. Basically, it means to be made whole, but this wholeness can mean being made well physically or spiritually, being delivered from physical bondage or slavery, being preserved, protected, etc. This breadth of meaning is the reason for the different translations of the same word, especially in the Gospels. If a person confesses, he is saved, or made whole.

The functional portion of this phrase is the activity called "confession." This word, in Greek, means to agree with someone, or to "say the same word" as someone else. We often think of confession as having to do only with sin. But this word covers a lot of territory in the Bible. We "confess" Jesus as Lord, that is, we agree with God that Jesus is Lord. We speak the confession of our faith. We can confess Jesus before men, and He will confess us before His Father. Confession is not limited to the activity of confession of sin.

And what does this confession, or agreeing with God, do for us? It brings wholeness. With the mouth he confesses (agrees with God), and so he is saved (made well). This breadth of application is not well understood by many Christians. God is not only interested in forgiving us, but also healing us of the consequences of our sin, when that is justly possible and wise. The process through which this occurs is the process of confession.

Like most unbelievers, before I met Christ my life was dominated by various lusts; like many other men, my mind was often occupied with sexual lust. After I became a Christian, my mind would often bother me as my thoughts would be interrupted by images from my past. Extra prayer, Bible study, and worship only seemed to make the matter worse, as I would experience a constant barrage of these thoughts while I was having my daily devotions. At that time I did not understand the principle of confession for healing, so I suppressed the thoughts whenever they came up. Once I learned that I could confess these thoughts and be free from their power, I began to speak out my agreement to God. I found that rather than returning, as the thoughts had always done before, the ones I confessed did not return to bother me. Remember that I was not confessing these thoughts as sin, because I had already been forgiven for my past life when I came to Christ. I was agreeing with God that what I had done and thought was wrong, and as I confessed, I was healed.

The damage that a person incurs when he is bitter and resentful can also be substantially healed through the process of confession. The person can make a list (perhaps during a time of prayer) of the people against whom he has been bitter. He can then go through the list before God, acknowledging that he was wrong to be bitter against them, and healing will come in the person's spirit and mind.

The application of this principle of confession has brought astounding changes in some counselees' lives. One woman who was extremely rejected as a child experienced a change of personality that was so dramatic that the people who lived around her could see a difference in her the very next day. She no longer gave off an air of "you should reject me, stay away from me" as she had done before. Her problems were not over, by any means, but the change was amazing.

So then, the root level, rejection by others, can be handled through repentance and confession—repentance to bring forgiveness of sins, and confession to bring healing.

The problem level, that is, rejection of self, is one that deserves a good bit of attention. Most men coming from a homosexual background have very poor, inaccurate self-images. A bad self-image is an unbiblical, untrue concept of one's identity and value. Self-loathing, often confused with a bad self-image, is the *response* of the person's emotions to the bad self-image. The person thinks that he is worthless, and his emotions make the appropriate response to that untrue thought. The result is self-loathing. The way to deal with self-loathing, which is very common among homosexuals, is to change the self-image, the unbiblical concept of the person's value.

When a person is rejected, he receives a strong unspoken message that he is worthless. "No one wants to be around me," he thinks, "so there must be something wrong with me. I'm no good, I'm worthless. That's why people reject me." This message is in complete opposition to what God says about the person. God says that we have been made in His image (Gen. 1:26), that we are made a little lower than God (Ps. 8:5), that He has crowned us with glory and majesty (Ps. 8:8), that we are more valuable than many sparrows (Matt. 6:26; 10:31), more valuable than a sheep (Matt. 12:12), and more valuable than the whole world (Mark 8:36–37).[2] For a person to think of himself as worthless

---

[2]Other principles also indicate that man is valuable: (1) God created us, (2) God called all that He made "very good," (3) God grieved over man's sin, (4) God moved in history to redeem man, which culminated in the cross, and (5), God determined to resurrect the physical body.

is both unbiblical and untrue.[3] But since homosexual men have had a whole background of rejection, they most often think this way about themselves.

One goes about changing a bad self-image to a biblical one, strangely enough, through *humility*. When properly understood, true humility will bring a person to an accurate assessment of his own value. The problem is that most people do not understand pride and humility, and some churches even teach a form of pride as if it were humility. They then encourage their members to be involved in this form of pride, not realizing that it will further damage the self-images of the people.

The basic essence of this kind of pride is dishonesty. When I think I am greater than I really am, I am proud. If I say I can do things I cannot do, I am proud. If I act as if I am more important than I really am, I am proud. The reason I am being proud is that I am being dishonest with who I am, what I can and cannot do, or what my value is. Most people are familiar with this form of pride. But if I think, speak, and act as if I am *less* than what I really am, what then? Am I not being just as dishonest, and therefore, just as proud? It may be the "pride of the worm," but it is pride nonetheless.

Humility, then, is to be honest, 100 percent honest with who we are, what we can and cannot do, and what our true value is. If I am an expert on the violin, it is not humility but rather pride to say, "Oh, it's really nothing." When people recognized that Jesus was the Messiah, the Prophet who was to come, He didn't make himself out to be more or less than what He was. He most often replied with the polite Hebrew response, "You said that." Jesus was 100 percent honest with who He was, so he was completely humble.

If an unbiblical, untrue concept of one's identity and value constitutes a bad self-image, a person goes about changing it by

---

[3]There are some Christians, these days, who would have us think that to attribute any value at all to man is a humanistic, anthropocentric worldview. They seem to think that if they call man valuable, they will denigrate the glory of God. But why should this be so? To say that man is valuable does not detract from God's greatness or glory. Actually, the opposite would be true. To say that God made something that was worthless is to attribute stupidity to an omniscient being. Please note, though, that to affirm the value of man is not the same as affirming the goodness of man. The Bible is quite clear that man, in his sin, is not good. But there is a difference between being *worthless* (a value-related statement in the realm of metaphysics), and being *unworthy* (a morals-related statement in the realm of ethics).

being humble: *Don't think anything that is not true about you according to the Word of God. Don't speak about yourself in any way that is out of line with what God's Word says about you or your value. And lastly, don't act toward yourself in a way that is not in accordance with your true value.*

Once, after a man asked my forgiveness for a sin, he said, "Yeah, I'm always doing things like that." I grabbed him by the elbow before he could walk away, and said, "Would you like to say that again?" He thought about what he had said, then rephrased the statement to, "I sometimes do things like that." Some people might think this is nit-picking, but the man's first statement was a lie, and God takes lying very seriously.

Humility, then, is the answer to a bad self-image. As the person persists in thinking, speaking, and acting toward himself in a biblical fashion, his concept of himself will change, his emotions will respond to that new concept, and he will begin to feel good about himself. Most homosexuals do not loathe themselves because they *are* awful people, but because, as a result of rejection, they *think* they are worthless. This is a result of rejection. Consequently, gaining a new and biblical self-image is a vital part of the person's healing.

The third level of rejection, rejection of others, must be viewed from two angles. When a person relates to others, their different kinds of actions require different responses. The problem with the rejected person, though, is that he tends to make the wrong response to others whether he is loved or rejected. The reason for these incorrect responses is directly connected to the person's bad self-image.

The rejected person uses his bad self-image as a standard to judge the motives of other people, and as a result becomes suspicious of any display of affection. If someone says "I love you," the rejected person will consult (unconsciously) with his self-image, compare the statement with his opinion of his own value, and conclude that the other person must be insincere, since the rejected person is "not worth loving." Thus, rejected people are suspicious of the love of others. They mistakenly believe that they are not worth loving, so if anyone expresses love to them, the other person must not be telling the truth. You can hear this psychological phenomenon expressed in statements like, "Well, they say that they love me, but you just wait. You give them three months to get to know me, and then they'll reject me for sure." In this kind of expression, the rejected person is telling us more about what he thinks of himself than what the other person is like. Thus, the person with a damaged self-image is suspicious of other people and rejects their love.

On the other hand, the rejected person may be rejected by others. When this happens, the person checks with his self-image, judges the expression to be appropriate ("I ought to be rejected, since I'm worthless"), and *accepts* the rejection of the other person. As odd as this may seem, it happens all the time.

"I can't figure out why I always want to go out with men who treat me like dirt," Marilyn said. "If a man treats me like a princess, I drop him as fast as I can. But if a guy is really nasty to me, I seem to like it. Why is that?"

"Well, Marilyn," I replied, "I think your response has more to do with what you think of yourself than with the actions of the men you date."

This woman's problem was her estimation of her own value. She did not believe that she was worth loving. When a man treated her as valuable, she simply could not believe that he was being sincere. If a man mistreated her, it fit her self-image, and she accepted the abuse. Thus, rejected people reject the love of other people, and they accept rejection—though deep down they don't like it. Eventually, they end up rejecting any kind of communication from others, because, as far as they're concerned, all communications contain some kind of negative message about their value.

At last the suffering person comes to believe that all other people are potential threats, whether the others love or reject him. He then interprets all communications as *rejection by others*. He has come full circle: (1) the person is rejected by others, so (2) the person rejects himself, and then (3) the person sees all others as potential threats, so (4) the person rejects others, but (5) the person *feels* that all others are rejecting him, and on it goes. If the counselee is to live a stable Christian life, he will have to learn to deal with both the love and rejection of other people.

When the rejected person is loved, he needs to learn to respond to that love correctly. There are three things that can help him to learn that the love of other people is most often sincere. First, he should *stop judging* the motives of other people. Jesus commanded us not to judge others, lest we be judged by our own standard (Matt. 7:1–2). The suspicion of the rejected person leads him into unfair judgment of the motives of others. So, he must obey God's command, and stop judging others. Second, he needs to learn to *trust others*. God says that "love believes all things" (1 Cor. 13:7), or love gives others the benefit of the doubt. The rejected person can choose to trust others, and needs to learn to do that. Third, the hurting person should learn to *accept others*. Every Christian is commanded to accept others as God has accepted him (Rom. 15:7). If the rejected person can learn to respond to these three commands from God's Word, he can effectively deal with the love of other people. Learning to accept the love of others will promote the healing process in his life.

But what is a person to do if he is rejected by others? What if other people hurt him? God gives us practical responses to rejection, too. First, the rejected person is to *bless the other person*. Jesus tells us to bless those who curse us (Luke 6:28). If another person speaks negatively about us, we are to respond by speaking positively about him (or to him). Second, the rejected person can *pray for the other person*. Again, Jesus teaches us to pray for those who abuse and persecute us (Matt. 5:44). When we have been hurt by others, praying for them can be a tremendous aid in not becoming bitter against them. Third, the person can *do good to them*. We are commanded to do good to our enemies (Rom. 12:20, 21). So, if the rejected person has opportunity, he should do good to the person who hurt him.

Bless them, pray for them, do good to them. These three things can help the rejected person handle hurt in a godly manner, thus stopping the cycle of rejection.

Breaking the rejection syndrome is extremely important to the life of the homosexually oriented counselee. Most men who come from a homosexual background go back to their lifestyles because they feel they don't "fit in." They don't feel accepted in a church, or in a Christian community, or by their Christian friends. They feel rejected, yet they have a need to be loved, and so they go to the solution they find most familiar—the gay community. In many cases, however, the Church did not reject the person. Rather, the person responded out of his background of rejection, and *supposed* that the Church rejected him, when it was really his own problem.

"Nobody here really loves me!" Phil shouted, his eyes darting in anger at everyone in the room. "You say that you love everyone, but no one has shown me love while I've been here."

"Phil," the pastor said, "that's not really true. People here really do love you. We're not perfect, and we make mistakes, but it is simply not true that nobody here loves you. Your problem is that you have trouble receiving our love because you were rejected in your past." The pastor kept trying to convince Phil that we loved him, but Phil's bitterness stood as a wall against every effort to reach him.

Unfortunately, this story has an unhappy ending. Phil continued to reject the love of others, blaming them for his problems, and eventually committed suicide. It could have been different if Phil had only learned to let others love him.

Problems with rejection develop in a person's life over a period of years. It is no wonder, then, that these problems are not easily overcome. But consistent application of the truth from God's Word to the counselee's life will bring change, and the difference is definitely worth the effort.

OVERCOMING CONDEMNATION

"Imagine," someone once said to me, "just imagine what it would be like if you had to feel guilty every time you became hungry! Think of it. What if you could live the rest of your life without eating, yet you were constantly hungry, and eating would be a sin against God? How would you feel?" Many men, after they leave a homosexual lifestyle, think they are guilty just for feeling sexual desire for other men, so they walk around with a heavy weight of condemnation on their hearts. As one man put it, "I feel as if God is always breathing down my neck."

Condemnation is probably one of the major killers in the Christian's life— a person has that awful feeling that something is somehow wrong between himself and God. God is against him, but he's not quite sure why. Or, he thinks he knows why God is angry, but he can't do anything about it. What a fix! Many homosexually oriented men face this dilemma. God says He loves them, and yet it is God who seems to demand that they not have the desires they so often feel.

The person with a homosexual orientation cannot afford to live under such pressure. The weight of condemnation will eventually lead him to discouragement, depression, difficulty in controlling his thoughts, even to lust and fornication. The problem is confusion, and the person can overcome condemnation if he can learn to make certain distinctions. The person must learn to distinguish between condition and behavior, temptation and sin, sexualization and lust.

1. *Condition and behavior.* For some reason, the difference between the homosexual condition (orientation, tendencies, proclivity, preference) and homosexual behavior seems easy for people to understand, but difficult to remember. One of my witnessing partners, after a year of witnessing in gay bars, still did not understand the full importance of this difference, and he could not clearly explain this difference to the men at the bar.

The homosexual condition, or sexual preference, is a psychological phenomenon. The person who has experienced the rejection process described in Chapter 4 is left with a strong desire for love, particularly male affection. These desires arise in the person due to the effect of the broken family pattern on the person's mind. Volition has nothing to do with the development or recurrence of these desires; the person did not choose to have them, and cannot simply choose to stop them. Since these desires are not chosen by the person, the person cannot feel responsible for them. Most men report that the feelings were just "there" when they came to understand themselves as sexual beings. This tendency, then, is a psychological reality that the person did not choose. He is not responsible for its existence, and he is not guilty for having it.

The behavior of homosexuality, on the other hand, *is* under the control of the person's will, and he is fully responsible to control his choices. No matter how strong his desire for male affection may be, there is still no excuse for disobedience to the Word of God. This disobedience may take the form of lust in the person's heart, or overt sexual acts, but the person is still responsible if he chooses to do these things. Whereas the homosexual *preference* is psychological, consisting of thoughts and feelings, the *behavior* is volitional, consisting of choices the person makes in response to the preference.

The difference between the condition and the behavior of homosexuality is vitally important to the homosexually oriented counselee. If the counselee cannot distinguish his thoughts and feelings from his choices, he will hold himself responsible for things that are not under the direct control of his will. Worse yet, he will feel that *God* is holding him responsible for things he cannot control. As a result, he will feel condemned when he is actually not guilty of any transgression against God's law.

One would think that a point so simple and yet so important would be readily remembered by a counselee. Alas, it is often not so. I have spent multiple hours covering this same territory

again and again, trying to help a discouraged counselee understand that he is not guilty for his feelings and desires. Then, two
counseling sessions later, I have to go through it yet again! Often
the person has spent so long thinking incorrectly about his problems that he finds it difficult to adjust to a new way of viewing
his situation.

The counselor must listen carefully to the statements of the
counselee. Sometimes the counselee will make open remarks
about his sense of condemnation. Sometimes the problem will be
obscure to the counselee, so he will make vague references to
feeling "heavy" or that "something is wrong" or maybe "God is
against me." At this point, the counselor should take the time to
probe for the thoughts behind these references. The counselee
may still be struggling with feelings of condemnation based on
untrue thoughts about himself and/or God, and may need to
work on learning to think the truth about his feelings and God's
attitude.

To avoid confusion for both counselor and counselee, the
difference between condition and behavior must be recognized
and kept in mind in every exchange. It may take time for the
Christian counselor to establish this distinction in his own thinking and to impress his counselees with its importance. But eventually the counselor will reap the reward of his efforts as he sees
his counselees free from confusion and condemnation.

2. *Temptation and sin.* The homosexual sexual preference provides an occasion for sin in a person's life, but the fine line between what is temptation and what is sin needs to remain very
clear in the person's mind. For instance, a homosexually oriented
man may attend a Bible study and meet another man to whom
he is attracted. Needing love, and thinking that this need can be
met in a sexual relationship with a man, the person is presented
with a temptation to meet this need in an ungodly, ineffective
fashion. Up to this point, though, there has been only the occasion to sin. The man's desires have presented him with an opportunity to break the law of God, but until a choice contrary to
God's law is made, the man has committed no sin. The same
principle would hold true of a heterosexually oriented man who
is attracted to a woman.

Most people find it easy to distinguish between temptation
and sin when the issues are sexual desire and fornication. The
distinction people find more difficult is the line between sexual
desire and lust. This difficulty arises because people forget that

not all of the states of their minds are under the direct control of their wills. Surely, *some* of the states of the mind are under the control of the will. But some of the states of the mind function apart from the will entirely. One cannot, for example, look at a red rose and choose to see a blue rose instead. Our perceptions of color have been fixed so that we do not have to choose to see colors a certain way. In the same way, the attractions people have for members of the same or opposite sex are not under the direct control of their wills. What they do with those desires can be righteous or unrighteous, but the desires in themselves are not evil. So, if a thought arises in a person's mind (in this case, a sexual attraction), the person can turn his thoughts to something else, and avoid sinning, or he can choose to continue dwelling on that thought in his mind, stirring up further desires, and commit the sin of lust.

One of the difficult aspects of this distinction is emotion. Our emotions are responses to what we think, what we do, and the circumstances around us. Consequently, whether we are only thinking about sinning (a temptation), or we choose to commit the sin, we can have the same reaction in our emotions. The intensity of the emotions may differ, but the quality of the emotions will be the same. Thus, after being tempted, we can feel as if we've sinned, when we have not. Therefore we must clearly define the difference between temptation and sin.

When the counselee complains of feelings of condemnation over his desires, the counselor may find it helpful to ask questions beginning with, "Yes, but did you choose to . . . " One might ask, for example, "Did you choose to go on dwelling on this thought to stir up your desires?" or "Did you become involved sexually with this person?" If the person's response is positive, he should be encouraged to repent of his sin. If the person's response is negative, he should be commended for his self-control. Forcing the counselee to make these distinctions in his mind will train him to differentiate between temptation and sin, sparing him much anguish in his Christian walk.

3. *Sexualization and lust.* Brian stared at me, his eyes wide, a look of shock frozen on his face. He evidently found it hard to believe that I had actually asked him the question. "But, but," he protested, "you want me to think about what part of a man's body I'm attracted to? Aren't you asking me to lust or something?"

"No, Brian," I said, "I am not asking you to lust. By thinking about what part of a man's body you're attracted to, you will learn how *not* to lust. Let's continue, and you'll see. Now, which part of a man's body attracts you first?"

Brian sat, still silent, either too shocked to speak or afraid to tell me what he was thinking. I could see he needed a little help, so I ventured a suggestion.

"Well, what is it? Are you attracted to the man's genitals?"

"Yes," he muttered, almost inaudibly. He still inspected me with suspicion, but began to shift his position and relax.

"Now," I said, "the most important thing is not what you are attracted to, but why. Now I want you to think about what you want to do with the man." Brian shifted uncomfortably in his seat, but remained silent. He was too embarrassed to reply.

"Oral sex, is that it?" I asked.

"Yes," Brian muttered again.

"Brian, you don't need to be embarrassed. Let's take a look at the desires that are behind this kind of thinking. In our culture . . ."

I went on to explain how in our culture a man's genitals are associated with his manliness. Whether this is proper or not is beside the point. It happens. So, we use a man's genitals to symbolize manliness. When the homosexual sexualizes his needs (cf. Chapter 4), he often associates a particular part of a man's body, as a symbol, with the need he is trying to fulfill. So, the desire to have oral sex with another man can be the expression of a basic need. The need may be for a sense of identity, power, value, competence, etc. By relating to the symbol, the man tries to meet a basic need by incorporation; that is, he tries to vicariously experience the qualities of another man by incorporating the *symbol* of that quality into himself, physically or relationally. Thus, the desire to incorporate another man's genitals in a sexual act is often the expression of a need for a sense of manliness, identity, power, significance, or competence. In the same way, an attraction to another man's chest may be the expression of a need for a sense of intimacy, closeness, affection, love, security, etc. The chest, or closeness to the heart, can symbolize love and security for the person. So, when the person sexualized his need for love, it became associated in the person's mind with that part of another man's body.

"Brian, are there other parts of a man's body that attract you?"

"A man's arms," he responded. Now that Brian saw where I

was going with my questions, he found it easier to answer. I could tell by the look on his face that he was already analyzing his thoughts.

"What is it about a man's arms that you find attractive? What do they symbolize to you?"

"Strength," he said.

"Now think about it a little bit deeper," I said. "What kind of strength?"

A small grin of recognition spread across Brian's face as he gained insight into his own needs and desires. "Emotional stability," he said, a note of revelation in his voice.

Brian felt emotionally unstable. After trying to have this need met vicariously through a relationship with another man, Brian began using the symbol of another man's arms to represent emotional stability. He became attracted to that symbol, thinking that the need would be met through the sexual symbol. This is sexualization. Now, Brian was learning how to *objectify* his needs, that is, he was learning to see the difference between the expression of a valid need and the sexualization of that need. Once Brian learned how to distinguish between real needs and their sexualization, he could work on getting those needs met in his relationship with God.

When Brian is strongly attracted to another man's body, he can make an objective, reasoned response. Perhaps Brian will be attracted to a man's arms. First, Brian can look away. Next, he can say to himself, "I am expressing a need for emotional stability." There may be different reasons why he is feeling emotionally unstable at that point. Perhaps Brian has disrupted a relationship and needs to seek reconciliation with that person. As he puts the relationship right, he will feel stable again. Maybe he has committed a private sin. If so, he needs to repent and confess his sin to God. He might not be able to pinpoint the exact reason for his feelings, but the most important thing is that he knows what needs he is expressing. Lastly, he can turn to God to meet his need.

With this new perspective on his problems, Brian also began to recognize the difference between the expression of a need and lust. This distinction kept Brian from condemning himself over every attraction to another man, since he recognized the attraction as a temptation rather than a sin. The Bible describes this principle when it states that "each one is tempted when he is carried away and enticed by his own lust" (James 1:14).[4] So, temptation to sin can come out of a person's valid desires.

The three primary steps in dealing with sexualization involve: (1) learning the difference between the expression of a sexualized need and lust, (2) objectification of that need, and (3) learning to get the valid needs met in a proper fashion. In order to help the counselee objectify his needs from the sexualization of those needs, I give the following assignment. I instruct the counselee to spend time thinking about his attractions to other men. He is then to list them concretely on paper. Next, he is to try to feel which needs he was trying to meet through those sexualizations, and write them in a second column opposite the first list. This exercise helps the counselee distinguish between the expression of real needs, which need to be met, and lust, for which the person needs to repent. This whole process, when properly instituted, can spare the counselee much unnecessary condemnation.

With a clear distinction in his mind between condition and behavior, temptation and sin, and sexualization and lust, the counselee is better able to determine those actions for which he is truly responsible, thus avoiding false guilt. As he learns to live a life free from condemnation, he will avoid the discouragement, depression, and anxiety that often plague those leaving a homosexual lifestyle. Putting those pitfalls behind him, he will more easily be able to establish a stable Christian walk.

A CASE OF THE INNOCENT SUFFERING

Frank had walked away for a moment, giving me a chance to ask God for understanding. "Lord, what can I say to this man? I'm not sure which direction the conversation should go."

God gave me a simple, profound answer, "Ask him if he prays."

When Frank returned, I asked him if he spoke to God.

"Well, I wouldn't say that I pray," he answered. "I would have to say that I send messages to God and he sends messages to me."

"Why don't you pray?"

"I'm afraid of what God will say to me," Frank said. "I'm afraid he'll tell me to stop living the way I'm living."

---

[4]The word *lust* here is not negative. It simply means "desire." This term is used for Jesus' own desire to eat the Passover with His disciples (Luke 22:15, translated as "earnestly desired" in the NASB).

I could not say, of course, what God would say to him if he prayed. God probably *would* tell Frank to leave his homosexual lifestyle, but that wasn't the point. The real problem was that Frank was afraid of God. He thought God had messed up his life by allowing him to have a homosexual orientation, and then told him not to engage in homosexual acts. As a consequence, Frank was resentful toward God, and his resentment kept him from praying.

Homosexuals often mistakenly assume that God hates them. With such a concept of God, it is little wonder that homosexuals find it difficult to come to God, and then after they do come, find it difficult to relate to God since they suppose that God is against them.

Unresolved bitterness toward God can kill a person's relationship with his heavenly Father. There can be many occasions for the development of bitterness, but most of the reasons revolve around the justice of God. If a person thinks that God has been unfair with him, dealt him a dirty blow, or tried to mess up his life, then the person cannot help but question the justice and goodness of God.

After coming to Christ, new Christians can have many questions concerning the character of God. One of the questions that bears directly on the problem of homosexuality is whether or not God had anything to do with the development of the person's sexual orientation. Did God plan it this way? If He did, then why does He forbid people to engage in homosexual acts? If God wasn't directly involved in the development of the sexual condition, then why didn't He stop it from developing? Many homosexuals ask, "Now that I have a homosexual orientation, what does God think of me? Will God help me with the problems arising from my sexual orientation? Do I have to change before God will relate to me as He does with other Christians? Does He really love me?"

Different kinds of questions require different kinds of answers. The question, "Why do the innocent suffer?" is an intellectual question that demands an intellectually satisfying answer. When a person's mind tells him that God may be untrustworthy, to tell the person just to "trust God" is a very lame, or lazy, if not irresponsible answer. There may be cases where a person's only recourse is to trust God, but when there are good, satisfying answers to an intellectual question, the person deserves to hear that answer.

When God made man, He made him in His image. Man is like God in that he can choose, think, and feel. Man also has some spiritual capacities resembling God's capacities—abilities such as devotion and intuition. Because man is like God, man must be free to choose to follow or disobey the law of love. Since the time of Adam and Eve, mankind has chosen to rebel against God, reaping as a consequence the fruit of that rebellion—the destruction of man and the earth. Although God has enough power and intelligence to be able to stop the rebellion and its consequences, He is not free *morally* to do so. If God took away the free will of man in order to stop the temporal suffering of the human race, He would, at the same time, take away the significance of man, since that significance depends upon man's freedom to choose. Thus, even though God never wanted anyone to sin or to suffer, He had to allow it, in that He could not *justly* stop it.

In the case of the homosexually oriented person, this general information applies specifically as follows. God never did, and still does not, want anyone to sin. When a family pattern breaks down, it is the result of two things: (1) the general effect of sin on the human race and (2) the sin of the people in the family.[5] Therefore, the effect that family patterns had on the mind of the sensitive child (i.e., developing a homosexual orientation) is directly or indirectly a result of sin. God never wanted it to happen, and is presently grieved over the situation, but He cannot justly stop it when it involves the free wills of humans made in His image. Thus man, not God, is at fault for the development of a person's homosexual orientation. The innocent party suffers due to the choices of other human beings. The child cannot automatically point the finger at his parents, claiming that it was their fault. It may have been indirect, more a result of the general effect of sin on the human race than a result of the specific sins of the parents. The important point is that it was not God's fault. God never wanted it to happen, He is presently grieved over the situation, and He loves the affected person just as much as He loves anyone else.

It may take some time for the counselee to grasp these concepts. The counselor and counselee will probably have many discussions centered around this topic. Once the counselee appropriates the truth into his thinking, he will be able to seek God's

---

[5]These two points were clarified and illustrated in Chapter 4.

forgiveness for his bitterness, stop blaming God for his problems, and see that God is willing to help him on a daily basis. The counselee's emotional reactions to the thought of God should also change, as the truth of the justice of God takes root in the counselee's thought processes. Some practical homework that will help the counselee more clearly comprehend the justice of God might include: (1) studying the justice of God from the Scriptures, (2) recounting and recording experiences from his life that illustrate the goodness of God to him, and (3) reading good books or listening to good teaching on the subject of "Why do the innocent suffer?" (See the suggested reading/listening list at the end of the book.)

THE LITTLE FOXES

"I didn't just go out and hop into bed with another guy," James explained. "Actually, I don't know exactly where it began. It was a long, slow process. I suppose it started with lust in my mind. That led to a habit of masturbation. Somewhere along the line I started looking at pornographic material, and that only stirred up more lust. Then came flirting with other men. Finally, I gave in to my lust and committed fornication. If I had known where it was going to end up, I probably wouldn't have let it get so out of hand."

The decline from a godly life to a life of selfishness seldom begins with an overt sin. Usually the Christian allows "minor offenses" to remain in his life, persistently resisting the conviction of the Holy Spirit, until he dulls his conscience and eventually engages in open rebellion. Since any sin, then, can lead to estrangement from God, it is important to resist all sin aggressively. The "little foxes" that can spoil the vines (Song of Sol. 2:15) need to be stopped before they completely destroy the vineyard.

Different developmental patterns produce different ideas about what will meet a person's needs. That is, depending on his childhood experiences, a person may feel that money will meet the need for security, or that getting married will meet that need. Someone else may feel that the need for a sense of value will come through fame and prestige. Yet another may feel that a true sense of competence will come through mastering a musical instrument. The list is endless, but the process is the same. As we grow up, we are presented with scores of false ideas about what will meet our basic needs for affection, identity, power, love, value, or competence. Consequently, different Christians fall prey to different temptations, because certain developmental patterns tend to produce different weaknesses in different people.

The rejection process that produces a homosexual orientation leaves the affected person open to particular temptations that others may not find difficult to resist. The following list of "little foxes" includes sins that all Christians will have to deal with at some time or another, but I have found in my counseling that these particular sins can be especially devastating for the homosexually oriented Christian. The counselee needs to be warned to be on guard against these sins, since they can so easily lead to more serious offenses.

1. *Bitterness vs. Forgiveness.* One man described homosexuals as having "bitterness collectors." What he meant is that homosexuals, as very sensitive people, seem to fall into the sin of bitterness quite easily. Homosexuals can find it easy to be hurt, easy to become bitter or resentful, and difficult to forgive. If a Christian harbors bitterness and resentment in his heart, his spiritual life will decay, and he will soon be involved in things he probably thought he would never do. Thus, the homosexually oriented Christian must be on his guard against bitterness. He must be quick to forgive and to restore relationships when necessary. Failure to maintain a forgiving attitude could result in the destruction of the person's spiritual life, so it is vital to deal with any bitterness before it causes severe damage.

2. *Selfishness vs. Giving.* The counselee should work on being "other-centered" rather than self-centered. Coming from a background of rejection and hurt, the counselee may feel that everyone and everything should revolve around him and his needs. He thinks about what people should do for him, but is not diligent to discover and meet the needs of others.

One counselee complained to me that he had been to church the previous Sunday and received nothing from the service. "Well," I told him, "if that was your attitude, I'm not surprised."

"What attitude?" he asked.

"You went to church expecting to receive rather than to give. If you had sought to meet other people's needs, you would have received as you gave. God says that if you water, you will be watered. You failed to receive because your attitude was selfish."

A self-centered life quickly withers and dies. We only flourish as we give to others. The counselee needs to be encouraged to maintain an "other-centered" attitude at all times. If he becomes self-centered, it is just a short step into self-pity, perhaps one of the greatest threats to vital spiritual life.

3. *Self-pity vs. Service.* The self-defeating, downward spiraling trap of self-pity can wreck a counselee's life faster than any other problem. Like condemnation, self-pity can quickly deaden spiritual vitality.

Self-pity is a constant rehearsing of selfishness. As the person feels sorry for himself, he nurses his selfishness, thinking only of his own needs. He feels that his own needs are not being met, and no one cares about him. The isolation and deep sense of need eventually drive the person to meet his needs, first in his mind, then in his actions—in the only way he knows how. He turns to lust in his mind, then to fornication, trying desperately to feel loved and accepted.

Self-pity is selfishness, and as such, the person must repent of it, forsake it, and confess it as sin. But beyond that, the person needs to replace this bad habit with a positive habit pattern. The focus of self-pity is inward. The person concentrates on his own needs and forgets about the needs of others. Once the person has repented of his self-pity, he should work on learning to serve others. Meeting the needs of others can help him to forget about his own problems, freeing him from self-interest.

Praise, worship, thanksgiving, and meditation on the Scriptures are also powerful tools the counselee can use to fight the battle against self-pity. Since the movement from self-pity to lust and fornication is extremely rapid, it is important that the counselee be on the alert against any self-serving thoughts, arresting them before they can "take hold" in his mind. A lot of pain, grief, temptation, and sin can be avoided, if the counselee will stop with the *first* thought of "poor me."

4. *Complaining vs. Thanksgiving.* Sins of the tongue are rampant in the gay community. Under the pressure of constant comparison, rejection, bitterness, and low self-image, homosexuals develop tenacious habits of gossip, slander, complaining, and backbiting. Upon coming to Christ, the new convert must learn new speech patterns. One of the most effective tools for breaking the habit of complaining is thanksgiving—thankfulness to both God and others for every blessing.

Thanksgiving has a positive, threefold effect on the thankful person. Thankfulness delivers the person from his *past.* As the person thanks God for his deliverance from lust and fornication, he reminds himself of the awfulness of sin and the privilege of freedom. Thankfulness roots the person in the *present*. Many people are waiting for "real life" to start—tomorrow. Real life always seems to elude them as they covet another time or circumstance. Thanksgiving forces a person to acknowledge the blessings of the present, and protects him from coveting the future as the answer to his problems. And third, thankfulness prepares the person for the *future*. Recounting the goodness and faithfulness of God cements God's true character in his mind, thus building faith that God will help him in the future just as He has helped him in the past. So, thanksgiving is good for the person's past, present, and future, besides acting as a wonderful antidote to the poison of complaining.

5. *Negative vs. Positive Speech Patterns.* "But I'm such a slut!" Jeff blurted out. "Why would you want to talk with a queer like me?"

"First of all," I said, "you are not a slut if you have left your homosexual lifestyle, so that statement is not truthful or accurate. Secondly, the term 'queer' is unhelpful to me, since I know that you are no longer gay, and it's unhelpful to you, since you're only using it to put yourself down. Now, let's work on developing positive, biblical speech patterns."

The low self-image of homosexually oriented counselees manifests itself in various forms of negative speech. Counselees will often make deprecating remarks about themselves or other people. They may complain about their jobs, their financial situations, their housing, their church, or their friends. Their outlook is often bleak, so their conversation follows suit. This negative talk should be confronted by the counselor every time it occurs.

In Ephesians we read, "Let no unwholesome word proceed from your mouth, but only such a word as is good for edification according to the need of the moment, that it may give grace to those who hear" (4:29). The term "unwholesome word" is not directly defined, but the meaning is indirectly implied in the remainder of the verse. Evidently, wholesome words are words that edify the hearer, they are appropriate or timely, and they give grace to the hearers. That would mean that unwholesome words are words that tear people down, are out of place, or inappropriate, and bring some form of bondage to the hearers. Since we are commanded to speak no unwholesome words, then every time a counselee tears himself or someone else down, we, as counselors, should confront this unbiblical activity. It is important, too, to point out to the counselee the reason for such behavior. He tears other people down to try to bolster his own sense of significance as a person, and he feels he needs to do this because he is not convinced of his own value.

Negative speech patterns and the negative thoughts that produce them are also the spawning ground for feelings of depression. The counselee cannot afford to be depressed, as this will make him more vulnerable to the temptations of lust and fornication.

So, if the counselor helps the counselee to pinpoint and change the negative thoughts that produce the negative speech patterns, he will be aiding the counselee to improve his self-image, avoid depression, and maintain a godly Christian walk.

6. *Laziness vs. Diligence.* Final responsibility for change rests on the shoulders of the counselee. The counselor can communicate many life-changing principles, but if the counselee fails to apply them to his life, there will be no change. Homework is the practical application of the theory discussed in a counseling session, but if the counselee consistently chooses to ignore his homework, no amount of counseling will help him. One of the chief reasons for avoiding homework is laziness, and one of the main reasons for laziness is *fear.*

In Chapter 3 we discussed the different kinds of fear that can be part of the homosexual's life. One of these fears was the fear of assertion. A man can develop a fear of asserting himself if his relationship with his father breaks down. If the father was too passive, the child received no praise for his efforts. If the father was too aggressive, the child learned that assertion provoked the anger of the father. Either way, the child will eventually learn that it is futile to exert effort to accomplish anything, and so becomes passive and lazy. In adulthood, the man may find it difficult to acquire new skills, meet new people, attend job interviews, or change his lifestyle. It is as if he feels the presence of an unseen father, constantly scrutinizing his every move, waiting to make some negative comment about the effort. Fear of retaliation produces a fear of assertiveness, culminating in passivity and laziness.

In this case, laziness is a symptom of the fear of assertion. The counselor can confront the problem on two levels. First, laziness is a sin, and the counselee should repent and seek God's

forgiveness. Second, the counselor and counselee should examine the roots of the laziness and take appropriate steps to correct
the foundational problems. It usually boils down to two distorted
concepts: the counselee's corrupted view of what fathers are like,
and the counselee's view of his own value and competence.[6] As
the counselee deals with his fears, his avoidance of homework
should subside. When he applies himself diligently to his homework, the changes in his life will encourage him to further effort.
This "snowball effect" will propel him into productive behavior,
thus curtailing periods of laziness and developing a responsible,
diligent approach to life.

7. *Pride vs. Humility*. Pride takes two basic forms: a person can
think, speak, and act as if he is either greater or less than he truly
is. Because both of these attitudes are dishonest, both constitute
pride. The counselor tends to see more of the second kind of
pride, the "pride of the worm," in homosexually oriented counselees. For this reason, the counselor must watch for negative,
deprecatory statements or actions.

The proud person consistently thinks and says things like: "I
don't know how I can make it with God. I'm such an awful person. I've always been a failure. How could God love me? I'm just
a jerk. I know I'll fall away from God sometime, and He will
finally give up on me." With these thoughts and words the proud
person prepares himself for defeat. He almost insures failure by
his attitude. Unless he conforms his thoughts, speech, and actions to the truth of God's Word, he probably *will* fail, but failure
is not necessary if the counselee can learn to be truly humble.[7]
Many other pitfalls could be added to this list of basic attitudes
that need to be carefully watched in the homosexually oriented
counselee. Due to the special needs of the person coming from
a homosexual lifestyle, he falls prey to certain sins more easily.
Once he gives in to these "little things," he quickly slides into old
habit patterns, usually lust and/or fornication, and loses the stability of his Christian walk. The Christian counselor must impress
the counselee with the seriousness of these "little foxes" in order
to protect him from more serious offenses.

---

[6]Chapter 7 provides information on how to change a father-image. The section
Dealing With Rejection in this chapter offers a discussion of how to help the
counselee improve his self-image.

[7]The section on rejection in this chapter gives instruction on how to practice
humility on a daily basis.

STAY BUSY

Boredom can pose a real threat to a person's spiritual life. People become involved in many unnecessary or sinful activities just because they are bored—overeating, oversleeping, gambling, drug abuse, alcohol abuse, pornography, masturbation, and fornication, to name just a few. The only way to avoid boredom is to be involved in positive, fulfilling activity.

The Christian probably finds his greatest fulfillment in serving others. Ministry to others can create a sense of satisfaction that few other things can produce. There are always needs that require someone's diligent involvement, so the counselee will not have to look far to find something to keep him busy.

Of course, staying busy should not be an end in itself. The counselee should want to serve God out of love for God, but serving God diligently *will* also keep a person busy. Then, as the counselee works to fill his days with helping others, he will not have time for the boredom, self-pity, depression and other ills that plague the inactive person.

TO MARRY OR NOT TO MARRY?

Should the homosexually oriented person marry? Will marriage help to heal the person with a homosexual condition? I am frequently asked this question, not just by Christian counselors, but also by my counselees. For the counselor, the question can be totally academic, whereas when the counselee asks, there are greater things at stake. Marriage is a lifetime commitment that cannot be made lightly, so the counselee must decide, before he marries, whether or not the step will be beneficial.

God commanded, "Let marriage be held in honor among all, and let the marriage bed be undefiled; for fornicators and adulterers God will judge" (Heb. 13:4). Holding marriage in honor does not logically imply, though, that everyone should automatically go out and get married. One counselor suggested that *the* answer for homosexuals was heterosexual marriage because the Bible says, "But because of immoralities, let each man have his own wife, and let each woman have her own husband" (1 Cor. 7:2). I find this thinking unhelpful for three reasons. First, in its historical context, it would seem that Paul is telling married people to be faithful to their spouses, thus avoiding fornication. This text does not seem to be a suggestion aimed at the single person.[8] Second, this counselor's reasoning implies that single people cannot be chaste, so the only answer to a problem with fornication is marriage. What ever happened to self-control? What about the example of the Lord Jesus? He never married, yet He maintained sexual purity. Third, this solution implies that the problem of homosexuality is entirely behavioral, having no psychological dimension. This counselor seems to think that if a homosexually oriented person marries, all his problems with homosexuality will disappear because he is having intercourse with a member of the opposite sex. Getting married, however, will not solve a person's psychological problems.

Many of the decisions that a Christian must make are not governed by clearly stated principles from the Bible. In these cases, the Christian's recourse is to God's specific guidance. God has many ways to speak to His children. The Bible is an objective, written revelation of the mind of God. Perhaps a good 90 percent of our guidance can be found in the principles of God's Word. But God can also speak directly to the hearts of His people by His Spirit. Although all subjective forms of guidance will have to be tested by the objective revelations of the Bible, the life of Christ, and creation, this does not invalidate the reality of specific guidance through the Spirit of God.

Whether or not to marry appears to fall into the realm of specific guidance. It will be up to the individual counselee, then, to seek God about that decision. After he feels he has guidance to marry, he will want to submit his ideas to other Christians for their counsel, prayers, and opinions. This will help bring objective confirmation, or negation, of his subjective ideas. Seeking objective confirmation is an important safeguard for anyone who is trying to discover God's will in a particular matter.

So then, the counselor does not need to feel obligated to give an opinion either way if a counselee asks, "Should I marry or not?" Counselor and counselee could discuss: (1) the advantages and disadvantages of marriage for the homosexually oriented

---

[8]Dr. Gordon D. Fee, a New Testament scholar with Regent College, Vancouver, B.C., Canada, affirms this historical exegesis. In his work, *Corinthians: A Study Guide* (Brussels: International Correspondence Institute, 1979), Dr. Fee states, "Therefore, verse 2 must mean, 'It is not good to abstain from sexual relations within marriage, because this will lead to temptations to adultery. Thus, let each married person continue in good sexual relations with his or her spouse' "(p. 130).

person, (2) the importance of discovering God's specific will, (3) the process of obtaining objective confirmation for subjective leadings, and (4) other matters generally related to the topic of marriage.

There are two extremes to avoid when discussing marriage with a counselee. If the counselee wants to get married, the counselor can help him to consider the decision and its ramifications. The counselor should not hold out false hope that marriage will solve the counselee's problems. On the other hand, if a counselee decides that he does not want to marry, that is also an acceptable alternative. He can remain single the rest of his life and still be perfectly within the boundaries of God's will. If, however, he is refraining from marriage out of fear, it will be necessary to confront and conquer that fear, so he can remain open to any options God may have for him. Since marriage is a matter of guidance, the counselor must be careful not to force the counselee in either direction.

THE BIGGEST PROBLEM?

Daniel sat quietly in the armchair across the room. He stared at his lap. After a while he looked up, desperation written on his face, and asked, "Do you think I can conquer these problems with homosexuality?"

"Yes, Dan, I believe you can. Not only that, but you will probably discover during our times together that homosexual temptations are really not your biggest problem."

"I don't understand," Dan said. His voice quavered, revealing his emotions.

"Homosexually oriented men often believe that their temptation to homosexual sin is their biggest problem. During counseling and the application of their homework, they often discover that there are other weaknesses in their lives that pose far greater challenges than the temptation to homosexuality. Men frequently comment to me that if they are controlling certain other problems, the temptation to homosexuality is easier to resist."

"I find that hard to believe," Dan said, "since my problem with homosexuality seems to be the biggest thing in my life right now."

"Well, give yourself some time to calm down, and to learn some things about yourself; then you'll see what the real problems are. Okay?"

Dan said, "Okay," but brightened only slightly.

After a few weeks of counseling, Dan started a session one day by saying, "Guess what! I found that what you originally said to me is true. My problem with anger is really bigger than my problem with homosexuality, and when I am diligent to keep my anger under control, I have very little difficulty resisting temptations toward homosexuality."

Dan had found out what many men with a homosexual condition discover. Their biggest problem is usually not the temptation to homosexuality, but rather some other attitudinal sin, which, when kept under control, lessens the power of homosexual temptation. Homosexuality appears to be the biggest problem when the person first comes for counsel, but as the counselee uncovers the roots of his troubles, he begins to see the real culprits in his life.

The results of this discovery are freedom and hope. When a person focuses all his attention on one problem in his life, he begins to feel as if that were the *only* problem he has. That one thing fills his whole field of vision, and everything else seems secondary. When the person comprehends that there may be bigger struggles in his life than the temptation to homosexuality, this knowledge frees him to see his life in better perspective. This freedom to view his life differently helps instill hope for change, one of the most necessary ingredients in successful counseling.

CHAPTER NINE

FIGHTING THE UNSEEN ENEMY

I think I'm losing my mind," Allan blurted out. His outburst brought our small-group meeting to an abrupt stop. As we stared at him in silence, Allan began trembling and weeping, still muttering about losing his mind.

I glanced around the room to see how the others were handling the situation. Since the faces of the group members registered fear and unbelief, I realized I had to do something quickly. I walked to where Allan was sitting, placed my hands on his head, and commanded the unclean spirit that was bothering him to leave him alone. Allan immediately stopped shaking and weeping, dried his face, and thanked me.

"This was a simple spiritual attack," I explained. "It could be stopped with a verbal command using the authority of Jesus." I then took advantage of the opportunity to give a short teaching on spiritual warfare and sensitivity to the spiritual world.

The Bible is very frank about the existence of the spiritual world and how it impinges on physical reality. The Christian does not think of this as unusual or weird, but as "the way things are." Angels, cherubim, seraphim, and demons appear frequently on the pages of Scripture. There are even some amazing descriptions of unnamed creatures, creatures with six wings and eyes all over them, who would probably scare to death any human who saw them (Rev. 4:8). Appearances of spiritual beings are not presented as extraordinary in the Bible, but are recorded as simple, historical events. Abraham served a meal to the Lord and two angels as if they were visitors from the tent next door (Gen. 18:1–8).

When the Christian counselor diagnoses what is happening in someone's life, he must seriously consider the spiritual aspect of reality. Failure to acknowledge this facet of life promotes distorted and ineffective counseling. Spiritual maladies require spiritual remedies, and attempting to handle a spiritual problem on a moral, psychological, or physical level can cause disaster. A person's spiritual life is just as real as these other aspects, and the counselor who ignores it could leave the confused counselee with problems that could have otherwise been solved.

Fear of involvement in spiritual matters will sometimes keep a counselor from delving into his counselee's spiritual problems. One common fear is the fear of imbalance. There have been so many extreme cases in the past few years that some counselors avoid dealing with anything spiritual for fear they will be branded as lunatics or fanatics. This fear is understandable, but it still should not hinder the Christian counselor from dealing with his counselees in truth, and the truth is that spiritual problems are real. If the counselor remains faithful to the truth revealed in God's Word, he will maintain balance in his counseling. The Bible acknowledges different kinds of problems with different solutions, and it is only when people stray from this message in the Bible that they become unbalanced.

Another major fear that counselors face is fear of the spiritual battle itself. That is, they are afraid to engage spiritual beings in battle using the authority of Jesus, either because they lack confidence in their own ability, or are afraid of being hurt in the battle. But these fears should not stop the Christian counselor. First of all, every Christian has been given authority over all the power of the enemy (Luke 10:19), and does not need to worry about whether or not he has enough authority. Second, Jesus has promised His disciples that nothing will injure them when they do spiritual battle (again, Luke 10:19), and so the fear of harm can be put aside.

A proper attitude toward spiritual battle is *conscious respect without fear*. It should be *conscious* because the counselor must never forget about or ignore the spiritual world. There should be *respect* because spiritual beings do have great power and can be dangerous if they are not confronted correctly in the authority of Jesus (Acts 19:13–16). And it should be *without fear*, because Jesus has promised the Christian authority and protection if he is serving Him. So, if we submit to the Lord Jesus and follow the instructions in His Word, we need fear neither the battle itself nor becoming unbalanced in our approach.

While ignoring the spiritual world is one trap the Christian counselor should avoid, on the other end lies the problem of assigning responsibility to the wrong party in a spiritual conflict. C. S. Lewis commented that the devil uses two extremes to deceive us. He will either encourage us to think that he does not exist, thus keeping us from recognizing his attacks, or he will make us believe that he is far greater than he is, on the same level as God, only evil, and all our attention will be focused on him, giving him more attention than he deserves.[1]

When a homosexually oriented counselee gets the idea that the devil or demons are responsible for his actions, the result can be disastrous. This kind of thinking quickly becomes an excuse for all sorts of disobedience—"The demons made me do it." Since this idea rids the counselee of responsibility, it appeals strongly to the person's fallen nature, and can be very difficult to change. Sorting out "who is responsible for what" can be a mammoth task once a counselee begins to blame demons for his actions. Thus, the Christian counselor must help the counselee distinguish between the influence of demons and the counselee's own choices, keeping in mind that demons can and do influence people, but that people are responsible for submitting to that influence.

It is not necessary to lose our balance when dealing with the spiritual world. We do not have to ignore demonic activity, treating it as if it were a moral, psychological, or physical problem. On the other hand, we do not need to "find a demon behind every bush," treating every problem as if it were demonic in origin. Faithfulness to God's Word will keep us from going to extremes, allow us to see the problems clearly, and help us to point our counselees toward biblical solutions for their various spiritual problems.

When a counselee is experiencing spiritual troubles, it is important to know both what the problem is and how the counselee can overcome it. Three general categories of spiritual difficulties include: (1) spiritual attack, (2) occult bondage, and (3) deliverance from demons. Once again, these problems are common to most Christians, but the specific application of the solutions will differ somewhat for the person with a homosexual condition.

---

[1]C.S. Lewis, *The Screwtape Letters* (New York: The Macmillan Company, 1961), p. 3.

SPIRITUAL ATTACK

One evening, my wife and I heard a faint knock at our front door. When we opened the door, Mary, a member of our community stepped in. She was pale, shaking, and mumbling something about losing her mind. We escorted Mary to a chair where she sat, put her head on the table, and wept. My wife and I looked at each other in bewilderment, wondering what might be the matter.

"Well, Carol," I said, "I guess we'll just have to ask God what's wrong."

As soon as we prayed we understood that Mary was under spiritual attack. We laid our hands on her, rebuked the unclean spirit that was bothering her, and the response was immediate. Mary became calm, looked up, smiled, and said, "Oh, hello. What am I doing here?" She evidently didn't remember walking to our house. After Mary relaxed for a bit, we instructed her in the use of her spiritual authority, so that if she should happen to have the same feelings again, she could stop them before they became overpowering.

As residents of an enemy-occupied planet, Christians can and do come under spiritual attack. Wicked spiritual beings, whether fallen angels or demons, will attempt to influence Christians to do evil. This influence may come in the form of evil thoughts, unusual spiritual experiences, or even physical sensations, but the intent is always the same—try to get the Christian to disobey God. In order to withstand these attacks, the Christian needs to know what authority he has, how to recognize when he is under attack, what kinds of weapons the enemy will use, and what kinds of weapons the Christian can use in response.

There are essentially three kinds of authority in the universe: (1) intrinsic, (2) delegated, and (3) usurped. Only God has intrinsic authority. He has authority based on His nature as God and His character. His nature and character qualify Him to be the governor of the universe, while our need to be ruled (due to our finiteness) gives Him the grounds of the right to rule. Thus, having the grounds and meeting the conditions of the right to rule, He has intrinsic authority. All other beings will either use delegated authority, delegated to them from God on condition of obedience, or they will have no authority. If this is so, then how do evil spiritual beings exert so much influence in the lives of humans, especially in Christians' lives?

A third kind of authority is *usurped* authority. Now, the devil and demons do not technically have authority, because they do not meet the conditions to receive delegated authority from God. But wicked spirits can exert influence or use power in any sphere of authority where the being who has responsibility for that sphere does not use his properly delegated authority. In other words, if a Christian fails to fulfill his responsibility to exercise his delegated authority, the enemy is allowed an opportunity to operate in that sphere of influence. An example of this would be the Christian father, the head of a family, who does not use his authority to protect his family spiritually. If he refuses, through ignorance or rebellion, to wage spiritual warfare for his family, then wicked spirits are free to influence his family in ways they would otherwise not be able to. This does not mean, of course, that the Christian father can protect his family from all spiritual attack. The man's responsibility for and authority over his family are not absolute. Only God has that kind of authority. But in the realm of the man's limited responsibility, if he does not express his God-delegated authority, the enemy has an opportunity to exert influence. So then, God has intrinsic authority, the Christian has authority delegated to him upon condition of submission to God, and evil spiritual beings usurp authority in order to accomplish their work.

The devil and demons usurp authority from other beings through the use of two very effective tools. In the book of Revelation, a description of the devil sums up the basic activities of the devil and demons. The devil is described as the "accuser of our brethren" who "deceives the whole world" (Rev. 12:9–10). Deception and accusation are all that evil spirits need to render other beings inactive. Through deception, the enemy will make the Christian think that he has no authority. Through accusation, the enemy will make the Christian think that he has no right to exercise his authority. Either way, if the Christian submits to this attack, and is intimidated into not using his own authority, the enemy is free to express his power in that sphere of influence.

Knowing when we are under attack from the enemy is one of the keys to effective spiritual warfare. How can a person tell if his thoughts are his own or have been influenced by a being from the spiritual world? The following observations cannot be taken as absolute, but they appear to be common experience with many Christians. First, a person's own thoughts are usually "traceable," that is, the person can think back through his thoughts to the starting point for those thoughts. Also, he can often uncover a stimulus from the external world that prompted that chain of thoughts. When a spiritual being influences the thoughts of a human being, the thoughts seem to interrupt the normal flow of thoughts with no antecedent, traceable chain. The ideas virtually "pop" into the person's mind with no apparent connection to the person's thought processes or surroundings. Second, the nature of the thoughts may give some indication of their source. If the content of the thoughts is contrary to the revelation of God's thoughts in His Word, that might indicate that the thoughts are not of human origin. Third, the timing of the thoughts can be crucial. If some nagging negative thoughts seem to appear only when the person is attempting to draw near to God (for example, during prayer, praise, or Bible study), this could be an attack of the enemy to keep the person from God. As stated before, these subjective observations cannot be taken as absolute, but many Christians have found these distinctions useful for recognizing thoughts that might originate in the evil spiritual realm.

In response to the deception and accusation of the enemy, the Christian has quite an arsenal of weapons. Just as the enemy has thousands of lies, which are all some form of deception, so the Christian has many weapons, but they fall into two basic categories. The Christian counters deception and accusation with truth and righteousness, respectively. So all of the Christian's weapons will be an employment of truth against the lies of the enemy, or righteousness against his accusations. The passage of Scripture that gives us the description of the devil as a deceiver and an accuser also shows us the antidote to those attacks. Rev. 12:11 states about the devil: "And they overcame him because of the blood of the Lamb and because of the word of their testimony." Christians can be right with God through the blood of Jesus, counteracting accusation, and they can handle truth as a mighty sword through the word of their testimony, counteracting deception.

Some of the specific weapons the Christian will employ against evil spiritual beings include: the authority of Jesus, the Word of God, prayer, praise, the gifts of the Spirit, and the fruit of the Spirit. If we consider each of these carefully, we see that each deals either with truth or righteousness. You can also see that most of these are applied verbally; when a person is assailed by deception from the enemy, in the form of evil thoughts for instance, the person must respond to those lies with the truth from God's Word, and he will usually do this verbally.

If a person is having a fairly normal day and his thoughts are suddenly interrupted by ideas like, "God doesn't love you anymore!" (deception), or, "You can't be pleasing to God" (accusation and deception), or, "God has left you, you're going to go to hell!" (again, both accusation and deception), the person is probably under spiritual attack. Now, people can have thoughts like this due to a damaged self-image, but then the thoughts will usually have some antecedents. In this case, when the person comes under attack, he can say something like, "Unclean spirit, I resist you in the authority of Jesus and command you to stop bothering me. God has said that He loves me and will never leave me or forsake me. Jesus has died for me and given me eternal life, so stop speaking to me and leave me alone, in the name of Jesus!" The application of truth and righteousness counteract the deception and accusation of the enemy.

The enemy's attack on a person will usually be directed toward the person's weak points. For the person with a homosexual condition, the major areas will include: rejection, bitterness, self-pity, lust, deception, and condemnation. There will also be numerous variations of these thoughts, but these categories represent the major battlefields for many homosexually oriented people.

First, thoughts of rejection sound like this: "Nobody here really loves you. They don't really care for you. They say they're concerned, but they're not telling the truth—give them a little while to know you and they'll drop you for sure. You'd better withdraw from them first, before you get hurt. You have to protect yourself because no one else will look out for you." When thoughts like these intrude on the person's normal thought patterns, the person is probably under attack. In this case, it is important for the person to respond with the truth that he is loved by God and by other people, that he can handle hurt even if it should happen, and that it is right to reach out to others rather than withdrawing. As stated above, the person should confront the enemy directly, verbally, and command the evil being to leave him alone.

Bitter thoughts sound something like: "They shouldn't have done that to me. I'll get them for that. I'll show them." Sometimes people will have whole arguments in their minds with other people. They think, "I would say this, and then he would say that.

Then I would give him a piece of my mind." Now, thoughts of this nature could be an indication of unresolved bitterness and resentment, which, as such, would need to be handled as a moral issue. But thoughts like these can also erupt in a person's mind with seemingly no cause. In that case, the person should consider the possibility of spiritual attack and take the appropriate action. Because of the rejection he has experienced in the past, a person coming from a homosexual background is especially vulnerable to attack in the realm of bitterness.

Thoughts of self-pity include: "Poor me, I'm all alone. I guess I'll have to do without friends for the rest of my life. People don't like to be around me, so I must be a real jerk. I'll just go somewhere to be by myself and sulk for a while." These thoughts could be symptomatic of a damaged self-image, or they could be the influence of a spiritual being. Again, once the counselee determines the source of the thoughts, he can take action to stop them. If they come from a bad self-image, he can work on thinking the truth about himself, but if they are an attack, he will need to perform the appropriate spiritual warfare to be free.

The fourth kind of attack involves two distinct aspects to an attack of lust as it concerns the person with a homosexual condition—one mental, and one emotional. The first problem enters the person's mind as a thought that he will never get his need for love met if he does not do it in a homosexual fashion. This thought challenges the truth that God both can and wants to meet the person's needs. In many men, it seems to be attended by an accompanying thought to commit fornication. Once again, this thought comes with no flow of thoughts leading up to it; it is suddenly "there" in the person's mind. The second aspect of the attack can take the form of very strong, although vague feelings of loneliness coupled with an intense desire for male affection. As I have asked counselees about the stimulus that may have produced such feelings, I have found that there is seemingly no pattern to this occurrence. The feeling comes suddenly, intensely, regardless of the mental or emotional condition of the counselee. This lack of pattern indicates that this is very possibly a spiritual attack, and many counselees have found that spiritual warfare can stop these feelings.

Fifth, the spirit of deception is very strong in the gay community, so it is not surprising that Christians from that background are attacked in that area. The original deception in the garden was that there would be no consequence for sin—"You surely shall not die." Those with a homosexual orientation will sometimes find their minds invaded with thoughts like: "How can it be so wrong? Why would God forbid people to love each other? God wouldn't really punish you if you had sex with someone—that's just a ploy by the heterosexual Christians to keep you under control and to spoil your fun. The Bible doesn't really say anything against homosexuality." Remember that these are not reasonings that come up logically in the person's thoughts. These are thoughts that burst on the person's mind for no apparent reason. When this happens, all the reasoning in the world will not help. The person must do spiritual warfare to overcome a spiritual attack.

Finally, Christians often face the attack of condemnation. At times, the feelings of condemnation are nothing more than the symptoms of a false concept of God or oneself, but sometimes the enemy plays a part in causing these irritating thoughts. Because the Christian strives to be sensitive to any sin in his life, he will value the conviction of the Holy Spirit. Many Christians struggle, though, with the difference between the Spirit's conviction and the enemy's condemning voice. One way to tell the difference between the two is to think about the focus of the thought.

First, the conviction of the Holy Spirit will always be specific. Sin is committed specifically, and so conviction of sin will also be specific. The Holy Spirit will remind the person that he thought, said, or did something contrary to the law of God. Second, the Holy Spirit always points the convicted sinner to the cross where the person can find forgiveness and freedom from his sin. Third, conviction always comes with a sense of joy and release as the person looks forward to forgiveness and cleansing from sin.

In contrast to these three points, the condemnation of the enemy is vague; it points the person to himself with thoughts like: "Look what you've done! You really blew it now! You're a real failure! God can never use you if you're like this! Condemnation leaves the person with a sense of hopelessness and despair. Thus, if the person considers the focus of the thoughts, he should be able to distinguish between the conviction of the Holy Spirit and the condemnation of the enemy.

So then, in these six areas—rejection, bitterness, self-pity, lust, deception, and condemnation—the homosexually oriented counselee must pay close attention to his thoughts. Although very subtle, spiritual attack is very real and can be extremely strong. It can also be very dangerous if the counselee is not guarding his mind carefully.

OCCULT BONDAGE

"I'm amazed at just how many of these men are involved in those kind of things," John said. John, the doorman at a gay bar, was referring to involvement in the occult. Although he disapproved of participation in the occult, he acknowledged that large numbers of gay men do engage in some form of occult practice. Men avidly discuss astrology, fortune telling, I-Ching, Eastern meditation, and even spiritism over a drink at the bar. Many of them hunger for true spiritual food, but their ignorance of spiritual matters allows the enemy to feed them a cheap counterfeit.

As a result of this widespread involvement in the occult, many Christians from a homosexual background experience a residual spiritual bondage. When someone participates in the occult, he opens his spirit to the evil spiritual world and consequently comes into spiritual bondage. After the person commits his life to Christ, he may have stopped his occult practices, but he could still suffer from troubling symptoms. It is tragic that so few Christian counselors know about and deal with occult bondage.[2] The bondage is fairly easily resolved, so there is little reason to allow a counselee to suffer from irritating, bewildering symptoms when he could be free.

The following is a list of common symptoms of occult bondage:

1. *Pride.* The pride symptomatic of occult involvement differs greatly from the sin of pride. Occult "pride" is a violent swing from feeling like the greatest person in the world to feeling like the scum of the earth—all in a matter of a few moments. Unlike the phases of bipolar affective disorder[3] that occur over a period of days or weeks, this occult symptom happens in a period of minutes. The extremes can be so violent that the person may feel he is superhuman one moment and doubt his own reality the next.

---

[2]This is especially disturbing in light of the abundance of biblical injunctions against occult practices. Passages like Ex. 22:18; Lev. 19:31; 20:6, 27; Deut. 18:10–12; 1 Chron. 10:13–14; Isa. 8:19–20; and Acts 16:16ff. make it very clear what God thinks of occult involvement, and this is only a short selection out of many references.

[3]Bipolar affective disorder, sometimes called "manic-depression," is a biophysical disorder that can severely affect a person's emotional state.

Martha sat on the couch, wringing her hands in her lap. She stared at her hands intently, never looking up.

"Do you sometimes think that you're not real?" I asked.

"Yes, sometimes I wonder if my body might be just an illusion," Martha said, her voice completely flat.

"This is a symptom of your involvement in the occult," I said. I explained to Martha how she could be free from this bondage by renouncing her involvement with occult practices. After counsel and prayer, Martha confessed her activities, spoke out her renunciation of the occult, and never again experienced the annoying sensations of unreality.

Martha's sensation that her body was unreal was symptomatic of her contact with the occult realm. In this case it was a form of inverted pride. Though some psychological phenomena appear similar to this, the counselor can learn, with a little practice, to recognize the distinct differences in symptoms.

2. *Times.* Funny feelings about times can be a symptom of occult bondage. A person may have strange, foreboding feelings about certain times of the month (e.g., the full moon), or days of the week, or times of the year, or certain numbers (e.g., the number 4 is evil).

"If I don't touch something three times, I feel uncomfortable with it," Liz explained. "Before I can sit on a chair, turn on a faucet, or open a door, I feel I have to touch it three times. This compulsion started in my life quite suddenly. Do you know why I feel like this?"

I checked for other symptoms of obsessive-compulsive behavior, and since some of the distinguishing marks were missing, I probed into the possibility of occult involvement. It soon became evident that Liz's "compulsion" was a symptom of occult bondage. As we prayed together, Liz renounced her occult practices and the compulsion left her life as quickly as it had entered.

3. *Marriage.* This symptom manifests itself as a feeling that marriage is somehow unholy or unclean. The attitude, then, is that no one should be married. It is not just that the person prefers not to marry, which a homosexually oriented person may do, but that it is unholy for *anyone* to marry.

4. *Foods.* When a person stresses abstinence from certain foods, especially meat, it would be good to check if the person has been involved in the occult. This is neither a preference ("I don't like meat"), nor a nutritional statement ("Too much red meat could cause cancer of the colon"), but a spiritual reaction.

Statements like, "You shouldn't eat animals—you wouldn't want to have the vibrations of a crab, would you?" are indicative of some form of influence from the occult world. It is always wise for the Christian counselor to ask his counselees why they are vegetarian.

5. *Unbelief.* "I just don't understand it," Carla said, "I've heard about Jesus, and I want to give my life to Him, but there seems to be something holding me back. Just at the time I want to believe, there seems to be a rope connected to my soul that pulls me away from Him." Carla was a white witch. The hindrance she was experiencing was a symptom of her involvement in the occult. Some people will feel a "pull" or "blockage" when they attempt to draw near to God, that is, a strong form of spiritually induced unbelief. Renunciation of the occult will deliver a person from this dilemma, and we will look at that process a little later.

6. *Forgetfulness.* An inability to remember truth can mark the life of a person from an occult background. Some people can hear the teaching or preaching of the Gospel, and then immediately forget everything they heard.

I handed a Bible to one of my counselees and asked him to read some verses of Scripture. When I took the Bible away from him, he couldn't even remember the general topic of the passage. This mental "fog" was a symptom of his involvement in occult practices. Immediately following the man's renunciation of the occult, he was able to read the Bible with comprehension and retention.

Another man complained of being able to hear what Christians were saying to him, but he couldn't make any sense out of the words. After the man renounced his involvement in astrology, he reported that he could understand the preaching of the Gospel. A few days later he gave his life to Christ.

The Bible says that "the god of this world has blinded the minds of the unbelieving" (2 Cor. 4:4), and unfortunately this blindness can continue into the believer's life if he does not renounce his occult practices.

7. *Headaches.* "I get these terrible headaches," Bill said.

"Oh? Do they occur at any particular time?" I asked.

"Well, yes they do," he said. "They seem to come on just before I start to read my Bible, or pray, or worship."

"Do you get them at other times, too?"

"No," Bill replied, "only at those times."

"Have you ever been involved in the occult?" I asked.

"Well, I did Eastern meditation for a year. Does that count?"

Obviously, it did count. Bill's headaches were an occult bondage that began during his involvement with Eastern meditation. As soon as Bill renounced his occult practices, the headaches stopped. There are other physical symptoms that can be an indication of occult bondage, so it is wise to carefully inquire about a person's spiritual history, especially if there appears to be no physical cause for the symptoms.

8. *Voices.* People hear voices for different reasons. With some, it is an indication of an extremely guilty conscience. With others, it could be a psychological disturbance. Many will hear voices as hallucination due to sleep loss, while others may have some chemical or enzymatic disturbance that produces this symptom. If these causes are lacking, though, there is another possible origin—occult bondage. Some people will hear voices as a result of dabbling with the occult, and if this is so, only deliverance from the bondage will solve the problem.

"It was difficult listening to your tape with all those people shouting in the background," Dave said.

"Where were the people?" I asked.

"In back of the coffee shop," Dave said, looking at me as if I should have already known.

"Dave, there were no people behind the coffee shop, and no one was shouting. What you were hearing was the voice of demons trying to stop you from listening to the tape."

As we prayed for Dave, it became obvious that he not only had occult bondage but that he also needed deliverance from demons. His hearing of voices had been a symptom of his heavy involvement in occult practices.

9. *Abilities.* Sometimes the supernatural abilities that people experience while involved in the occult can continue into the person's Christian life. One lovely Christian woman was still able to do automatic handwriting[4] after being filled with the Holy Spirit. She thought the ability came from God, but could not figure out why it brought such fear into her life. After she renounced the practice she lost the ability, but she also lost the fear of the dark that had plagued her for months.

10. *Feeling unforgiven.* A person may meet all of the conditions of salvation, and yet experience a sense that he is not forgiven.

---

[4]The practice of yielding one's hand to a demon to receive messages from the spirit world.

This is not the typical doubt of salvation that can be remedied by trust in God's Word. In this case, there is a heavy oppression and a feeling of being "cut off" from God.

"I know I've done what I need to to give my life to Christ," Tom said, "but I just can't shake the feeling that I'm still rejected by God." I tried to counsel Tom in the usual fashion, thinking that he was having the same doubts that many new Christians experience. None of this worked, though, and I sat in silence, wondering how I could help my new brother.

Just then, Dave, one of the other team members, entered the room. After I explained the situation to Dave, he turned to Tom and asked, "Have you ever been involved in the occult?"

"Well, I was a witch for three years."

"That'll do it," Dave said, and proceeded to lead Tom in a prayer of renunciation.

As soon as Tom stopped praying, he looked up, smiled, and said, "Now I can sense that I am forgiven. I have a witness in my spirit that I am a child of God." Tom's symptom was originating from his past involvement in the occult, and no amount of counseling would have cured him.

This brief list of symptoms should give the counselor an idea of what he is looking for when the counselee has an occult background. There are many other symptoms, of course, and the counselor can compile a list in his notebook as he encounters different symptoms along the way.

FREEDOM FROM BONDAGE

The Book of Acts contains one of the clearest examples of how the early Christians dealt with the occult:

> Many also of those who had believed kept coming, confessing and disclosing their practices. And many of those who practiced magic brought their books together and began burning them in the sight of all; and they counted up the price of them and found it fifty thousand pieces of silver. (Acts 19:18, 19)

This passage of Scripture outlines four distinct steps in the process of deliverance from occult bondage. Though someone could read the passage and obtain a general idea of what to do, an expanded explanation will help clarify the exact procedure and importance of the steps.

1. *Submission to the lordship of Jesus.* Notice that the people

mentioned in the Scripture had already believed. They had believed the message of the Gospel and had given their hearts to
Christ.

Some Christians think that once a person becomes a believer
there is no need to deal with the past. They imagine that the past
is somehow completely gone, and that what a person did before
his conversion can no longer affect him. This approach is both
unbiblical and unrealistic. The command to make restitution assumes that a person must deal with his past. Restoring broken
relationships presupposes that the person is responsible to rectify
his past actions. And the text mentioned above assumes that
Christians will deal with previous occult involvement.

The first step, then, is to submit to the lordship of Jesus. The
person must give his life to Christ and be ready to do whatever
Jesus commands.

2. *Confession to God.* Since involvement in the occult is a sin
against God, the troubled person must confess his sin to God and
ask His forgiveness. Some counselees will protest that they did
not know at the time that the activity was a sin. Careful scrutiny
of the person's past will probably reveal, though, that the person
did feel, at least intuitively, that there was something basically
wrong with occult involvement. When the person resisted this
intuitive impression, he violated his conscience, and so incurred
guilt. The idea that occult practices are sinful may not have been
worked out objectively in the person's mind, but he still sinned
if he went against his intuitive moral understanding. Consequently, it is necessary that the person confess his involvement
to God as a sin and seek God's forgiveness.

3. *Renunciation.* The phrase "disclosing their practices" means
that the people made a public renunciation of their involvement
in the occult. Because of their new-found faith in Christ, they
were willing to speak out publicly against their former practices,
declaring them to be evil, and forsaking them forever.

The importance of this step may not be obvious to many who
have never dealt with the occult realm before. The word "occult"
means secret or mysterious. The secrecy can refer to the activity
itself or to the knowledge gained from participation in that activity. Either way, if a person performs the occultish method, or
receives and uses knowledge gained through such a method, the
person has been involved in the occult. The power behind occult
bondage is its secrecy, and public renunciation breaks the bondage because it exposes the secret method or knowledge.

A few practical steps to help facilitate the renunciation could include:

a. Making a list of the person's specific involvement. A general renunciation of the occult is usually ineffective. In order to be specific, the person can pray for revelation and then write down his individual acts of participation in occult practices. Prayer for revelation is important because one of the symptoms of occult bondage is forgetfulness. The person has probably forgotten his specific dabblings with the occult, but prayer can release the person's memory. Once the person has a list, he can go on to the next step.

b. Renounce each contact individually. Urge the person to be specific. Do not let the person say, "I renounce seances in the name of Jesus." Insist that the counselee renounce each occasion when he participated in a seance. Different instances can produce different bondages, so it is vital that the person be specific.

c. Pray for healing for the person who is renouncing the occult. Jesus said that believers can lay hands on the sick and they will recover (Mark 16:18), and the person affected by occult bondage needs healing. Although most symptoms will disappear upon renunciation of the practices, some residual effects may require the prayers of other believers for their alleviation.

4. *Destruction of any physical remnants.* A person's involvement in the occult may have included the use of many physical objects. Some of these remnants can include: ouija boards, tarot cards, the book of I-Ching, books on the occult, jewelry with occult symbols (e.g., astrological signs), a pen used in automatic handwriting, even clothing. Almost any physical object could be used in connection with the occult, so it does not matter what the object is—its importance lies in its occultish use. In the passage from Acts, magic books were the remnants the people destroyed as they renounced their occult practices. A fire is a convenient way to handle all four steps if necessary. If the person is not yet a Christian, he can make a public pronouncement of his acceptance of Christ at the bonfire. Then, he can confess his sin to God, renounce his involvement in the occult, and burn any remnants he may have brought along.

After the person has been released from occult bondage, it will be important to instruct the person to continue in obedience to God. Consistent Christian living is the protection from future problems with the occult. Daily Bible study, prayer, worship, and fellowship will strengthen the person, making it more difficult to return to his former practices.

I know that any good Christian book on the occult will teach these general principles. I have found, though, that because of the rise of interest in the supernatural in our society, the Christian counselor must be aware of and equipped to handle occult bondage. A large percentage of homosexuals participate in occult practices, so it is becoming more important to check for these problems and to know how to resolve them.

DELIVERANCE

"I finally became sick and tired of it, Mike!" Bill lamented. "Every time I turned around, somebody was trying to cast a demon out of me. Why don't people understand that problems with homosexuality aren't always caused by a demon? People would try to deliver me and then expected I would have no more problems with temptation. I finally gave up on deliverance and realized that my problems were psychological. I wish other people in the church could see that, too."

One should not assume that all homosexuals need deliverance from spirits of homosexuality any more than one would assume that all thieves need deliverance from spirits of robbery. Whether people will or will not have demons is not a precise science, so the only recourse for the counselor is to diagnose the problems as they appear, and respond accordingly. Those who assume that all problems with homosexuality are demonic in origin only confuse their counselees and leave them in a hopeless state. The counselee will be confused because he will overlook the psychological aspect of his problem, thinking that demons are always to blame. He will feel hopeless because he is always at the whim of other beings, never gaining control of his own choices. Thus, it is a great disservice to any counselee to teach or even imply that all of his problems are demonic.

If, in the course of counseling, however, the need for deliverance becomes apparent, the Christian counselor should not hesitate to initiate the actions necessary to help his counselee. The symptoms of many problems can mimic demonic oppression, so the counselor will need to exercise discernment in his diagnosis. When he is sure that the problem is demonic, he should proceed with the only solution—deliverance.

TELLING THE DIFFERENCE

Distinguishing between demonic disturbance and other common problems is likely the biggest hindrance to accurate treatment. One has to diagnose the problem before he can treat it effectively. Since some moral, psychological, physical, and emotional problems can be imitated by demons, the counselor must be sure he is actually dealing with a demon before he attempts deliverance. Such procedure would not only be ineffective but would also be very confusing for the counselee. The following practical points may make the task a little easier for the counselor:

1. *Apply the normal Christian disciplines.* As Christians, our spirits are disciplined through prayer, our souls through meditation, and our bodies through fasting. If the counselee has applied these disciplines in a concerted effort to overcome his problem, the source could possibly be demonic. Demonic problems do not submit to regular Christian discipline.

2. *Note when the problem seems the worst.* If the counselee is applying Christian discipline and making a strong, deliberate choice to resist in the time of temptation, the habit patterns should weaken under this treatment. The timing of the problems could be an indication of their origin, though, so if the counselee can note when the problems occur, it may help the counselor pinpoint the source. If the problem becomes worse just before the person prays, reads his Bible, worships, witnesses, or has fellowship with other believers, this could signal a demonic influence.

3. *Confess the problem to others.* Confessing a non-demonic problem to others brings the situation "into the light" and usually produces greater freedom. A truly demonic bondage will not submit to such treatment, however, so confession can be a useful indicator in the diagnostic process.

If the counselee has applied the above three steps and still suffers from the same symptoms, there is a good possibility that the problem is demonic. One additional step that could prove helpful is to pray that God will cause the demons to manifest themselves. Both counselor and counselee can pray that God will "place pressure," as it were, on the spirits, forcing them to make themselves evident.

THE PROCESS OF DELIVERANCE

Once an accurate diagnosis has been made, and the counselor is persuaded that the problem is indeed demonic, the counselor can arrange a time to administer deliverance to the counselee. The counselor may want to invite others to pray with him, since team ministry is often more comfortable and effective than individual ministry. As the counselor (or team, as the case may be) begins the time of deliverance, there are some general guidelines that can help things move along more smoothly and effectively.

1. *The counselee must remove the demon's legal right to stay.* Unconfessed sin gives a demon moral grounds for remaining in a person. Unless this ground is removed through confession, casting out the demon could prove quite difficult. It is probably best to handle this step as a form of homework before the actual deliverance session.

2. *The counselee should desire deliverance.* Although this is not always necessary or ascertainable, the cooperation of the counselee can greatly facilitate the process of deliverance.

3. *Identifying the demon may help.* Although not absolutely necessary, this step does sometimes aid in the process of deliverance. Once a demon's name is known, it seems to make the demon's influence weaker, making it easier to cast it out. Jesus asked some demons for their names, others He knew through the Holy Spirit, and others He simply called "unclean spirits" and cast them out by that name. So, it is not always necessary to know a demon's name, but it can help in some instances.

4. *Someone must confront the demons directly and command them to leave.* The process of deliverance is actually quite simple. A Christian, using the authority Jesus has given him, commands the spirits to leave the afflicted person. There will often be some form of manifestation, often something related to the person's mouth (coughing, slavering, vomiting, screaming, shouting), and then the spirit departs. After ejecting one spirit, the team moves on to the next, until the person is completely free.

5. *The counselee's own will can be used against the demon.* Again, this is not absolutely necessary, but it does help in some cases. If a person has a spirit of lust and says, "I renounce you, spirit of lust, in the name of Jesus, and command you to leave me alone," it could hasten the process of deliverance.

The counselor could uncover many kinds of demons during the time of deliverance, but there is a general pattern governing which kinds he is likely to discover in certain people. A person is usually indwelt by those demons that coincide with the kind of sin that allowed them to enter. In other words, if a person was deeply involved in the occult, he is more likely to have spirits of witchcraft, divination, or sorcery. If a person has had an uncontrolled temper, he could have spirits of anger, murder, violence, or suicide. Homosexuals, because of their lifestyle, tend to require deliverance from spirits of resentment, bitterness, rejection, lust, masturbation, fornication, deception, or confusion. People usually have demons according to the sins they have committed. The important thing is to see that the person is delivered and learns to live in freedom.

After the counselee's deliverance, he should be encouraged to follow good Christian discipline in order to maintain his freedom. He should be directed to live by the Scriptures, praise God, pray, guard his thought life, cultivate good Christian friendships, and submit to other members of the Body of Christ.

Some counselees will ask, "Just what should I expect to gain from a time of deliverance? What will it do for me?" This is a good question, since many people assume that deliverance is a panacea for all spiritual ills. What does deliverance really do? Well, there are some things that it does not do. Deliverance does not solve relationship problems, it does not bring about any character development, it does not renew the person's mind, and it cannot take the place of a good relationship with God. Deliverance performs one necessary function: it removes a negative influence from the person's life, aiding the person to continue, unhindered, with the normal processes of Christian growth.[5]

---

[5]The suggested reading/listening list at the back of the book lists additional materials dealing with the subject of demons and deliverance.

CHAPTER TEN

RELATING TO THE BODY OF CHRIST

Man's greatest need is God. Yet most human beings sense the desire for human love before they appreciate their need for relationship with God. While God is capable of meeting our basic needs directly, He created us with a desire for the companionship of other humans. This is clearly evidenced in Adam's sense of loneliness (Gen. 2:18–25). God's answer for Adam was the creation of Eve, a suitable companion. Eve was suitable for (or corresponding to) Adam, because where Adam had a need to relate to another of his own kind, Eve was able to fulfill it. The mental, emotional, physical, and relational needs Adam felt could be met in his relationship with his companion. These needs are a part of every human being's makeup, so the desire for human companionship persists, even when the basic need for God is satisfied.

Most of the desires of the homosexually oriented person are the same basic human longings that all people have—the desires for communication, friendship, intimacy, affection, understanding, etc. He needs other Christians as fellow believers and as humans, so it is not strange that he should expect to get his needs for companionship and friendship met in the body of Christ. He will continue to have the needs; if he does not get his needs met in the Christian fellowship, he will eventually go somewhere else to fulfill them. Just how he will meet his needs becomes an important issue to the person with a homosexual preference.

Counselees will often ask how much they should share with other people. They are also concerned about how much physical

171

affection they can show without breaking God's law or offending others. Sometimes they want to know if a close, committed relationship with a Christian family could bring healing through a process of "reparenting."

PARTICIPATION IN A LOCAL BODY

Although each person becomes a Christian through his own personal choice to follow Christ, God does not reconcile us to himself as individuals. Rather, God brings us to himself as a body.[1] Consequently, there is no place for the "lone ranger" in the body of Christ. We are all "members of one another,"[2] so independence from other Christians is both disobedient and dangerous. Refusal to join a local fellowship of Christians usually indicates some form of pride, rebellion, or fear on the part of the hesitant person. Due to his disobedience to God's Word,[3] this believer puts himself in a spiritually vulnerable position. "Lone ranger" Christians always get "picked off" first.

After ascertaining that the counselee is truly converted, some of the counselor's next questions should be, "To which body of believers are you submitted? Where do you receive your spiritual food? To whom are you responsible? Who has pastoral oversight in your life?" These and similar questions will quickly reveal the counselee's attitude toward spiritual authority. The responses can vary from a cheerful, "Oh! I'm a member of such-and-such church. I really enjoy the fellowship and good Bible teaching there," to "I don't go to church. I don't think I need to go to church to be a good Christian. It's just Jesus and me. That's all I need." The latter attitude of independence and rebellion provides a breeding ground for all kinds of problems. Thus, if the counselee expects to attain stability in his Christian life, he will need to change his attitude and submit himself to a local Christian body. Once the counselee has changed his position, the counselor can help him find a fellowship where the Bible is preached, Christ is glorified, and the people truly love one another.

The homosexually oriented counselee usually requires a good deal of oversight. If he is not accountable to someone, he may flounder when he comes under strong temptation or spiri-

---

[1]Eph. 2:16.
[2]Eph. 4:25.
[3]God commands us to submit to one another (Eph. 5:21), and to submit to the elders in the local assembly (1 Pet. 5:5; Heb. 13:17).

tual attack. Thus, for his own safety, it is important that the person be an active member of a stable Christian fellowship. Instruction, encouragement, exhortation, and rebuke all play a part in the normal Christian lifestyle, and these are only available to the person who is committed to other believers. The independent person forfeits the privilege of this input from the lives of others.

Gary had seen me for counseling over a long period of time, but always seemed to vacillate in his Christian walk. After not seeing him for a few months, I ran into him one day at the wedding of a mutual friend.

"Hi, Mike!" Gary said, his voice exceptionally cheery.

"Hello, Gary. How have you been?"

"Actually, Mike, I've been doing just great lately." Gary seemed more peaceful than I had ever seen him.

"And to what would you attribute your improved condition?" I asked.

"To something you tried to tell me about long ago," he said, "but I guess I just wasn't ready to listen at that time. I finally became a committed member of a good local church, and the experience has changed my life. I'm more stable in my Christian walk now because I have people who love me and will hold me accountable for the things I do. It has been very good for me."

Another valuable aspect of this submission is the opportunity the counselee has to contribute to the spiritual lives of other Christians. Giving is a necessary ingredient in spiritual growth, and a committed church member has more opportunity to give than does the spiritual drifter.

So, if the counselee is not already a committed, submitted, functioning member of a local Christian fellowship, the counselor and counselee should work together to find a body the counselee can join. After the counselee is a faithful member of a Christian group, he may develop questions about how he is to relate to his brothers and sisters. How much of his struggles should he reveal? How free can he be to show physical affection with others? Since these relationships can help or hinder the young Christian's spiritual life, he will not want to jeopardize his Christian walk through unwise behavior.

WISDOM IN COMMUNICATION

As a committed, submitted member of a local church, the counselee will probably still have questions about how he can wisely reveal his struggles to his fellow believers. In an effort to be transparent and vulnerable, the counselee may suppose that it is right to communicate everything about his life with anyone in the church. But this is a mistaken idea of what it means to be transparent and vulnerable. To be transparent means to be *willing* to communicate everything, should that be necessary, but it is not always wise to disclose everything to everybody. Some people might not be able to handle the information responsibly, others may not understand, and still others could become frightened. The result of such unwise communication could be rejection, the one thing the counselee does not need from his brothers and sisters. Vulnerability is the *willingness* to share even if the person could be wounded in the process. The person should not ignore blatant maliciousness, though, in his desire to be open with other people. It is wise for the counselee to consider the maturity of the people with whom he plans to talk. The following questions may help the puzzled counselee to determine whether he should share in a given situation:

1. *With whom will he share?* Is the person mature enough to handle the information in a responsible fashion? Does the person need to know about the counselee's struggles? This will probably be determined by whether the listener would be a part of the solution or a part of the problem. It is not wise to share with everyone, since not everyone can handle the information properly. It is seldom wise to share with an entire body of people unless the Lord has specifically led the person to do so. Since the counselee cannot know everyone in the church, he will probably get some unexpected negative reactions, and, depending on the maturity of the counselee, this could spell disaster for his spiritual life. It would be nice to think that every Christian could always handle the struggles of his homosexually oriented brothers and sisters, but alas, this is not so. The church is not perfect.

2. *How much should he share?* The extent of the communication will be determined by the reason for the sharing. A good rule to follow is to say only what is pertinent to the problem at hand, that is, tell the other person only what he needs to know to help. Some people feel that they must share everything with everyone or they are not being honest. This kind of communication is usually guilt motivated, and stems from a misconception of the Christian's responsibility to be truthful. The Bible says, however, that the *fool* utters all of his mind;[4] it is unwise to say everything

---

[4]Proverbs 29:11 (KJV).

that comes into one's head. Because unrestrained sharing could result in misunderstanding, rejection, and breakdown of relationship, the counselee should consider carefully what he will and will not say.

3. *When will he share?* The timing of the communication can be as crucial as the content. Sometimes this is difficult to determine, but if the recipient is in a vulnerable emotional state (had a bad day, had an argument with his boss, is depressed over his own circumstances), it would probably be wise to wait until another time to share. If a person is having problems with his own life, he will likely find it difficult to understand and empathize with someone else's difficulties. So, the counselee should pick his time carefully.

4. *Where will he share?* Although this is not as crucial an aspect as some of the above, the setting of the conversation could significantly influence the outcome of the communication. If the counselee goes out to have coffee with his pastor, there will be limitations on what the person can disclose, just because they are speaking in a public place. Then again, if the details of the information will not be extensive or intimate, a restaurant may be just the right place for a "lighter" conversation. Though it is not terribly important, the counselee may nonetheless want to consider the location when he is contemplating sharing his struggles with someone else.

5. *Why does he want to share?* The motivation behind a person's sharing can hinder or further the effectiveness of his communication. After a long abstinence from honest interpersonal contact, the deep needs of the hurting person can influence him to act like an emotional "sponge" or "leech"; that is, he tries to drain as much attention and affection as possible from the other person. This overreaction reveals the sharer's selfish motivation. Since the listener will sense the speaker's selfish attitude, he will probably withdraw emotionally to protect himself, thus limiting the effectiveness of the dialogue. While it is acceptable to talk about one's needs in order to receive counsel and support from a friend, there is no need to place an emotional burden on the other person. So, if the counselee wants to get the most out of his sharing, he should carefully examine his own motives before he communicates.

This last question brings up the important issue of expectations. What should the counselee expect from the Christians around him? Unrealistic expectations can cause untold disappointment, so it is good for the counselee to consider what he should and should not expect from others. The homosexually oriented person sometimes naively believes that every Christian will love him, accept him, and fully understand his struggles.

Unfortunately, the responses of other Christians may be anything but loving. Instead, the counselee may be faced with unbelief, rejection, or downright horror as he reveals his background and difficulties.

"George," the director said, "could you please come into my office?"

George wondered why his boss should sound so grave. George was a member of a large, well-known Christian organization. In all the time he had worked for him, George had never heard the director use that tone of voice. George tried not to show his apprehension as he entered the director's office.

"I'm afraid we're going to have to let you go," the director said.

"But why?" George protested. "I don't understand."

The director became even more somber. "One of the brothers here said that you asked for prayer. He said that you were being tempted in the area of homosexuality. Is that right?"

"Well, yes it is," George replied. "Is there something wrong with asking for prayer?"

"George, we just can't have people with your problem on our staff."

"But why?" George protested again. "If I had been a married man asking for prayer because I was tempted to commit adultery, would you have fired me then?"

"Well, no, George, but this is . . . well, it's just different."

George protested again, but it did no good. George was summarily dismissed, wondering what all the talk of Christian love and acceptance actually meant when people could treat him this way.

When a person receives reactions contrary to his expectations, he may be confused at first, but it will not take long for confusion to turn to disappointment, discouragement, bitterness, resentment, or anger. He expects the body of Christ to have the same reactions as God, and perfection is too much to ask from fallen human beings. This is not meant to imply that Christians should not *try* to react as God would. Of course, they should. It is only a recognition that, in spite of their good intentions, they are still not perfect, and it is foolish for a man to trust another person as he would trust God. So, if the counselee can gain a realistic perspective before he shares, it will spare him much pain and disillusionment in his Christian walk.

If the counselee is displaying wisdom in his communications with other believers, he will likely enjoy close friendship with a number of other people, and these friendships will probably involve a certain amount of physical affection. Just how the homosexually oriented person can show physical affection without falling into trouble will eventually become an important issue to the counselee. An honest discussion about the need for affection and how that need can be properly met should be a scheduled part of the counseling process.

SHOWING AFFECTION

As a child grows up, he moves from the concrete to the abstract in his understanding. This progression applies to most, if not all, aspects of human development, and the need for affection also follows this pattern. When first born, an infant's basic needs are physical—air, water, sleep, food, shelter, but also affection. If a baby is not touched and held, the infant can wither and die, even though the child's nutritional needs are fully met. As the child grows, his need for affection increases, each aspect becoming more abstract than the preceding. The first level is physical. Later, the child senses a need to see love expressed through the actions of others. When the child begins to understand language, the need for love expressed in words begins to manifest itself. Still later, the whole range of attitudes and motives becomes important to the child. A closer look at these four levels will help illustrate the point.

First, the child needs to receive affection physically. The child requires the loving touch of his parents or appropriate guardians. Playing with the infant is another way to express physical affection. If the child is hurt, a hug is usually the first way the child understands the concern of the parent. A little later, child training, or discipline, when properly administered, will be interpreted by the child as a loving act. This need for physical contact starts in infancy, perhaps even before birth, and continues throughout the person's life. The form of the affection may vary from time to time, but the need continues.

Second, the child will need to experience love through the actions of people around him. These are "tokens of love" to the child. The presence and attention of the parents is one form of love in action. Providing for the child's basic needs also communicates love to the child. Giving and receiving of gifts is yet another way the child will see love acted out. This need to see love through the actions of others overlaps, chronologically, with the need for physical affection, as if it were a "layer." As with the former need, it begins, but does not cease.

Third, when the child begins to understand and use language, he will experience a need to give and receive love verbally. Appreciation, compliments, instruction, encouragement, and even rebuke can all play a part in the verbal expression of love to another person. Now the child experiences the need for affection in three areas—physical, action, and verbal.

Fourth, the child will eventually come to understand attitude and motivation. Once this insight has developed, the attitudes of other people will become important to the child. Respect, concern, loyalty, patience, and sympathy can all be used to communicate love on the attitudinal level. As with the former stages, this need is added to the previous ones so that the child now senses a need for affection on all four levels.

If these needs are properly met throughout the person's life, the development of the person's personality should proceed normally. The great tragedy is that many people are not loved when they are young, their normal needs for affection are not met, and their personalities evidence that lack of love. In some cases the needs are not met at all, in others, the need is greatly hindered, and in still others, the child learns to accept rejection or abuse *as* love, so the process is actually reversed.

In the case of the person with a homosexual preference, the rejection process has left the person with a great need for affection. It is reasonable for the person to expect that his need for affection will be met, at least partially, through the members of the body of Christ. The vital question for this person, then, is how he will give and receive affection in a godly, beneficial manner. Most counselees do not have trouble learning how to share affection on the action, verbal, and attitudinal levels. Their biggest struggle seems to arise as they attempt to give and receive affection physically.

Instead of learning how to do things correctly, people tend to swing to one extreme or another. Because things can go wrong when people share affection, some people try to be so careful that they share no affection at all. Not only do they show no physical affection to others, they try to insure that no one else in the church will display physical affection. This again is an over-reaction. A more reasonable, balanced approach teaches people how to share physical affection correctly rather than forbidding the practice entirely.

Here are a few guidelines that can help the counselee give and receive physical affection with others without getting into trouble:

1. *Fear God.* The fear of the Lord is to hate evil (Prov. 8:13). To the extent that the person fears the Lord (hates evil), he will be free to share affection with others. If, at any time, the person comes close to doing something wrong, his hatred of evil will protect him. The difference between lusting and loving, or getting and giving is very clear in the mind and heart of the person who hates sin. Even a tainted motive will bring a response in the person's sensitive spirit. So, the more the person fears God, the freer he can feel to share affection with others.[5]

2. *Use discernment.* The person who desires to share physical affection properly needs to show discernment in three areas.

First, the person should consider the personal standards and background of the person receiving the affection. Sometimes the recipient's former experiences can influence the extent and variety of affection he is willing to receive. If a man has had some hurtful experiences with male affection in the past, the person who shows him affection should be considerate of his special background and feelings.

Second, we must always be sensitive to the culture of the other person. Some cultures are generally more open with the expression of physical affection (e.g., the Italian culture), while others are more reserved (e.g., the German culture). Thus, if a man tries to hug another man, and the person rejects the affection, it may be nothing more than a cultural reaction. In that case, the man giving the affection needs to be sensitive to the culture of the other person.

Third, a person must consider the circumstances around him when he shares affection. The setting can determine what amount and kind of affection would be acceptable. Thus, what is permissible in one circumstance may not be in another. Greeting a close friend with a kiss on the cheek may be an appropriate display of affection in private. But this same greeting could be

---

[5]The fear of God is further discussed in Chapter 7.

misunderstood in a public place. In this one must be discerning of the circumstances.

So then, one needs to be sensitive to the recipient's personal preferences, the person's cultural background, and the present circumstances when sharing physical affection.

3. *Don't judge another person's motives.* This point applies more directly to receiving affection than to giving it, but the counselee may find it valuable from time to time. When someone shares affection and the person on the receiving end feels uncomfortable, it is important that the receiver not judge the giver's motives. The reason for the feelings may lie on either side, so it is unfair to assume that there was something wrong with the giver's motives just because the receiver felt uncomfortable. Rather than judging the person and rejecting him (as many people would do), it would be better to ask the person a question about his motives. Honesty will then protect both parties. If the giver honestly believes his motives were pure, the receiver should accept the person's assessment and trust his motives. Pulling back from affection rather than communicating about it will almost always be interpreted as rejection by the giver.

Once, when a Christian friend from a homosexual background hugged me, I felt uneasy about the brother's motives. When he finished, I asked him if he felt his motives were pure. He acknowledged that he was being selfish in his communication of affection, so we both bowed our heads and he asked God's forgiveness for his selfishness. After the prayer I told him, "Now, I want you to hug me again, and I want you to do it right." The second hug felt completely different from the first, and it left both of us feeling comfortable with the exchange. Now, many people would have withdrawn their affection from this brother at the first hint of impurity, but that is certainly not what another brother deserves. People need to learn how to show affection correctly, and to do that, others must trust their motives and allow them to try, even if they should stumble some in the process.

4. *Take other people's affection seriously.* The communication of affection involves a certain amount of risk. The person who shares physical affection runs the risk of being misinterpreted, judged, or rejected by the receiver. Showing love is serious business, and how someone handles that love reveals what he thinks of the person who sent it. Consequently, the response can send a message of love and acceptance or of coldness and rejection.

Even the person's sense of self-worth is at stake, since the person usually assumes that if he is valuable, the other person will receive his love. Thus, it is extremely important to take another person's display of affection seriously, or the person may conclude that both he and his love are worthless. A simple "thank you," or "thank you for your friendship," will let the person know that both he and his affection are appreciated.

5. *Don't let fear keep you from obeying the Bible.* God's Word commands Christians to be kind, tenderhearted, compassionate, and affectionate with their brothers and sisters.[6] Unfortunately, though, many believers refrain from any display of physical affection with members of the same sex. People adopt a "hands off" policy because they fear that their affection may be interpreted by others as indicative of some problem with homosexuality. Even people who are generally affectionate with members of the opposite sex will often be distant (physically) where a member of the same sex is concerned. But Christians should not submit to this social pressure to conform to an ungodly standard. Yes, believers should be sensitive to the culture and circumstances when showing affection, but they should not be so afraid of what others think that they disobey God to avoid criticism. Physical affection, shown properly under biblical guidelines, will attract others (whether believers or unbelievers); it will not drive them away.

6. *Don't be afraid of tempting others.* Sometimes people are afraid that if they show affection to someone who comes from a homosexual background, they will provide that person with an occasion for stumbling. This is a concern stemming from love, since tempting one's brother or sister would certainly be unkind. In most cases, however, there is no basis for this fear, since, when physical affection is shared in a godly, appropriate fashion, the person will not be tempted, but rather edified.

Being curious about this very point, I once asked a brother if affection from other men tempted him. His answer surprised me. "Mike," he said, "I'm not tempted when men show me affection, but rather, when men don't share affection with me. If they won't touch me, I interpret that as rejection, and it is much easier to deal with any feelings that result from affection than to deal with rejection. Once I feel rejected, it is easier to submit to

---

[6] Eph. 4:32; Col. 3:2; 1 Pet. 3:8; 2 Pet. 1:7; c.f. also 2 Cor. 7:15; Phil. 1:8; 2:1; and 1 Thess. 2:8.

the temptation of lust and fornication, since I feel unloved and start looking for love in all the wrong places. I would rather have to handle affection than rejection anytime." It appears, then, that *not* showing affection could cause bigger problems for another person than *showing* affection would. Even if problems should develop, integrity, the fear of God, and the conviction of the Holy Spirit will still be in operation, and the difficulties can be resolved. Thus, Christians need not let fear of becoming a stumblingblock keep them from showing others the physical affection they need.

At this point, some of the readers may be asking themselves if this "need" for physical affection is a real need. This question arises because many of the readers have had normal family backgrounds, and their basic need for the affection of their parents was met in childhood. The person with a broken family pattern, though, will have an overexaggerated sense of need for affection, since the need was not met in the proper family setting. The man with a homosexual orientation, then, can have a need for male affection that other people may not understand. Even if the counselor cannot empathize with the counselee's need, still he should try to understand, and aid the counselee to meet this need in a godly, proper manner. Hopefully, these six guidelines can direct the counselee in his efforts to give and receive physical affection in a godly, acceptable fashion.

EMOTIONAL DEPENDENCY

When two people participate in a close relationship, it is possible for them to develop an unhealthy emotional attachment to each other. This unhelpful joining is a serious problem that commonly disturbs the homosexually oriented counselee (or other emotionally needy counselees). This attachment, or emotional dependency, can severely limit the spiritual and emotional growth of both parties. If the counselor discovers that the counselee is involved in such a relationship, it will be necessary to instruct the counselee how to break this dependency wisely.

This is an extremely important topic—one that could easily constitute another chapter in this book. Since some excellent material on the subject has already been written by Lori Thorkelson, I will not try to duplicate her work, but will rather, with her kind permission, include the entire contents of Lori's booklet, *EMOTIONAL DEPENDENCY: A Threat to Close Friendships*, as an appendix to this book. Any counselor who deals frequently with people from a homosexual background will want to order multiple copies of this excellent booklet to use as handouts. Ordering information is included in the appendix.

COMMUNITY LIVING

Learning to relate properly to members of the body of Christ is foundational to the Christian life. Sometimes, though, a person's living situation is not conducive to establishing and maintaining good working relationships with other Christians. An issue of some importance, then, is whether or not the counselee should change his living situation in order to gain closer contact with other believers. There are two sides to this point, the negative, that is, where the counselee will *not* live, and the positive, where the counselee *will* live.

First, where should the counselee *not* live? The three basic aspects of this question include: the home, the neighborhood, and the work environment.

1. *The counselee should not continue living with a homosexual partner.* This thought will not always cross the mind of a new believer, so the counselor must ask the counselee about his home. The decision as to which party will move out is something the counselee and his (or her) roommate will have to determine. The counselor can help the counselee by discussing the relevant factors in the situation, the alternatives, and the ramifications of the various choices. Though the counselee will make the final decision, the counselor should point out the biblical absolutes applicable to the various steps in the decision-making process. Outlining the whole decision on paper can sometimes aid the counselee in clarifying his thoughts. The major point, though, is if the counselee continues to live with someone who is pursuing a homosexual lifestyle, it will probably not be long before the counselee returns to his sinful behavior patterns.

2. *The counselee should avoid a neighborhood composed mainly of homosexuals.* Some major metropolitan areas have whole residential districts where the majority of the residents are homosexual. Because the Christian is commanded to abstain from sin and any situations that could lead to sin,[7] it would be wise for the counselee not only to move out of a home situation that could become

---

[7] 1 Cor. 15:34 and Rom. 13:14.

a temptation but also remove himself from a "gay" neighborhood if at all possible.

What a person sees around him every day profoundly affects the way he thinks. His mind quickly adapts to the lifestyle that is consistently modelled before him, and those who imagine that the stable Christian will not be affected by his environment are deceived.[8]

When my wife and I worked on a crisis-intervention team in a largely homosexual area of San Francisco, we were immersed in a "gay" atmosphere. After ten weeks of constantly seeing gay "couples," I one day beheld a mixed couple on the street. The sight of a man and a woman together, arm in arm, struck me as rather odd. Then I realized that it was my reaction, not the couple, that was odd, and it had taken only ten weeks for that distorted environment to affect my thinking.

Christians already have a tough enough time resisting temptation just because they live in the world. If the person from a homosexual background is confronted with his past lifestyle every time he opens his front door, a stable Christian walk will be all the more difficult to maintain. So, to protect the counselee from unnecessary temptation, he should consider even the neighborhood where he will or will not live.

3. *The counselee may find it necessary to change his work location or even his occupation.* A person's work environment has a profound influence on his thinking, values, relationships, and habits. Although it is not always possible to change the counselee's work environment, it should be a point to consider when discussing his living situation.

"Where did you say you were working, Jerry?" I asked.

"I'm working as a disc jockey in a gay bar," Jerry said matter-of-factly. "Do you think there's something wrong with that?"

"It might just cost you your spiritual life," I said. "Isn't that enough?"

After he responded with a weak, "I suppose," we went on to discuss Jerry's employment alternatives.

Is the environment a healthful one? Can it be changed? Can the counselee find a new job? Should the counselee be trained for a new occupation? Some of these alternatives are radical, and the consequences need to be carefully weighed before making a decision, but "major surgery" may be the only option for saving

---

[8]1 Cor. 15:33.

the person's spiritual life. Again, the final decision will fall in the counselee's lap, since he must learn to be responsible for his own life, but a discussion about the alternatives and their implementation could help the counselee clarify his position.

In contrast to where the counselee should not live, we have the second point—where the counselee *can* live. The three major options open to the counselee include: living alone and maintaining close relationships with the members of a local church, sharing a living situation with another Christian, or living in an intentional community.[9]

1. *The counselee can live alone but have close contact with other Christians.* Although this is a possible option, it never seems to work out well for the young Christian. It requires a very strong person, indeed, to live alone and constantly resist the temptation to look for love in the wrong place. Not only is the person alone, and is therefore more likely to suffer from loneliness, but the person is also likely to receive calls and visits from people who will encourage him to return to his former lifestyle. When that happens, it is always good to have another Christian around to support the person through prayer, fellowship, and exhortation. Without that extra support, the person will find it more difficult to resist temptation, and he may eventually fall into ungodly practices. So, although living alone is one alternative, it is probably not the best in most cases.

2. *The counselee could live together with another Christian.* There are many benefits to this arrangement. First, it offers spiritual protection for the counselee because the other Christian is available for prayer, fellowship, Bible study, encouragement, and rebuke (if necessary). Second, it can be financially advantageous, since the cost of living can be divided. Third, there is accountability to at least one other person, so the actions of both parties are not completely autonomous. Fourth, loneliness is not such a big problem, since they have each other for company. And fifth, the Christian atmosphere in the home will provide a place of refuge from the work environment, should that be necessary.

3. *The counselee could move into an intentional community.* This is probably the preferable living situation for the person leaving a homosexual lifestyle. The amplification of encouragement, support, fellowship, friendship, prayer, worship, and Bible study

---

[9]The term "intentional community" means a group of people living together by design, having one purpose. This might be under one roof or several, but the living accommodations would be close in proximity.

that transpires in a community of believers provides a new believer with an environment conducive to spiritual growth. Just as young plants need a greenhouse environment to become well established, so the young Christian needs extra spiritual input to solidify his recent commitment to Christ. Since the person exiting the gay community is leaving behind a well-organized support group, it is best if he enters another support group as soon as possible, and the intentional Christian community provides just such a place. Out of all my counselees, the ones who lived in community grew the most spiritually and remained the most stable. So, if the counselee can move into a Christian community, he will have a better chance at developing good Christian character and resisting the temptation to return to his former lifestyle.

THE MUSLIM CONNECTION

My friend Doug and I were in a bar witnessing, and as we talked together during a quiet time, Doug asked, "Mike, have you ever thought about the similarities between witnessing to homosexuals and witnessing to Muslims?"

"Well, actually, the thought has never crossed my mind," I said. "But go on, explain what you mean."

"It seems," Doug continued, "that homosexuals and Muslims face the same decisions when they come to Christ. They both have to leave a brotherhood, a brotherhood that offers the person total support as long as he is faithful to the other brothers. Both homosexuals and Muslims have a worldview that differs significantly from the Christian viewpoint. In most cases, the language, or at least the vocabulary, is quite different. And, both will probably face persecution from the brotherhood they forsake. Maybe that's why former homosexuals do better in a Christian community than they do living on their own. It could also explain why convincing a homosexual to leave his lifestyle is so difficult at times. He is leaving much more than just a sinful habit pattern—he is leaving an entire community, a culture, a way of life, and the trauma involved could make it more difficult to come to Christ."

I found that a most interesting thought. Another friend of mine, a missionary who works with Muslims in North Africa, wrote in a letter, "There seem to be many similarities with homosexuals. Muslims feel that their religion is a part of them—a part of their identity—just as homosexuals feel their homosexuality is something that is 'part of them.' " He went on to say that Muslims find it difficult to give up their religion because their Islamic beliefs are so intimately intertwined with their identity and culture.

This letter confirmed what Doug had suggested. There are many similarities between the gay and Muslim communities, and this comparison may help explain why homosexuals have a hard time coming out of their lifestyles, and why they require constant support from a loving community. Perhaps in the future, people who witness among homosexuals will be able to learn effective principles of evangelism from missionaries to the Muslim world.

REPARENTING

Before I close the chapter, I would like to mention one more issue that people sometimes raise. I am often asked if reliving a proper family environment can be beneficial to the person who suffered from the rejection process. This "reliving" is often called "reparenting" or "recapitulation" (i.e., repetition) of the family experience. In a reparenting or recapitulation arrangement, the counselee takes the position (or plays the role) of a son or daughter, while another person (usually older) plays the part of the parent. The purpose of the "reparenting" is to give the counselee the chance to experience a proper family atmosphere with the hope that psychological healing may result from the positive experience. Many people testify to the restoration they received as a result of a casual or formal recapitulation. However, the issue is questionable, maybe even objectionable, in some people's minds, so it would be good to mention some of the possible questions and suggested answers related to reparenting.

1. *Is it necessary?* There may not always be a need for reparenting. Much recapitulation happens naturally between the counselee and certain members of the body of Christ. The counselee cannot help viewing and treating certain older, more stable Christians as parent figures, especially if the person has any position of authority in the counselee's life.[10] If these relationships have developed naturally, and the effects of reparenting are appearing in the counselee's life, why establish a formal arrangement? In some cases it may be beneficial to clarify or declare a

---

[10]For example, elders often become "father figures" for people in their congregation.

relationship that developed casually, since this could hasten the healing process by objectifying the principles involved. For example, if the counselee knows that he is treating another person as a father, he is better able to discern what kind of help he should or should not expect from the person. This knowledge may also help him understand why he reacts to this "father figure" the way he does.

2. *Is it feasible?* There are some cases when it is appropriate and helpful to establish a formal parent/child arrangement, though many factors can influence the way the relationship will progress. Probably the most obvious and important factor will be the ages of the parties. If the counselee is young—sixteen or under—becoming part of a biblically ordered Christian family could be highly beneficial. Some important modelling could occur as the child learns what it means to be part of a proper family, and to submit to loving, stable parents. If the counselee is older, becoming part of a nuclear family may be awkward, unnatural, and inconvenient.

Another important factor will be the living situations of the parties involved. Sometimes a family simply cannot take in another member, no matter how much they may care for the person. The older counselee may be living on his own and holding down a job, making it impractical to move into someone else's house. One possible alternative to the live-in option is the arrangement of a looser friendship where the contact is regular, but not necessarily daily.

3. *Is it proper?* Reparenting should only be conducted if the relationship between the parties is godly. Impure motives, inappropriate affection, and unnatural attachment create emotionally dependent relationships rather than edifying friendships. If the reparenting arrangement (whether casual or formal) is ungodly in any way, it should be treated as a potentially dangerous situation, and abandoned.

If reparenting appears to be necessary, feasible, and can be conducted in a godly fashion, it could be very beneficial to a struggling counselee. The counselor and counselee will have to discuss the various factors to determine whether the counselee should pursue a formal reparenting arrangement. Close monitoring of the relationship will help prevent problems and insure greater benefit from the arrangement. The counselor should be especially sensitive to any refusal to discuss the relationship, since this secrecy could indicate the development of an emotional dependency. As long as appropriate controls are applied, the parties involved need not fear the establishment of a potentially beneficial relationship.

CHAPTER ELEVEN

A WORD TO THE STRUGGLER

One day you awakened to your sexuality and knew that you were different. Other young people around you were becoming interested in the opposite sex, but you found the attention and affection of the same sex attractive. You were suddenly aware of all kinds of desires, aspirations, longings, even cravings, but yours were different from everyone else's. This was all very puzzling to you, since you didn't choose to have these desires, they were just "there."

But wondering and curiosity quickly gave way to hurt, frustration, and fear when you realized that jokes about "fags," "fairies," and "fruits" were directed at people like you. So, you began to hide your feelings, trying to understand, trying to protect yourself, and at the same time, longing desperately that someone would love and accept you.

You probably spent most of your time hiding. You hid from other people, from yourself, you even tried to hide from God— all to no avail. Your hiding was understandable since you were sensitive, so easily hurt, and there were so many people who could hurt you. You longed to be friends with someone who would listen and understand, but the more contact you had with others, the more you realized they couldn't handle your problems. You reached out to be friends, only to be rejected because other people became afraid. How many times have you taken the brunt of homophobic reactions?

Maybe you grew up in a church that condemned homosexuals. The very people you expected would help you understand yourself became your enemies. You heard the things they said about "your kind" and knew from the start that you could never share your deepest feelings with them. Finally, you turned away—away from your family, away from the church, away from God. All you really wanted was unconditional love, but where could you find it?

Then someone did come along, offering the kind of love you sought. Along with that love came the whole gay scene, and for a while it gave you what you thought you wanted. You received affection, attention, and companionship, but it was frequently predicated on sex. It didn't take long to become hooked—sexually addicted—and the habits perpetuated themselves. After a while, you realized that the gay community was not what it claimed to be. There was just as much rejection, bitterness, resentment, greed, gossip, and lust as in straight society. You finally learned that people are people, regardless of their sexual orientation. The honeymoon was over, and you settled down to the tiresome routine of the gay lifestyle.

One day, in the midst of your monotonous existence, some little spark went off in your mind. Maybe it was a fragment of a song you learned in Sunday school. Perhaps it was a bit of a sermon you heard. Or, it could have been the influence of a Christian who displayed the love of Christ, accepting you for who you were, loving you unconditionally. It could have been any number of things, but you recognized it as the voice of God. God was speaking to you of His love.

You probably thought about it for a long time before you made your decision. You had so much to consider. Would you lose your only way of having your need for love met? Could Jesus really compensate for the affection that you would surrender? Would you have to lose your desires and change your way of thinking before God would accept you? There were so many questions.

Finally you took the step. You surrendered your life to Jesus Christ, trusting His promises, and became one of God's children.

For a while, you flew on the emotions of your new-found relationship with Christ. Everything was wonderful, life was new, and you almost forgot about your homosexual desires. Eventually, though, you learned that you couldn't live by your emotions, and you had to face the reality of living by God's Word alone. Once more you became aware that you had all kinds of desires you didn't want and couldn't understand. What did God think of you? Did He still love you even though you wanted to relate sexually to the same sex? Did He really understand, or were those only nice ideas without any substance?

Maybe this is where you find yourself right now. Deep in your heart you love God and want to do what is right, but there are so many battles. You struggle with feelings that won't go away, your mind doesn't want to stay on what is pure and holy, and your selfish habit patterns relentlessly assert themselves. You know this isn't God's best for you, but you don't know how to obtain it. Will you have to go on forever with unfulfilled needs and cravings that cannot be righteously satisfied? Sometimes you honestly wonder if you can go on any longer.

By now, you are skeptical of "instant cures," and it is good that you are, because there aren't any. Deliverance from demons, prayer for inner healing, fasting, Bible reading—all promised immediate release from homosexual desire, but none completely solved the problem. Even a testimony of someone who claims to be "completely healed" can leave a sick feeling in the pit of your stomach. Sure, maybe God does completely, immediately heal some people, but what about the ones He doesn't heal? Does He care for them? Does He still love them? You know that living for Christ is the only way to real happiness. You don't want to hurt God, or forsake Him, but you still have your desires. If God loves you and has the answers to your problems, why is it taking so long to become well?

I hope that some of the following suggestions will help you in your struggles. I don't claim to offer any miracle cures, but if you can come to stability in your Christian walk, the path home will be easier to travel. Remember, psychological healing takes time, sometimes a long time, but any change that brings you freedom is worth the effort.

First, be careful that your goals in life are biblical and realistic. God does not demand that you be healed, happy, or heterosexually oriented. These things are all by-products of other activities, and as such, should not be targeted as suitable goals for your life. You cannot directly choose these results, so your heavenly Father has not set them up as standards in your life. God commands you to be holy in all your behavior (1 Pet. 1:15–16), and as a just Father, He is only requiring of you what He requires of every other human being. You are supposed to abstain from lust and fornication, but so is every person in the human race. That you are tempted toward the same sex rather than the opposite makes no difference—God's standard is just the same for you as for every other person. There is no partiality with God (Rom. 2:11). Your desires and temptations do not have to change in order to please Him; He accepts you just the way you are.

If you do sin, it is not the end of the world. If you lust or commit fornication, you should repent, ask forgiveness, and go on with your life. Wallowing in self-pity, or thinking that your situation is unique, or imagining that you are beyond hope is only a manifestation of pride, so repent of that attitude, humble yourself, and continue following God.

Your goals need to be biblical (obedience, not healing), but they should also be realistic. People change slowly, so give yourself time to change. You will not attain a stable Christian life in a week or a month, so don't give up after six months, thinking that God has forsaken you, and that it is useless to keep on trying. Be patient, and you will eventually see God's character developing in your life.

Second, resist any condemnation in your life. Temptation is not sin, condition is not behavior, and sexualized needs are not lust (Chap. 8). Keep these distinctions clearly in mind, refusing to allow yourself, other people, or the enemy to feed you lies. Deal with sin concretely, repenting and seeking forgiveness, but resist any vague, uneasy feelings of guilt. You cannot live under a burden of condemnation for very long before you weaken and yield to temptation. So, stay strong by living in freedom from false guilt. There is no condemnation to those who are in Christ (Rom. 8:1).

Third, remember how God views you. He does not stand over you with a whip, demanding that you change to please Him. He is not waiting until you become heterosexually oriented to be intimately involved in your life. Rather, as your loving Father, He longs to help you in your daily circumstances, hurting when you hurt, rejoicing in your victories, and answering your prayers with delight. Work on correcting your "father image" (Chap. 7), and refuse any thoughts about God's character that do not line up with God's Word. As *you* see what *God* is really like, it will be easier to perceive how *He* views *you*.

Fourth, be sure you work through the issue of the justice of God. You are an innocent person suffering because of the choices of other people. Your homosexual orientation was not your choice, but neither was it God's choice. As a fallen creature in a fallen world, you can suffer as an innocent party, but God did not want this for your life, just as He never wanted any sin, disease, or death to exist. That was man's fault. Other people's choices also play a big part in the speed of your healing. Your choices are significant because of their consequences, and if God eliminated the consequences of your choices, He would also eliminate their significance. This not only applies to your choices, but also to the choices of those who hurt you. God cannot simply eliminate the consequences of other people's choices just because those choices are affecting you adversely. Don't get me wrong. God can heal, but only if the healing is consistent with His character and wisdom.

These thoughts may be new to you, so it may take some time to work them through. They are very important, though, and you owe it to yourself to take the time to see how God is completely free of blame in the development of your sexual condition. If you don't take the trouble to think this through, you may struggle in your relationship with God because you will view Him as unjust when that is not really the case.

Fifth, learn to think of yourself biblically (Chap. 7). God describes us and defines our value in His Word. The problem with this is that our concept of ourselves seldom comes from the Bible. Mostly, we pick up our idea of our self-worth from people around us, and this image is usually false. Thus, the homosexually oriented person tends to view himself in a particularly negative light since the world has such a distorted idea of what homosexuality is all about. Self-image correction will be invaluable to you as you strive to follow Jesus consistently, so learn to think of yourself according to the description God outlines in His Word.

Sixth, learn to get your basic needs met in Jesus. You long for love and a sense of value as a person, and Jesus wants to meet these needs, but you must spend time with Him daily if you hope to experience this fulfillment. If the foundation of a building is weak, the whole building will be shaky. The foundation of your Christian life is your communication with Jesus through prayer, worship, Bible reading (or study), and obedience. Neglect these fundamentals, and your whole life can go wrong. As you spend quality time with God, your basic needs for love, affection, security, value, self-worth, and a sense of competency will be fulfilled, and the temptation to meet these needs through homosexual activity will become easier and easier to resist.

Seventh, and lastly, don't give up! As I said before, change comes slowly, but it does come. Don't submit to feelings of futility, thinking, "Why bother? I haven't changed yet, so why should I go on trying?" Though it may take time, change is possible, so it is definitely worth the effort to keep on going. God is for you, not against you, and He can see you through to victory over sin and a life that glorifies Him in every respect. Just give Him a chance to help you. He really does care.

APPENDIXES

EMOTIONAL DEPENDENCY: A Threat to Close Friendships

By Lori Thorkelson

Mary had spent long hours with Sarah, counseling her and helping her through the struggles of being a new Christian. They seemed to have a great friendship with lots of common interests and a mutual love for the Lord. Sarah felt Mary understood her better than anyone ever had. Even Sarah's husband, Bill, could not provide her with the closeness she experienced with Mary. Mary and her husband, Tom, had a fulfilling marriage, but Tom's sales career kept him away from home often. A loving person, Mary willingly invested her time and care in Sarah, who really seemed to need her. It was rewarding for Mary to see Sarah growing in the Lord, and she enjoyed Sarah's obvious admiration.

The shock came when Mary and Sarah found themselves emotionally and physically involved with each other. Neither woman had ever been aware of homosexual feelings before. Both of them loved God and cared for their husbands. Their friendship had appeared to be Christ-centered, as they frequently prayed and read the Bible together. If what they were doing was wrong, why hadn't God stopped them? Why hadn't they seen the danger signals along the way? Now that they were so closely involved, they could not imagine being apart. "What are we going to do?" they wondered.

WHAT IS EMOTIONAL DEPENDENCY?

Long before Mary and Sarah were involved homosexually, they had entered into an emotionally dependent relationship. Emotional dependency is *the condition resulting when the ongoing presence and/or nurturing of another is believed necessary for personal security.* This nurturing comes in many different forms of input from one person's life into another's:

- attention
- listening
- admiration
- counsel
- affirmation
- time spent together

Emotionally dependent relationships may appear harmless or even healthy at first, but they can lead to destruction and bondage greater than most people can imagine. Whether or not physical involvement exists, sin enters the picture when a friendship becomes a dependent relationship. If we have been enjoined to seek first the kingdom of God, making the Lord Jesus Christ the center of our doing and being, then transgression has taken place when a relationship—any relationship—is made central to existence instead of God. God must be the provider of personal security because a human being ends up doing so only imperfectly.

To differentiate between the normal interdependency that happens in wholesome relationships and an unhealthy dependency, we will look at the factors that make up a dependent relationship: how and why it gets started and how it is maintained.

CHARACTERISTICS OF A DEPENDENT RELATIONSHIP

We all have a deep need, placed in us by God, for intimate friendships. How do we know when we are meeting this need legitimately? Is there some way to recognize when we have crossed the line into dependency? Here are some signs that an emotional dependency has started to form.

When either party in a relationship:

- experiences frequent jealousy, possessiveness and a desire for exclusivism, viewing other people as a threat to the relationship.
- prefers to spend time alone with this friend and becomes frustrated when this does not happen.
- becomes irrationally angry or depressed when this friend withdraws slightly.
- loses interest in friendships other than this one.
- experiences romantic or sexual feelings leading to fantasy about this person.
- becomes preoccupied with this person's appearance, personality, problems and interests.
- is unwilling to make short- or long-range plans that do not include the other person.
- is unable to see the other's faults realistically.
- becomes defensive about the relationship when asked about it.
- displays physical affection beyond that which is appropriate for a friendship.
- refers frequently to the other in conversation; feels free to "speak for" the other.
- exhibits an intimacy and familiarity with this friend that causes others to feel uncomfortable or embarrassed in their presence.

There are some significant differences between a healthy friendship and an unhealthy relationship. A healthy relationship is free and generous. Both friends are eager to include others in their activities. They experience joy when one friend hits it off with another. In a good friendship, we desire to see our friend reach his or her full potential, developing new interests and skills. A dependent relationship is ingrown, creating mutual stagnation and limiting personal growth. In normal relationships we are affected by things our friends say and do, but our reactions are balanced. When we are emotionally dependent, a casual remark from our friend can send us into the heights of ecstasy or the pits of grief. If a close friend moves away, it is normal for us to feel sorrow and a sense of loss. If one of the partners in a dependent relationship moves, the other is gripped with anguish, panic and desperation. A healthy friendship is joyful, healing and upbuilding; an emotional dependency produces bondage.

SET-UPS FOR EMOTIONAL DEPENDENCY

Emotional dependency comes as a surprise to most people. Like Mary and Sarah, they do not see the problem coming until it has a hold on them. However, dependencies do not happen in a vacuum. Definite elements in our personalities and situations can set us up for binding relationships. Sins and hurts from the past leave us vulnerable, too. Having an awareness of these set-ups helps us know when we need to exercise special caution in our relationships.

Who is susceptible? Anyone can fall into a dependent relationship given the right pressures and circumstances. However, there are a few common personality patterns that consistently gravitate toward each other to form dependencies. The basic combination seems to be the individual who appears to "have it all together" teamed up with one who needs the attention, protection or strength the other offers. Variations on this theme include:

- counselor/person with problems
- "in control" person/one who needs direction
- parent/child
- teacher/student

Although these pairs appear to include one strong person and one needy person, they actually consist of two needy people. The "strong" one usually has a deep need to be needed. As often as not, the one who appears weaker actually controls the relationship. I have talked with people who have been "weak" in one relationship and "strong" in another, and sometimes these elements are not apparent at all. A balanced friendship can turn into a dependent relationship if other set-ups are present.

When are we most vulnerable? Certain times in our lives find us feeling insecure, ready to grasp whatever security is available to us. Some of these include:

- life crises: relationship break-up, death of someone close, loss of a job.
- transition periods: adjusting to a new job, moving to a new home, getting engaged or being newly married, starting college, becoming a Christian.

- peak pressure periods: finals week, deadlines at work, personal or family illness, holidays such as Christmas or Thanksgiving.
- being away from the familiar and secure: vacation, camp, conferences, prison, military service.
- times of boredom and/or depression.

The best way to avoid trouble is to recognize our need for special support during these times and plan ahead for these needs to be met in healthy ways. This might include sharing our burdens with a small prayer group, scheduling a series of appointments with a counselor or pastor, increasing our contact with family members and, most important, cultivating our relationship with Jesus through special quiet times. Also, there is nothing wrong with letting our friends know we need their support! Problems only develop when we lean too much on one particular friend to meet all our needs.

ROOTS: WHY ARE WE PRONE TO DEPENDENCY?

In a dependent relationship, one or both people are looking to a *person* to meet their basic needs for love and security, rather than to Jesus. Unless underlying spiritual and emotional problems are resolved, this pattern will continue unbroken. Typical root problems that promote dependency include:

- covetousness: desiring to possess something (or someone) God has not given us.
- idolatry: when something or someone is at the center of our lives rather than God.
- rebellion: refusing to surrender areas of our lives to God.
- mistrust: failing to believe God will meet our needs if we do things His way.

Sometimes hurts from our past leave us with low self-esteem, feelings of rejection, and a deep unmet need for love. Bitterness or resentment toward those who have hurt us also open us up for wrong relationships. These sins and hurts need to be confessed and healed before real freedom can be experienced. This can happen through confession and prayer, both in our personal times with the Lord and with other members of the body of Christ.

Emotional dependency is a painful thing to discuss. Most of

us have experienced this problem. None of us are exempt from the temptation to draw our life and security from another person, especially when that person is handy and cooperative. Dependent relationships can form in opposite-sex and same-sex friendships. They can happen between married couples and between parents and children. But in the heart of the Gospel there is the message of truth that can free us from self-seeking relationships. For a lot of us, that really is good news!

MAINTENANCE THROUGH MANIPULATION

Manipulation is an ugly word. None of us likes to believe we could ever be guilty of this activity. Yet when emotionally dependent relationships form, manipulation often becomes the glue that holds them together.

My working definition of manipulation is *attempting to control people or circumstances through deceptive or indirect means.* Webster's Dictionary describes manipulation as being insidious, which means:

- treacherous: awaiting a chance to entrap.
- seductive: harmful but enticing.
- subtle: developing so gradually as to be well established before becoming apparent, having a gradual but cumulative effect.

There are a variety of forms of manipulation, but here are some that I've seen used to begin and maintain dependent relationships:

- finances: combining finances and personal possessions such as property and furniture; moving in together.
- gifts: giving gifts and cards regularly for no special occasion, such as flowers, jewelry, baked goods and gifts symbolic of the relationship.
- clothes: wearing each other's clothing, copying each other's styles.
- romanticisms: using poetry, music or other romanticisms to provoke an emotional response.
- physical affection: body language, frequent hugging, touching, rough-housing, back and neck rubs, tickling and wrestling.
- eye contact: staring, giving meaningful or seductive looks; refusing to make eye contact as a means of punishment.

- flattery and praise: "You're the only one who understands me." "I don't know what I'd do without you." (Proverbs 29:5 says, "Whoever flatters his neighbor is spreading a net for his feet.")
- conversational triggers: flirting, teasing, using special nicknames, referring to things that have special meaning to both of you; in the company of others using language that excludes by creating a secret, double conversation that only the two of you understand.
- failing to be honest: repressing negative feelings or differing opinions.
- needing "help": creating or exaggerating problems to gain attention and sympathy.
- guilt: making the other feel guilty over unmet expectations: "If you love me, then . . ." "I was going to call you last night, but I know you're probably too busy to bother with me."
- threats: threats of suicide and backsliding can be manipulative.
- pouting, brooding, cold silences: when asked "what's wrong," replying by sighing and saying, "Nothing."
- undermining partner's other relationships: convincing him others do not care about him; making friends with partner's friends in order to control the situation.
- provoking insecurity: withholding approval, picking on partner's weak points, threatening to end the relationship.
- time: keeping the other's time occupied so as not to allow for separate activities.

These are common ways manipulation is used to hold dependent relationships together. Some of these things are not sinful themselves. Honest praise and encouragement, giving of gifts, hugging and touching are important aspects of godly friendship. Only when these things are used for selfish ends— to bind or control another, to arouse responses leading to sin— do they become manipulative.

WHY ARE DEPENDENCIES HARD TO BREAK?

Even when both parties realize a relationship is unhealthy, they may experience great difficulty in breaking the dependency. Often those involved will begin to separate, only to run back to each other. Even after dependencies are broken, the effects may linger on for some time. Let's look at some reasons why these attachments are so persistent.

There are benefits. We usually do not involve ourselves in any kind of behavior if we do not believe it benefits us in some way. As painful as dependency is, it does give us some gratification. The fear of losing this gratification makes dependent relationships hard to give up. Some of the perceived benefits of an emotional dependency include:

- emotional security: a dependent relationship gives us the sense that we have at least one relationship we can count on. This gives us the feeling of belonging to someone.
- intimacy: our need for intimacy, warmth and affection might be filled through this relationship.
- self-worth: our ego is boosted when someone admires us or is attracted to us. We also appreciate feeling needed.
- relief from boredom: a relationship like this might add excitement and romance when life seems dull otherwise. In fact, the stressful ups and downs of the relationship can be addictive.
- escape from responsibility: the focus on maintaining the relationship can provide an escape from confronting personal problems and responsibilities.
- familiarity: many people do not know any other way of relating. They are afraid to give up the "known" for the "unknown."

We can't see it as sin. The culture we live in has taken the truth "God is love" and turned it around to mean "Love is God." In modern history romantic or emotional love is viewed as a law unto itself; when you "love" someone (meaning: when you have intense romantic feelings for someone), anything you do with that person is "OK." Viewed in this light, dependent relationships seem beautiful, even noble. Dependent attachments can be easy to rationalize, especially if there is no sexual involvement. Genuine feelings of love and friendship might be used to excuse the intense jealousy and possessiveness present in the dependency.

Also, we may not be able to see how a dependent relationship separates us from God. "I pray more than ever," one woman told us. What she didn't mention was that she never prayed about anything *but* her dependent relationship. Sometimes people say, "This friend draws me even closer to God." What usually has happened is that the emotional dependency has given them a euphoric feeling that masquerades as "closeness to God." When the friend withdraws even slightly, God suddenly seems far away!

Root problems are not dealt with. We might end a dependent relationship by breaking it off or moving away. However, if we still have unhealed hurts, unfilled needs or an unrepentant heart, we will fall right into another dependent relationship or return to the one we left. Dealing with the surface symptom rather than the real problem leaves the door open to future stumbling.

Spiritual influences are overlooked. When we ignore the Holy Spirit's correction, we make ourselves vulnerable to satanic oppression. Those who willingly enter dependent relationships become candidates for spiritual deception. Wrong begins to seem right to them, and truth begins to sound like a lie. When breaking free from dependent relationships, we sometimes overlook the importance of spiritual warfare: prayer, fasting, and deliverance. If emotional ties have gone deep into a person's life, especially if sexual sin has been involved, there's the need to break the bonds that have formed between the two people. When dependency has been a lifelong pattern, ties need to be broken with all past partners as well. If the spiritual aspects are not dealt with thoroughly, this sin pattern will continue.

We don't want to give up our sin. Counselors know the frustration of going through all imaginable steps of counseling, support and spiritual warfare on behalf of a counselee only to realize this individual has no interest in changing. People in dependent relationships sometimes say they want out, but they really want to be relieved from the responsibility of doing anything about the problem. They hope talking to a counselor will free them from the pressures of their conscience. Meanwhile, their desire and intent is to continue having the dependent relationship. Sometimes the bottom line is this: an emotional dependency is hard to break because the individuals involved don't want it to be broken.

THE PATH OUT OF DEPENDENCY

The tendency to draw our life and security from another human being is a problem nearly everyone faces. However, it is only after we encounter repeated frustration and sorrow in emotionally dependent relationships that we hunger for something more satisfying. We long to find contentment and rest in our relationships with others, but how do we break the old patterns?

Before we start exploring the different elements in overcoming dependency, we need to grasp an important truth: *there is no formula* that leads us to a transformed life. Lifelong tendencies toward dependent relationships cannot be changed by following "ten easy steps." Jesus Christ desires to do an intimate and unique work within each of us by the power of His Holy Spirit. Change will come as we submit to Him and cooperate with that work.

The guidelines we are considering here illustrate ways God has worked in various people's lives to bring them out of emotional dependency. Some of the suggestions apply to gaining freedom from a specific relationship, others pertain to breaking lifelong patterns. All represent different aspects of a whole picture: turning away from forms of relationships rooted in our sin nature and learning new ways of relating based on our new natures in Christ.

Making a commitment to honesty. Dependencies are often hard to break because of the deception that sets in; we can't see dependency as sin. This deception is broken when we are *honest with ourselves*, admitting we are involved in a dependent relationship and acknowledging our dependency as sin. Then we are ready for *honesty with God*, confessing our sin to Him. We do not have to hide our confusion, our anger, or any of our feelings. We just need to pour out our hearts to Him, asking Him to give us the willingness to obey His will in this matter.

The next challenge is being *honest with another person.* We can seek out a mature brother or sister in Christ and confess to them, "Look, I'm really struggling with my feelings toward my partner on the evangelism team. I'm getting way too attached to her. Could you pray with me about this?" As we "walk in the light" in this way, we can be cleansed and forgiven. If we are aware of specific ways we have manipulated circumstances to promote the dependent relationship, we can ask forgiveness for these actions, too. The deeper the honesty, the deeper the cleansing we will receive.

In choosing someone to share with, the best choice is a stable, trustworthy Christian who is not emotionally involved in the situation. This person can then intercede for us in prayer and hold us accountable, especially if we give him or her freedom to periodically ask how things are going. Extreme caution needs to be used in sharing our feelings with the one we are dependent on. I have seen regrettable results when one brother (or sister) has shared with another in an intimate setting, "Hey, I'm really attracted to you. I think I'm getting dependent." It's better to seek the counsel and prayer of a spiritual elder before even considering this step, and, even then, we need to ask the Lord to shine His light on our motives.

Introducing changes in activities: Gradual separation. It's easy to begin planning our lives around the partner in the dependent relationship. Often this may include being involved in the same church. Quitting that church just because the other person is there is not the best solution. A parting of the ways must take place, however, and that may incorporate involvement in individual activities and only getting together in group situations. Placing ourselves unnecessarily in the presence of the person we are dependent on will only prolong the pain and delay God's work in our lives.

Allow God to work. This sounds so obvious, but it's not as easy as it seems! After we confess to God that we are hopelessly attached to this individual and are powerless to do anything about it, we invite Him to come in and "change the situation." The Lord never ignores a prayer like this. Some people begin to confront us about this relationship, but we assure them we have it all under control. Our friend decides to start going to a different Bible study, and soon we find a good reason to switch to the same one. The Holy Spirit nudges us to get rid of certain record albums, but we keep forgetting to do it. We ask God to work in our lives, but then we do everything in our power to make sure He doesn't! I've learned from my own experience that thwarting God's attempts to take someone out of my life only produces prolonged unrest and agony. Cooperation with the Holy Spirit brings the quickest possible healing from broken relationships.

Prepare for grief and depression. Letting go of a dependent relationship can be as painful as going through a divorce. If we acquaint ourselves with the grief process and allow ourselves to hurt for a season, our healing will come faster. If we repress our pain and deny ourselves the time we need to recover, we will carry around unnecessary guilt and bitterness. Some people have said that they found the Psalms to be especially comforting during this time of "letting go."

Cultivate other friendships. Even if it's difficult, scary, and our hearts are not in it . . . we need to do it. Our feelings will catch up later, and we will be glad we have made the investment in the lives of our new friends. The Lord will choose relationships for us if we will let Him. Willingness to accept the friends He gives us will deepen our relationship with Him as well. He knows just the relationships we need to draw out our special qualities and chip off our rough edges.

Discover God's vision for relationships. If we love another person as God loves him, we will desire to see that man (or woman) conformed to the image of Christ. The Lord wants to bring forth qualities in us that reflect His character and gifts that enable us to do His work. Andy Comiskey of Desert Stream in Santa Monica, California, has said: "At the onset of any friendship, we must choose a motivation. Either we mirror a friend's homosexual desirability or his/her new identity in Christ. This may sound tough, but our willingness to be disciplined emotionally might just make or break a friendship. When we exchange another's best interest for our own neediness, we run the risk of losing the friendship." If we desire an exclusive emotional involvement with this friend, then our desires are in conflict with what the Lord wants. We need to ask ourselves, "Am I working with God or against Him in this person's life?"

Resolve the deeper issues. The compulsion to form dependent relationships is a symptom of deeper spiritual and emotional problems that need to be faced and resolved. Self-analysis is the least effective way to uncover these problems. The most effective way is to go directly to Jesus and ask Him to show us what's wrong. "If any of you lacks wisdom, he should ask God, who gives generously to all without finding fault, and it will be given him" (James 1:5). Another effective way is to go to those God has placed in positions of authority over us and submit to their counsel and prayer. For some, a long-term counseling relationship will help us face the sins we need to repent of and the hurts that need healing. For others, a small covenant group that meets regularly for deep sharing and prayer will help tremendously. Sometimes personal prayer and fasting draws us to God and breaks sin bondages in a way nothing else will. The desire to find our identity and security in another human being is a common sin problem with a myriad of possible causes. Confession, repentance, deliverance, counseling and inner healing are means the Lord will use to bring purity and emotional stability into our lives. The healing and forgiveness we need are ours through Jesus' atonement. We can receive them by humbling ourselves before Him and before others in His body.

Prepare for the long haul. Sometimes victory escapes us because we prepare for a battle rather than a war. Whether we are trying to gain freedom from a specific attachment or from lifelong patterns of dependency, we need to prepare for long-term warfare. We need to know ourselves: our vulnerabilities, the types of personalities we are likely to "fall for," the times when we need to be especially careful. We need to know our adversary: know the specific lies Satan is likely to tempt us with and be prepared to reject those lies, even when they sound good to us! More than anything, we need to know our Lord. We need to be willing to believe God loves us. Even if we cannot seem to feel His love, we can take a stand by faith that He does love us and begin to thank Him for this fact. As we learn of God's character through His Word, we can relinquish our images of Him as being cruel, distant or unloving. A love relationship with Jesus is our best safeguard against emotionally dependent relationships.

IS THERE LIFE AFTER DEPENDENCY?

Though overcoming dependence may be painful for a season, it is one of the most curable ailments known to man. Often people are so healed that they cannot even conceive of the extent of their former bondage to dependent relationships.

The immediate reward in giving up a dependent relationship is peace with God. Even in the midst of pain over the loss of the dependency, we experience peace, relief and joy as our fellowship with God is restored. "It's like waking up after a bad dream," one woman told us.

Peace with ourselves is another blessing we receive. It's much easier to like ourselves when we are not scheming and striving to maintain a relationship we know God does not desire for us. When we have relinquished a dependent attachment, we are no longer tormented with fear of losing the relationship. This, too, brings peace to our hearts.

In the aftermath of dependency, we discover a new freedom to love others. We are members of one another in the body of Christ. When our attentions and affections are wrapped up totally in one individual, other people in our lives are suffering for it. They are not receiving the love from us God intends them to have.

Individuals who have given up dependent relationships say they discover a new caring and compassion for people that's not based on sexual or emotional attraction. They find they are less critical of people and less defensive. They begin to notice that their lives are founded on the real security found through their relationship with Christ, not the false security of a dependent relationship.

And, finally, overcoming dependency brings us a freedom to minister to others. We can lead others only where we have been willing to go ourselves. When we are no longer rationalizing wrong attachments, we have new liberty in the Spirit to exhort and encourage others! Our discernment becomes clearer, and spiritual truth is easier to understand and accept. We become clean vessels, fit for the Lord's use.

In our desire to remain free from this problem, we need to remember that hiding from people is not the alternative to dependency. Dependency is a subtle counterfeit to the tremendously rich and fulfilling relationship the Lord intends for us to have through Him. If we are trying to overcome the sin of dependency, let's remember that Jesus is not harsh with us. He will teach us to love people in a holy way, and He knows that this takes time. There is a battle between the flesh and the spirit in every area of our lives—relationships are no exception. But Jesus is the one who is bringing His body together, and we are learning. "I am confident of this: that He who began a good work in you will carry it on to completion until the day of Jesus Christ" (Phil. 1:6).

About the Author

Lori Thorkelson Rentzel was on staff seven years with Love in Action International, a Christian outreach to those overcoming homosexuality.

In addition to writing for the Love in Action newsletter, Lori counseled friends, parents and spouses with homosexual loved ones. She has taught seminars on "Help for Friends and Families" and "Emotional Dependency" and has been a regular workshop leader at the annual EXODUS International educational conference.

Now a full-time homemaker, Lori lives with her husband Rudy and daughter Rebekah in San Rafael, California.

Ordering Information

Copies of this appendix are available in booklet form from: Exodus International, P.O. Box 2121, San Rafael, CA 94912; 415/454–1017. Single copies are $1.50, including shipping. Bulk rates are available upon request.

WITNESSING TO THE HOMOSEXUAL

J esus commanded us to "beseech the Lord of the harvest to send out laborers into His harvest" (Luke 10:2). The gay community is one portion of the harvest field that the Church has neglected too long. Some Christians who emphasize reaching the whole world for Christ will shudder at the thought of witnessing to a homosexual, and this lack of compassion for homosexuals has kept the gay community from hearing the good news of Jesus Christ. It is time for the Church to repent, to be filled with God's love for all people, and to seek wisdom for effectively reaching unbelieving homosexuals.

BEFORE YOU GO

Proper preparation is essential to any witnessing effort, but the task of reaching homosexuals for Christ can require some extra equipping for the Christian worker. A missionary to a foreign country would want to have a burden for the people, he would pray for them, and he would find out all he could about their language, culture, dress, history, etc. In the same way, the person who ministers in the gay community will want to have the right heart attitude, he should intercede, and he needs to be informed about the people he desires to reach.

1. *Attitude*: A person can sense whether or not other people truly love him. This perception may result from observation of other people's actions, or it may come from an intuitive response in the person's spirit. Sometimes a Christian says he loves everyone, but sends gays a subliminal signal of rejection due to deep-

seated attitudes of pride, revulsion, or disgust that he harbors toward homosexuals. In any case, if a homosexual senses that the Christian does not love him, reaching him with the Gospel may be nearly impossible. It is imperative that the Christian witness have a sensitive, gentle, loving attitude toward homosexuals, and this attitude can come only through brokenness and sharing God's heart for these people.

The best way to learn God's attitude toward homosexuals is to pray, asking God to share His heart with you. As you pray, God will communicate His burden for homosexuals to your heart, mind, spirit, and emotions. Once you have experienced God's love for gays, your attitude toward them will never be the same. When I first take a friend to a gay bar to witness, I ask him to stay in one place to pray for the first twenty or thirty minutes. He asks God to break his heart for the men he is trying to reach. I have often returned to find my friend weeping because God has shared His burden with the man's spirit. Once this happens, the person's attitude toward gays is forever altered. I have also seen the other reaction in some Christians. A few of the men who came to the bar became angry and refused to allow God to put His burden in their hearts. These men were unable to witness all night long because the Holy Spirit could not anoint their proud, stubborn hearts. As one person put it, "God will not give you His mind until He has given you His heart." So, if we open our hearts to God, He will allow us to feel His love, His burden, His concern for homosexuals.

2. *Intercession.* Praying for the people you are evangelizing will prepare you as the evangelist, the people you are attempting to reach, and the circumstances surrounding your witnessing.

Difficulty in witnessing is often the result of prayerlessness. If you intercede consistently, your mind will be sensitive to the voice of God while you witness, and you will have greater wisdom for each person, knowing exactly which portions of God's Word to bring into the different conversations. Also, sensitivity to the spiritual world comes through prayer, and being able to sense what is happening in the spiritual realm is crucial to effective evangelism.

If you pray for the people you speak to, their hearts will be better prepared to receive the message of the Gospel. Pray that they will be convicted of their sin. Pray that they will meet Christians everywhere they go. Pray that God will remove the spiritual blindfold from their minds,[1] giving them an understanding of His love for them. As you pray, God will guide you specifically, giving you revelation of what He wants to do in their lives.

If you pray about the circumstances, God will move to arrange situations for more effective witnessing. One night, a brother on our witnessing team prayed that God would make cars break down in front of the bar if He wanted those people to hear the Gospel through us that evening. Later that night, that same brother had a long, exciting conversation with an honest young man. When the brother asked the man why he came to the bar that night, the man replied, "Oh, I wasn't planning on coming in here tonight, but my car broke down in front of the bar. Since I can't get it fixed tonight, I decided I may as well stop in for a drink before I go home." Some people might say this was purely coincidental, but it was not. It was the direct intervention of God in the affairs of men. And why did it happen? It happened because someone prayed. Unbelievers often call these events coincidence, but I have found that if I stop praying, the coincidences stop happening. Another evening, Dan prayed that he would meet someone who had been specifically prepared to hear the Gospel. Later, as Dan conversed with one of the men in the bar, the man seemed surprised that he had encountered a Christian.

"Why should that surprise you?" Dan asked.

"Well," the man said, "within the last few weeks I lost my father and another close relative, so death is very real to me right now. Besides that, for the last two nights I have had dreams about Jesus and my need for Him."

Because God loves us and all those we witness to, He longs to orchestrate this kind of situation. Sometimes, though, we do not have because we do not ask (James 4:2). Intercession is vital to evangelism, so be sure to pray for yourself, the people you talk to, and the circumstances. It could mean someone's spiritual life or death.

3. *Information.* In the Introduction I mentioned how information can help us have compassion for other people. Besides producing greater understanding and compassion, better information can make the Christian more effective in his witnessing effort. Being informed helps the person to know what to say and

---

[1] This is a necessary part of our spiritual warfare in witnessing because "the god of this world has blinded the minds of the unbelieving" (2 Cor. 4:4).

not say, what to do and not do, and how to avoid hurt or embarrassment for himself and the person he is trying to reach.

Jerry had never been to a gay bar before. As I was showing him the layout of the bar, Jerry walked only a few inches behind me, obviously amazed and maybe a little apprehensive about what he saw. At one point, Jerry leaned over my shoulder and exclaimed in a loud voice, "Is that a cop?" Evidently, it shocked him to see a man in a policeman's uniform in a gay bar. A number of people stopped and stared, while the man in the uniform began to laugh.

"No," I said, trying to be discreet, "that is not a policeman. I'll explain it to you later."

"Oh," Jerry said, "did I say something wrong?"

Fortunately, this incident was comical rather than hurtful. It was understandable that Jerry would not know that a uniform is sometimes used as part of a person's "sexual paraphernalia," but still, this little incident could have been avoided if Jerry had quietly asked me a question rather than speaking so the whole bar could hear. A little information could have saved a lot of embarrassment.

Just as any good missionary would study the people group he is striving to evangelize, so the person who wants to reach out to the gay community should study the topic of homosexuality. There are many good books and tapes on the Christian market dealing with the subject (see Appendix C). Some of the most important points to study will include: theories as to how the homosexual orientation develops; the feelings, desires, and aspirations of the homosexually oriented person; some of the special vocabulary used in the gay community; what the Bible says about the topic, and how to refute the "gay theology"; how to help the homosexual see his need for God; how to help the person with a homosexual condition to establish a stable Christian lifestyle. Not all of these topics will appear in every volume, so it will be important to collect a variety of study aids.

Having an academic knowledge of homosexuality is a good place to start, but the subjective experiences of the individual homosexual can greatly modify the application of this information. Consequently, the personal experiences of people who have left the homosexual lifestyle can be invaluable in gaining an understanding of the "inner workings" of the homosexual. An excellent way to examine these experiences is spending time with brothers and sisters who have come from a gay background. If the person is approached in a sensitive manner, he or she should not mind being interviewed, if that information can aid someone else to bring the Gospel to homosexuals. So, collecting data from Christians who have left the lifestyle can be a great help toward understanding homosexuals.

Another good way to learn about homosexuals is to be around people who are still living a gay lifestyle. Some people never give themselves the chance to understand homosexuals because they never spend time with them. We can go to places where they congregate, do things with them, try to become friends with some of them.[2] Personal contact with homosexuals will help you understand their specific needs. The more exposure you have to homosexuals, the more you will understand about how they think and what they need, and this increased knowledge will help you witness to them more effectively.

Before you go somewhere to witness to gays (e.g., gay bars, gay discotheques, health clubs that cater mainly to gays, streets frequented by male homosexual prostitutes), find out as much as you can about the place itself. Is it casual or formal? This may determine how you dress. Is it frequented by men or women only, or is it mixed? This will influence the makeup of your witnessing team. Sometimes, the first visit to one of these venues will be solely to collect information, but that can actually be advantageous, since people are not threatened by someone who is dependent on them for information. So, don't be afraid to go somewhere just to observe and learn. This new data will give you direction in prayer, greater understanding of the needs of the people, and ideas for creative strategies for telling them about Christ.

WHILE YOU WITNESS

Reaching a specific group of people with the Gospel requires a specific strategy. Although many of the cultural traits of the gay community will be the same as the surrounding heterosexual society, some of the differences make it necessary to adjust the witnessing procedure. Here are some hints that will be helpful

---

[2]Some people might question this step because they wonder about spending time with unbelievers. But I have never found it necessary to compromise my Christian convictions to be in contact with homosexuals. Picnics, sports, going to movies, or going out to eat are just a few of the ways we can spend time with them in a wholesome manner.

for evangelizing in the gay community.

1. *Be a friend.* Low-key friendship evangelism is one of the most effective ways of sharing the Gospel with gays. After dealing with a lifetime of rejection and hurt, many homosexuals are suspicious of other people, so the first thing they want to know is whether or not the Christian really cares for them. This obstacle can be overcome through friendship. Of course, the Christian should be a friend because it is right to do so, not just to tell the other person about Christ. If a homosexual (or anyone else, for that matter) suspects that the Christian is being friendly with ulterior motives, the person cannot help but feel manipulated by the Christian. But if the homosexual senses the believer's sincere love, it will open him up, not only to the Christian's friendship, but also to the Christian's message.

There are places and times that strategies like street preaching and tract distribution are quite effective. In a casual setting such as a gay bar, though, this kind of evangelism is seldom beneficial. Even the *presence* of a Bible can cause trouble. Whether or not one uses tracts or the Bible will depend on the circumstances, the group of people involved, and the depth of relationship the Christian has with the other people. For instance, if the Christian is invited to a gay beach party, he will have freedom to share his faith according to the relationships he has developed. If he is standing in a gay bar, he should be more careful, since he is working on starting relationships. Or, if the Christian is handing out tracts on the street and initiates a conversation with a homosexual, he will need to express great sensitivity, since there is no basis for mutual trust. The greater the degree of friendship, the deeper the level of trust, and this trust will generate greater freedom to share the Gospel.

2. *Share Christ with the person.* Wanting the very best for someone is part of what it means to be a friend. Since the Gospel is the power of God unto salvation, the Christian who befriends another person will want to share the Good News of Jesus with his friend. The homosexual's greatest need is for Christ and His forgiveness, so to withhold this most vital information from the person would violate the friendship.

Sometimes the homosexual will want to be friends, but only on the condition that the Christian does not share his faith with him. This kind of friendship would be neither desirable nor edifying. The Christian must not compromise his faith for the sake of friendship. When the Christian is faced with this alternative, he must reply tactfully, trying to maintain the friendship without being pressured into an awkward position.

Greg sat across the table from me, picking at his half-eaten dinner. He broke his silence by stating, "Mike, to be honest with you, I'm afraid of you."

"Thanks for being honest, Greg; what are you afraid of?"

"I'm afraid," he said, "that you will try to preach to me about Jesus, and I don't know if I want to hear about religion."

"Well, Greg, I want to continue being your friend, so we'll have to come to some kind of understanding about this. I don't want to cram religion down your throat—I know you wouldn't like that, and I don't want to hurt you. On the other hand, though, I am a Christian, and Jesus is the most important person in my life. So you have to expect that I will want to talk from time to time about someone who is very dear to me. If you had a lover, and I asked you to never speak about him in my presence, it would be very awkward for you, wouldn't it? Well, it's the same way with me. If we are going to be friends, I have to have the freedom to talk about the most important person in my life. I promise that I will try to be sensitive to you, and I won't try to force something on you that you don't want, but I will not promise that I won't talk about my friend and lover, Jesus. OK?"

Greg agreed to those stipulations and we continued our friendship.

If we are committed to loving homosexuals and being their friends, we cannot withhold from them the very truth that can set them free. All of our communications need to be sensitive and friendly, but we must not put ourselves in the position of never talking about Christ. This would be a great disservice to any person, but especially to those we call our friends.

Most of the time, while talking about Jesus, the Christian can simply ignore the sexual habits of the other person. Some Christians can talk with a drug addict and ignore his drug habit while they talk about the man's need for Christ. Those same Christians, when speaking with homosexuals, somehow feel they must confront the person about his or her sexual lifestyle right from the start. If a Christian feels under "compulsion" to immediately confront the person, he should consider examining his motives. Self-righteousness rooted in pride usually lies at the base of such behavior. In this case, the Christian is not confronting sin because that is in the other person's best interest, but because the Christian wants everyone to know that he is against such things and would never even *think* of doing anything "that bad." Or, it could be that the Christian is afraid and goes on the offensive to defend himself. But whether it is pride, or fear, or both, the drive to confront the homosexual about his lifestyle is usually founded in some distorted motivation. The subject of homosexuality and Christianity will come up soon enough and often enough that the Christian need not bring it up compulsively. So, in general, the believer can relax, be a friend, and treat the homosexual as he would anyone else.

3. *Define your terms.* The difference between homosexual condition and behavior is a foreign concept to most Christians, so learning to work with this idea can take some time. But it is not only Christians who fail to distinguish between orientation and behavior—many homosexuals also make no distinction between how they think and what they do. Consequently, one of the important steps to take while witnessing is to define these terms very carefully.

Because the homosexual has thought so long in terms of "I'm gay," combining orientation and behavior in his mind, he will consistently confuse these issues while he speaks. It is up to the Christian at that point to gently remind the person that there is a difference, and that the person may draw wrong conclusions if he fails to recognize this distinction. For example, the homosexual may say, "I'm sure God must hate me because I'm gay. But that's what I am and I can't change, so God will just have to accept that." This fusion of metaphysics (being) and morals (choice) causes the person to adopt an incorrect view of God's character, making it harder to come to Him. If the Christian can help keep this difference clearly before the homosexual's mind, the person will eventually understand that God loves him as a person, while not accepting his rebellious behavior, and that there is real hope for change.

4. *Begin with the positive.* Homosexuality is need-motivated. The homosexual's behavior is an attempt to meet his basic needs for a sense of identity, self-worth, affection, security, and love. When he hears a Christian say that he must forsake his homosexual lifestyle to know God, it sounds like: "If you give up your way of having your need for love met for the rest of your life, God will accept you." This is not good news to the homosexual, and any attempt to preach the Gospel from this perspective is doomed to failure. But since the homosexual is concerned about meeting his basic needs, that is a very good place to begin talking.

The person's needs will fall into one of two major categories. Either he is striving to meet a need for identity, self-worth, value, or power, or he is looking for love, affection, security, and dependency. Once you know the person's basic need, you can tell him how God has arranged for the fulfillment of these needs. When he understands that there is a valid, godly way to have his needs met, repentance will make sense to him. If homosexuality is an ineffective, destructive way to meet needs, and God has provided an effective, constructive way to get those needs met, then it makes sense to leave the homosexual lifestyle to enter a life of greater fulfillment. Attacking the problem from the other direction only produces resistance and contention, so why not start with the positive?

To witness to the homosexual, then, we need to be a friend, share Christ with the person, carefully define our terms, and begin with the positive, not the negative. These are only general guidelines, not a method or technology for witnessing. These principles are also very selective, since most of the guidelines for witnessing to heterosexuals will apply to the homosexual as well.

WHEN YOU RETURN

After you witness to someone in the gay community, your task is far from over. Planting seed is important, since if you never sow, you will never reap, but watering and weeding also play an important part in bringing in the harvest. Here are a few suggestions regarding what to do after you witness.

1. *Pray for yourself.* People do not commonly equate sharing their faith with spiritual warfare, but the witnessing Christian is in direct conflict with the powers of the enemy. Paul says that "our struggle is not against flesh and blood, but against the rulers, against the powers, against the world forces of this darkness, against the spiritual forces of wickedness in the heavenly places" (Eph. 6:12). However, Christians often imagine that they are struggling with flesh and blood when they witness rather than spiritual forces. This oversight encourages spiritual slackness, and in this unprotected state, the Christian can fall prey to the schemes of the enemy.

One demonic tactic that Christians experience is what I call the *Galatian kickback.* Galatians 6:1 says, "Brethren, even if a man is caught in any trespass, you who are spiritual, restore such a one in a spirit of gentleness; each one looking to yourself, lest you too be tempted." I used to believe that the temptation mentioned here was pride. Now, it is true that if I am one of the "spiritual ones" who restores others, I might be tempted to be proud. However, I found through much counseling experience that this temptation is much broader and much more subtle than that.

When a Christian ministers to someone else, whether he is witnessing to unbelievers or counseling Christians, the person is involved in a form of spiritual warfare. He attacks the spiritual world inasmuch as he sets people free from spiritual bondage. This confrontation will not go without notice, however, and the Christian will in return come under attack from evil spiritual beings. The interesting thing about this counterattack is that it comes in like kind to the problem the Christian was solving. In other words, if the Christian was ministering to a person with a lust problem, the Christian may experience a temptation to lust later. If the Christian witnesses to a person bound by anger, the Christian is liable to find himself tempted to lose his temper easily in the next few days. He can even find himself tempted by things that were never a problem in his life before (e.g., I have never taken drugs, but I found myself becoming very curious about drugs after I counseled someone with a serious drug problem).

A friend of mine, also a counselor, came to me one day with an unexplainable depression. As we prayed, I felt God said that the depression was not his. I asked him if he had counseled a depressed person recently, and he replied that just the night before he had helped a depressed, suicidal counselee. He failed to protect himself through prayer after the counseling session, and left himself open to attack from the spiritual world. As soon as we prayed, the depression lifted. I wonder sometimes how many depressed counselors have left the ministry because they do not understand this principle.

Prayer is the answer to the Galatian kickback, but it is not just a general covering in prayer—the prayer needs to be specifically directed against the very problems that the Christian has handled. If the Christian ministered to a bitter person, he will need to pray to be protected from bitterness. If he helped a gossip, he will need to pray for protection from sins of the tongue. Whatever the problem of the other person, the believer who confronts the problem needs to pray for protection from that very temptation. Failure to perform this simple spiritual exercise could result in great spiritual harm, so remember to pray for yourself after you witness to others.

2. *Pray for the people you contact.* Jesus said that the seed we sow in people's hearts can be snatched away by the enemy. Consequently, we need to pray that this seed will be protected and nurtured by the Holy Spirit. Pray that the person will understand what he has heard. Pray that he will remember the message, that he will be convicted of his sin, and that he will meet other Christians who will confirm the word he has already heard. If you pray for the person by name, this will help you remember the person's name the next time you meet him. Success in witnessing is largely due to prayer, so don't forget to pray for the people to whom you witness.

3. *Try to see the person again.* The homosexual's special needs and reservations make it necessary to spend large amounts of quality time together. Since friendships take time to develop, trust builds slowly, and understanding blossoms gradually, repeated contact with the person is the only way to insure lasting results.

Extending hospitality to the person is one way to show acceptance and concern. Invite the person to your home for dinner, for a party, or for a casual evening of playing games. Opening the door of your home communicates love without saying a word. As the homosexual feels comfortable in your home, he will probably become more open to your message, too.

Going places together affords another good opportunity to show love and share your faith. Taking a hike, visiting a museum, or going sightseeing will give you ample time to become better acquainted and discuss pertinent issues.

Yet another way to spend time together is to do things with the person. Maybe you have a mutual hobby, a sport you both enjoy, a car to fix, or even a yard to tend. It doesn't really matter what the activity is, as long as it gives you an opportunity to get to know each other.

Lastly, don't give up! The gay community is a very difficult field to sow: it requires extensive weeding and watering, and the harvest is often small. Nonetheless, every person is worth more than the whole world, so if one person is reached, the whole effort is worthwhile. In due season we will reap if we do not faint (Gal. 6:9).

SUGGESTED READING/ LISTENING LIST

Note: The inclusion of a book or tape in this list does not imply my total agreement with all of the ideas of the author or speaker.

BOOKS OR BOOKLETS ON THE TOPIC OF HOMOSEXUALITY:

Bradford, Brick, et al. *Healing for the Homosexual.* Available from Presbyterian & Reformed Renewal Ministry, 2245 NW 39th St., Oklahoma City, OK 73112.

Cook, Colin. *Homosexuality: An Open Door?* Order from H. A. Fellowship Services, P.O. Box 7781, Reading, PA 19603.

Drakeford, John. *A Christian View of Homosexuality.* Broadman Press, 127 9th Ave. N., Nashville, TN 37234.

Hurst, Ed and Robbi Kenney. *Homosexuality: Laying the Axe to the Roots.* Order from Outpost, 1821 University Ave. So. #S-292, St. Paul, MN 55104.

Johnson, Barbara. *Where Does a Mother Go to Resign?* Bethany House Publishers, 6820 Auto Club Road, Minneapolis, MN 55438.

Lovelace, Richard. *Homosexuality: What Should Christians Do About It?* Fleming Revell, 184 Central Ave., Old Tappan, NJ 07675.

Moberly, Elizabeth. *Homosexuality: A New Christian Ethic.* Attic Press, Rt. 2, Stony Point, Greenwood, SC 29646.

Rekers, George. *Growing Up Straight.* Moody Press, Chicago, IL.

Thorkelson, Lori. *Emotional Dependency.* Available from Exodus International, P.O. Box 2121, San Rafael, CA 94912.

Also, many excellent pamphlets and sheets on a wide variety of subjects are available from Love In Action, P.O. Box 2655, San Rafael, CA 94912. Write requesting a list of literature and prices.

Books on the General Topic of Counseling:

Adams, Jay E. *Competent to Counsel, The Christian Counselor's Manual*. Presbyterian and Reformed Publishing Company, Phillipsburg, N.J.

Backus, William. *Telling Yourself the Truth, Telling Each Other the Truth, Telling the Truth to Troubled People*. Bethany House Publishers, 6820 Auto Club Road, Minneapolis, MN 55438.

Basham, Don. *Deliver Us From Evil*. Chosen Books, a division of Fleming H. Revell Company, Old Tappan, NJ.

Crabb, Jr., Lawrence J., Ph. D. *Basic Principles of Biblical Counseling, Effective Biblical Counseling*. Zondervan Corporation, Grand Rapids, MI.

Dawson, Joy. *Intimate Friendship with God: Through Understanding the Fear of the Lord*. Chosen Books, Fleming H. Revell Company, Old Tappan, NJ.

Suggested Tapes for Additional Listening:

AVAILABLE FROM PILGRIM TAPES:

Dawson, Joy. *A Series of Messages on the Fear of the Lord.*

Saia, Michael R. *Homosexuality* (a four-tape series including two tapes on homosexuality, one on witnessing to homosexuals, and one on rejection).

Healing of Father Image (a message esplaining how a father-image is corrupted and how the affected person can develop an accurate image of God as Father).

Counseling (an eight-tape series on the presuppositions and preparation of the Christian counselor, the process of counseling, and the pitfalls of the counselor).

Why Do the Innocent Suffer? (two tapes that will help the homosexually oriented person understand how God is completely just in the light of the person's sexual orientation).

For a free catalog of over 1200 titles or other ordering information, write to: Pilgrim Tapes, P.O. Box 296, Sunland, CA 91040-0296.

AVAILABLE FROM EXODUS INTERNATIONAL:

Exodus International sponsors an annual training conference, featuring classes that cover many aspects of ministry to those overcoming homosexuality. Tapes of these classes from past conferences are available. For a complete listing, write to Exodus International, P.O. Box 2121, San Rafael, CA 94912.

APPENDIX D

MINISTRY REFERRAL LIST

EXODUS INTERNATIONAL
REFERRAL AND AFFILIATE LIST
(Used with permission)

ABOUT EXODUS

EXODUS International is a worldwide coalition of Christian outreaches to those overcoming homosexuality and related sexual issues. The EXODUS network was formed during the first conference in Anaheim, California, in September 1976. Over 60 ministries in North America are now part of EXODUS.

Note: This list is divided into two parts: the referral agencies and the affiliate agencies. *Referral agencies* meet the following requirements: agreement with Exodus doctrine and policy; the ministry has been in existence for at least two years; the director has been free from immoral sexual behavior for at least two years, has been in communication with an Exodus board member for at least six months, has attended a regional leadership meeting or national Exodus conference, and is active in a local church and has spiritual accountability there; the ministry has a policy-making board or governing body with the power to remove or change leadership if necessar.

The *affiliate agencies* have not completed the paperwork for approval by the Exodus board. *They are listed here for your convenience. Exodus does not take any responsibility for counsel received from an affiliate agency.*

This list is updated monthly. For a current copy, write to: Exodus International, P.O. Box 2121, San Rafael, CA 94912.

REFERRAL AGENCIES

Arkansas

Love in Action—Church of the Air, P.O. Box 9914, Little Rock, AR 72219. 501/565-1084. Aud Booher, director. Radio & prison ministry (KAAY radio); in-person, phone & correspondence counseling; literature; newsletter; inner healing seminar.

California

Desert Stream, 1415 Santa Monica Mall #201, Santa Monica, CA 90401. Andy Comiskey, director. 213/395-9137. In-person counseling; literature, tapes; newsletter; speaking engagements & seminars; Bible studies; 20-week discipleship series; group meetings for wives; AIDS resource ministry.

New Creation Ministries, 1020 E. McKinley, Fresno, CA 93728. 209/264-6125. Bud Searcy, director. In-person, phone & correspondence counseling; literature, tapes; newsletter; speaking engagements & seminars; group counseling; group for parents; group for spouses.

Hotline Help Center (EXIT Ministry), P.O. Box 999, Anaheim, CA 92805 (Los Angeles area). 714/778-1000. Joan DeGennaro, EXIT administrator. 24-hour phone counseling; in-person & correspondence counseling; literature; speaking engagements & seminars.

Love In Action, P.O. Box 2655, San Rafael, CA 94912 (San Francisco area). 415/454-0960. Frank Worthen, director. In-person, phone & correspondence counseling; literature & tapes; newsletter; one year live-in program (January to December); church seminars; weekly group meetings (men only); women's group meetings (weekly); support group for spouses (bi-monthly); speaking engagements; Bible studies.

Colorado

His New Creations, P.O. Box 3128 Littleton, CO 80161 (Denver area). 303/770-4648. Mary Lebsock, coordinator. On sabbatical for one year. Will serve as a referral center for the Denver area.

Florida

Eleutheros, 1298 Minnesota Ave., Suite D, Winter Park, FL 32789 (Orlando area). 305/629-5770. Sy Rogers, director. In-person & correspondence counseling; literature & tapes; newsletter; speaking engagements; group counseling meetings; seminars; support group for spouses; group for parents.

Worthy Creations Ministry, 3601 Davie Blvd, Ft. Lauderdale, FL 33312. 305/463-0848. Thom Rogers. In-person, phone & correspondence counseling; literature & tapes; videotapes; newsletter; evangelism; speaking engagements & seminars; Bible studies; group counseling; parents group; spouses group; live-in AIDS facility ("Victory House").

Georgia

Challenge, P.O. Box 371289, Decatur, GA 30037 (Atlanta area). 404/243-5020. Bob Middleton, leader. In-person, phone & correspondence counseling; group counseling; speaking engagements; Bible studies; support group for parents; support group for spouses.

Katapauo, P.O. Box 13962, Atlanta, GA 30324. 404/636-5924. Joel Afman, director. Individual and group counseling; literature; speaking engagements.

Hawaii

Pacific Community Church, 2875 Pacific Heights Rd. Honolulu, HI 96813. 808/536-5750. Dean Dyk, pastor. In-person counseling; audio tapes & videotapes; speaking engagements & seminars; fellowship & acceptance in a local church body.

Illinois

Jesus People USA, 4707 N. Malden, Chicago, IL 60640. 312/561-2450. Dawn Herrin, Pastor; Neil Taylor, elder-pastor. This ministry mainly offers live-in discipleship for those coming from a counter-culture street background. Besides individual counseling, members participate in Bible studies and community outreaches.

Maryland

Regeneration, P.O. Box 9830, Baltimore, MD 21284. 301/661-0284. Alan Medinger, director. In-person, phone & correspondence counseling; literature; newsletter; speaking engagements & seminars; group meetings for ex-gays; support group for parents; support group for spouses.

Michigan

Hyperniken Ministries, 4362 Cascade Rd. SE #102, Grand Rapids, MI 49506. 616/942-2063. Vern Dunmire, director. In-person, phone & correspondence counseling; newsletter; speaking engagements & seminars; Bible studies; group meetings for ex-gays; support group for spouses; support group ("Support of Love") for parents and friends.

Reconciliation Ministries, P.O. Box 482, Wyandotte, MI 48192 (Detroit area). 313/281-0773. Jack Hickey, director. In-person, phone & correspondence counseling; literature, tapes; videotapes; newsletter; speaking engagements & seminars; Bible studies; group counseling; H-Anon meetings for parents & spouses.

Minnesota

Outpost, 1821 University Avenue So., #S-292, St. Paul, MN 55104. 612/645-2530. Ed Hurst, director. In-person & correspondence counseling; literature & tapes; newsletter; evangelism; speaking engagements & seminars; newsletter for wives; group meetings for ex-gays; Bible studies; support group for parents; support group for spouses.

Nebraska

Standing By, c/o Indian Hills Community Church, 1000 So. 84th St., Lincoln, NE 68510. 402/483-4541; 402/464-9004. Alice Hayman, Bill Noel. Group meetings. Correspondence and in-person counseling.

New Hampshire

Redirection Ministry, P.O. Box 3740, Manchester, NH 03105. 603/625-8190. Paul Demers, director. In-person & phone counseling; literature; videotapes; street evangelism; group counseling (monthly); Bible studies; correspondence counseling; speaking engagements & seminars.

Ohio

Spring Forth, c/o College Hill Presbyterian Church, 5742 Hamilton Ave., Cincinnati, OH 45224. 513/772-7725. Hal Schell, director. In-person phone & correspondence counseling; literature; speaking engagements & seminars; Bible studies; group counseling.

Oklahoma

Restoration Outreach, P.O. Box 745, Owasso, OK 74055 (Tulsa area). 918/272-2931. Wanda and Jerry Harris, directors. In-person, phone & correspondence counseling; literature, tapes; videotapes; speaking engagements & seminars; Bible studies; group for parents & spouses.

The First Stone, P.O. Box 1367, Bethany, OK 73008 (Oklahoma City area). 405/720-2437. Frank & Peg Rogers, directors. In-person, phone & correspondence counseling; literature & tapes; speaking engagements & seminars; group counseling meetings; Bible studies; radio program; AIDS hotline.

Pennsylvania

Day One Ministries, 1213 Chew St., Allentown, PA 18102. 215/282-4164. Earl Miller, director. In-person, phone & correspondence counseling; literature, tapes; videotapes; newsletter; speaking engagements & seminars; group counseling; group for parents; group for spouses.

Harvest, P.O. Box 53486, Philadelphia, PA 19105. 215/985-4031. John Freeman, director. In-person, phone & correspondence counseling; literature; newsletter; speaking engagements & seminars; Bible studies; group meetings for ex-gays; discipleship; evangelism; counseling for wives.

Texas

Christian Coalition for Reconciliation, P.O. Box 66130, Houston, TX 77266. 713/521-3317. Michael Newman, director. In-person, phone & correspondence counseling; literature; newsletter; speaking engagements & Bible studies; group counseling; parents group.

Washington

Metanoia Ministries, P.O. Box 33039, Seattle, WA 98133. 206/793-3500. Douglas Houck, director. In-person, phone & correspondence counseling; literature; newsletter; speaking engagements & seminars; Bible studies; group counseling; parents group; spouses group.

Canada

New Beginnings, Box 1030, Station F, Toronto, Ontario M4X 2T7. 416/921-6557. Pat Allan, director. In-person, phone & correspondence counseling; literature & tapes; Bible studies; group meetings for ex-gays.

Europe

For current information on ministries, contact: **True Freedom Trust**, P.O. Box 3, Upton, Wirral, Merseyside, England L49 6NY. Martin Hallett.

South Pacific

For current information on ministries, write: **Liberty**, 15 Eagle Terrace, Torwood, Brisbane, Queensland 4066, Australia. Peter Lane.

AFFILIATE AGENCIES

The Exodus board does not take responsibility for any counsel received through the agencies listed in this section.

Afiliate agencies meet the following requirements: agreement with Exodus doctrine and policy; director has been free from immoral sexual behavior for at least one year; director has attended a regional leadership meeting or national Exodus conference; director is active in a local church and has spiritual accountability there; person overseeing the ministry has written a letter of recommendation on behalf of the ministry director.

Alabama

Streets and Alleys, P.O. Box 19631, Birmingham, AL 35219. 205/870-5673. Tom Nelson.

Arizona

True Perceptions, P.O. Box 36494, Tucson, AZ 85740. 602/882-4753.

California

Cornerstone, P.O. Box 5, Antioch, CA 94509. 415/757-1517. Bob Carlson.

Desert Stream (Inland Empire), P.O. Box 813, Claremont, CA 91711. (serving Pomona, San Bernardino & Riverside counties) 714/624-6065. Shawn Corkery.

Exile Ministries, P.O. Box 9458, Fresno, CA 93792. 209/224-9211. Arnie Lloyd.

Friends Who Care, P.O. Box 23293, Pleasant Hill, CA 94523 (Oakland area). 415/934–3056. Mary Christ. Group meeting.

New Creations, c/o Metro Christian Center, 3135 W. Warner, Santa Ana, CA 92799 (Los Angeles area). 714/540-4331. Joe Dallas; Jack Felton.

Pure Life Ministries, P.O. Box 1932, Fair Oaks, CA 95628. 916/635-1866. Steve Gallagher.

Wisdom's Way, P.O. Box 171086, San Diego, CA 92117. 619/286-4690. Michael Hastings. Counseling; evening discipleship classes.

Colorado

Where Grace Abounds, P.O. Box 11056, Denver, CO 80211. 303/595-9099. Mary Heathman.

Florida

Banner Ministries, 1101 S. Flagler Dr., W. Palm Beach, FL 33401. 305/833-3621. Douglas Hilzey.

Living in Liberty, P.O. Box 1487, Oldsmar, FL 34677 (Tampa area). 813/855-2025. Norman Troutman.

Illinois

Beyond Rejection Ministries, P.O. Box 156, Rockford, IL 61105-0156. 815/963-0303. Rebecca Tennant.

Kansas

Freedom at Last, P.O. Box 13314, Wichita, KS 67213. 316/267-8779. Michael Babb.

Massachusetts

Transformation Ministries of Boston, P.O. Box 1313, Back Bay Annex, Boston, MA 02117. 617/445-1787. Peter Robicheau Jr.

White Stone Ministries, % Ruggles Baptist Church, 874 Beacon St., Boston, MA 02215. 617/266-3633. Chris Greco, Linda Frank.

Michigan

New Hope, 5550 Oakland Dr., Kalamazoo, MI 49002. 616/375–7936. Randy Streich.

New Jersey

LIFE Ministry—New Jersey, 491 Alps Rd., Wayne, NJ 07470. 201/694-2938. Wayne Doyle.

North Carolina

Imago Dei, c/o Frank Courtney, Myrtle Grove Presbyterian Chruch, 800 Piner Road, Wilmington, NC 28403. 919/791-6179. Frank and Jeanne Courtney.

Ohio

Prodigal Ministries, P.O. Box 11277, Cincinnati, OH 45211. 513/861-0011. Joseph Miller.

South Carolina

Everlasting Freedom, P.O. Box 967, Mauldin, SC 29662 (Greenville area). 803/297-3223. John and Lynn Cooper.

Texas

Emmanuel Ministries, 18675 Jones Maltsberger, San Antonio, TX 78247. 512/496-2100. Kathy Ryan and David Park.

He is Able Ministries, P.O. Box 3769, Austin TX 78764. 512/462-2343. Susan Harris.

Washington

Transformation Ministries, P.O. Box 55805, Seattle, WA 98155. 206/364-2306. Carrie Wingfield.